This book is number

.....376...

of a limited edition

of one thousand copies

.....Paul Broadhurst.....

SECRET SHRINES

In Search of the
Old Holy Wells of Cornwall

PAUL BROADHURST

*First published by the author in a finely-produced
limited edition in 1988.*

*This edition published 1991 by
Pendragon Press, Box 888,
Launceston, Cornwall, England.*

ISBN 0 9513236 0 1

*Printed and Typeset in Great Britain by
Penwell Print Ltd., Kelly Bray, Callington, Cornwall.*

*Colour separations by
Peninsular Repro Services Ltd., Exeter, Devon.*

for the Queen of the night
and of the day

Acknowledgements

My sincere thanks to John Michell, whose boundless enthusiasm for the Earth Spirit is truly inspirational. Thanks also to Colin Wilson, for providing magical connections and not a little synchronicity. Thanks too, to Penny and Phil Harris, Pete Bailey, Mark Valentine and many others who have offered encouragement and stimulating conversation. Without the work of Thomas Quiller Couch, this volume would not exist, as it was the chance discovery of his book on the old wells that led directly to this present work, if one is inclined to accept the notion of chance, that is.

A great debt is also owed to his friend J. T. Blight, who recorded these old places before the upheavals of the twentieth century changed the countryside for ever, and whose evocative engravings add so much charm to the current book. But perhaps most of all, my thanks must go to Jane, whose quiet support nurtured the project from infancy, instilling it with confidence to go out into the wide world.

Contents

PART TWO

NOTE: *The terms Man and Mankind are used throughout the book as a generic description of humanity as a whole, and should not be taken to infer the superiority of the male of the species. As the book progresses, it should become apparent that the whole emphasis is towards a re-establishment of the great feminine principle, as recognized by the Nature religions of the past and their reverence for the Earth Goddess.*

List of Illustrations

COLOUR PLATES

by Paul Broadhurst

BLACK AND WHITE PHOTOGRAPHS

OLD SKETCHES AND ENGRAVINGS

Holy Well

Good salts in the well tonight.
Go and drink.
Close eyes and dream of the Milky Way,
the Worm of Middle Earth.
The moon is full.
Open eyes and look into well.
See the moon,
open mouth of glowing worm,
pumping sap into trees,
opening spirals of water,
pulling tides of sea and blood.
Drop in a coin.
The serpent in the well,
the snake in spring,
turns round
and walks like water.

Christine Rhone

Forethought

T HAS often been observed that, despite remorseless change and the attendant cataclysms of earthly existence, history seems to repeat itself. Yet we now find ourselves at a crucial stage where a complete re-appraisal of our attitudes to the planet is rapidly becoming no romantic ideal, but a practical necessity. It is becoming increasingly apparent that in destroying the life-support systems of the biosphere we have shown myopic ignorance which could well prove suicidal if we cannot make the quantum-leap in consciousness to understand that planet Earth is nothing other than a vast living body of which we are a part.

Until recently, such ideas were confined to the realms of the poetic and mystical. They are now, however, beginning to be taken seriously by scientists since the surfacing of the 'Gaia hypothesis', which demonstrates clearly that the Earth reacts exactly like an evolving organism, which maintains the conditions necessary for growth and evolution in ways which we are only just starting to grasp. But history has come full circle. For this concept of the planet as a living, breathing body is merely an echo of the way Mankind approached the Earth for thousands upon thousands of years, and which guided the attitude of early peoples to the Universe around them. It is only in comparatively recent times that the great Nature religions that were the living demonstration of this interaction between the human species and its environment were supplanted by different modes of thought which made us forget the reality, and veiled it from our senses. It is, perhaps, high time we began to see clearly, and with modern minds, that which was understood intuitively by the peoples of earlier times.

And so looking at what might first appear to be obscure remnants of archaeological interest only takes on a deeper significance, for most of the remains of the days of the Nature religions have dissolved back into the elements from which they were made. Little exists today to remind us of those days before written records, but what little does still defy time and the destroying hand of man takes us right back to the concept of the biosphere as an entity that is intelligent and alive. The problems of the modern world find answers in the remote past, and history turns full circle like the ancient symbol of the serpent swallowing its own tail.

Trying to understand the significance of this idea leads us into strange areas of the mind that are alive with re-discovery. The superficiality of twentieth-century life yields to ideas and attitudes that permeate our collective being and take us back into a world full of almost mystical rapport with the environment. Some may see it as the quest for the Grail, others as a sort of psycho-analysis that strips away current conditioning to give us a more lucid view of our proper place amongst the enigmas of existence. Whatever the effect upon the mind, dwelling on these matters may well help us to come to terms with the crucial re-alignment of attitude that would now seem pivotal to our continued habitation of planet Earth.

Introduction

John Michell

IT IS a real pleasure to have been asked to introduce SECRET SHRINES, because here is a book I can recommend to literally everyone. One reason is obvious at first sight. Paul Broadhurst is, amongst other things, a professional photographer, and his lovely pictures of the Cornish holy wells explain immediately why many people regard these humble monuments as the most beautiful and moving of ancient places. It is not easy to photograph them adequately. Their magic qualities ebb and flow with the seasons and are most apparent under certain conditions of light and weather, which have to be waited for. There is also the difficulty of finding many of these wells. Several which had been lost or forgotten for a generation or more are rediscovered in this book. Others have vanished without trace. Yet almost 200 holy wells are still known in Cornwall and the Scillies, and with them is preserved the ancient, sacred spirit of the west. They are the true wealth of this country. In their pure waters the old people found healing and inspiration. To modern visitors they offer respite and peace of mind, and they serve also as repositories of natural wisdom to enlighten the future. A book such as this, which reveals the beauty and spirituality of our holy wells and the importance of maintaining them in their natural surroundings, is therefore of great value. That is the second reason for recommending it.

A third reason is that it is written by an enthusiast who is both learned and humorous. We are told of his adventures in quest of forgotten springs, share his excitement at new discoveries and are entertained by his thoughts and theories. At the same time we are fully informed on the histories, lore, legends and literature of the old wells. Many of them are certainly of prehistoric origin. In early times they were resorted to by wandering tribes for communication with the spirits of nature on which their lives depended. By unknown rituals and invocations, performed at the appropriate seasons when the waters were at their most potent, they procured the fertility of animals and plants, and the traditions they founded have never wholly been forgotten. Many items of holy well lore, their seasons of efficacy and their various uses for healing or divination, may derive from Britain's earliest, mesolithic inhabitants.

The first, semi-historical characters associated with Cornwall's holy wells were the Celtic saints. The Celtic church was apparently little more than a reformation of Druidism, assimilating its doctrines and customs and adopting the old pagan shrines. This caused it in the seventh century to be suppressed by the Church of Rome, but stories of the mystical, hermetic holy men and holy women of the Celtic church, reflecting those of their Druid predecessors, were lovingly preserved into the Middle Ages and are still remembered in the names and legends of the holy wells which they sanctified. Even John Wesley, whose preachings persuaded the Cornish people to forget most of their native tales and traditions, could not undo their natural veneration for the spirit in sacred waters.

Modern medicine, piped water and the radical influence of secular ideas and economics on country life led to the neglect or loss of many holy wells. At no time, however, were they entirely without friends and protectors. On Cornwall's north coast in 1843 the Vicar of Morwenstow, Robert S. Hawker, poet, visionary and opium eater, won a lawsuit against a local landowner to gain possession of St. John's holy well. This he restored together with its neighbouring well, St. Morwenna's. His young protege, the Penzance artist John T. Blight, included the figure of Hawker at St. John's well in his book of Cornish crosses and antiquities, published in 1858. This was the first illustrated work on holy wells, and Blight's picturesque drawings, mostly reproduced in this book, have never been surpassed. One of Blight's informants was Thomas Quiller Couch, whose notes on Cornish holy wells were published in 1894 as the first book entirely devoted to the subject. It has since been followed by A. Lane-Davies's *Holy Wells of Cornwall* (1970) and J. Meyrick's *Pilgrim's Guide to the Holy Wells of Cornwall* (1982). SECRET SHRINES is thus the third such book to have appeared in less than 20 years, a testimony to the rapidly growing interest in these rustic holy places. This interest is now catered for by a magazine, *Source*, which reports on the holy wells restoration movement throughout the country.

The modern holy well renaissance is clearly in reaction against the processes which caused their decline and which are now threatening the last vestiges of local culture and the beauty and fertility of the entire countryside. Paul Broadhurst is well aware of this, and his book is a gentle but inexorable argument for the resanctification of the landscape beginning at the sources of its living spirit, for a land which loses its spirit together with its sacred places is no longer decently, humanly inhabitable. This is no mere personal opinion but a message which comes direct from nature and steals unbidden into the minds of silent visitors to the secret shrines of the earth goddess. At such places, traditionally adapted for communication with spirit, the deity makes known her moods and desires, which correspond to those of humanity. Every living thing, human, animal and vegetable, craves the fulfilment of its nature, and the same may apply to every element in creation, from the earth itself to the humble spring of water. Over a desecrated holy well, as over a mistreated child, hovers a scream of anguish. To bring help and comfort to any such is to turn darkness into light, a feat of spiritual alchemy which those who visit holy wells can perform to the benefit of themselves and the whole of nature. The process of healing the earth, and curing the sickness within ourselves, could begin with the reconsecration of our secret shrines.

To think about the past
is not merely to shut out the present
and the future, for all are inextricably
linked by the eddies and currents of time.
To dwell on the attitudes of our ancestors is not
so much a dry and dusty exhumation of old bones as
a strange adventure of the mind, alive with the
power of old memories. And in travelling back
through the centuries, we stumble across
elements of our own nature that are
obscured by a world far removed
from the raw harmony of those
ancient days. . . .

Visions and Veils

Colin Wilson

N 1944, Robert Graves wrote a book of such apparently wild eccentricity that, in spite of his established reputation, it was turned down by a number of publishers, one of whom hinted, in a rejection letter, that Graves had gone off his head. *The White Goddess* was eventually accepted by T. S. Eliot and published in 1948 by Faber and Faber. The critics received it with bafflement. What were they to make of a book that argued that poetry came into existence in some remote 'Matriarchal age', when the Moon Goddess was the most powerful of all divinities, and that the human race has been going downhill ever since the priestess matriarchs were replaced by priest patriarchs? Was it a joke? Or perhaps an allegory? Or just an extraordinary piece of self-assertion by a paranoid poet? Graves records with satisfaction that one publisher who turned it down with particular rudeness was soon after found hanging in his garden, wearing ladies' underwear, while T. S. Eliot received a Nobel Prize and an O.M. in the same year. . . .

In the forty years since its publication, the thesis of *The White Goddess* has been recognized as a profound insight into human history and human psychology. What Graves had understood was this: that the kind of knowledge taught in our universities is as crude and impersonal as a railway timetable. We have forgotten that there is a *totally different kind of knowledge*, and a totally different kind of knowing. And this was not just a cranky theory, but an intense conviction based on personal experience. One of Graves' fellow pupils at his public school was a boy called Smilley. One day, when the mathematics teacher had set them a complicated problem, Smilley had simply written down the answer; asked how he did it, Smilley replied 'It just came to me.' The master accused him of cheating and sent him to be caned. And eventually, Smilley was 'cured' of his odd ability to 'see' the answers to complex problems 'in a flash'. Graves knew Smilley's powers were genuine because he himself had had a brief experience of the same thing; one day, sitting on the grass-roller behind the cricket pavilion, he suddenly 'knew everything.' He explains (in the autobiographical story 'The Abominable Mr Gunn) that it was some kind of shift of awareness, an odd way of 'looking sideways' at disorderly facts to make order out of them. This 'mystical' way of seeing lasted about twenty four hours, until he tried to explain it on paper; then it went. But Graves remarks that this insight was 'a sudden infantile awareness of the power of intuition, the supra-logic that cuts out all the routine processes of thought and leaps straight from problem to answer.' In *The White Goddess*, Graves calls this intuitive way of knowing 'lunar knowledge', and the kind of intellectual calculation taught at universities 'solar knowledge.' He has no deep objection to solar knowledge, but feels that it is important for us to recognize that it is younger and cruder than 'lunar knowledge'.

In the mid-1960's, a scholar named John Michell stumbled on a series of discoveries that were closely related to Graves's insight. He discovered, to begin with, a little book called *Feng Shui* by the Rev. E.J. Eitel, about the ancient Chinese science of 'wind and water', whose purpose was to establish harmonious relations between people and their natural surroundings. In a reprint of Eitel's book, Michell remarked that 'at the time Eitel was writing (1873), the triumph of materialistic philosophy and science . . . was so apparent that it was scarcely possible for a rational European to express any serious interest . . . in Feng-Shui. Yet, as Eitel records, the Chinese were amazed that the Europeans, so advanced in other respects, were ignorant of Feng-Shui, which they regarded as the foundation of civilized life. According to Feng-Shui, the earth is a dim mirror of the powers of heaven—another version of the old hermetic doctrine 'As above, so below'—and man must somehow 'open himself up to these powers in the way that a great pianist must open himself up to the music if he wishes to express its very essence.

Michell also rediscovered the work of the retired English brewer Alfred Watkins: the notion that the network of footpaths and farm tracks that criss-cross rural England connect all kinds of 'sacred sites' such as churches, standing stones, ancient tumuli, and so on. Watkins believed they were the trade routes of ancient man, and that the men originally responsible for them were of priestly rank. Michell went further, and suggested that these 'trade routes' were far more than that (as Watkins himself came to suspect at the end of his life)—that they were the 'lines of earth force' that the Chinese adepts of Feng-Shui called Lung Mei, or 'dragon paths'. Michell's book *The View Over Atlantis* (1972), although quietly received, was to become one of the most influential books of the decade, as well as a kind of Bible for intellectual hippies. The idea that had so much appeal to these heirs of the Beat Generation was that there must have been some remote time—symbolized by Atlantis—when man had a far more harmonious and direct relationship with nature—a kind of Golden Age. Paul Broadhurst expresses it (in Chapter Six of this book): 'In the early days of human development there seems to have existed a totally different relationship between the mind of man and its environment. The differentiation that clearly marks out the individual from his surroundings today was not so pronounced in those early times, and Man could feel the power of the essential 'one-ness' of things.'

It would, I think, be a mistake to assume that stone age man went around embracing trees and gazing in rapture at the stars—he was too busy with the struggle to keep alive. But I believe it is also fairly certain—using the analogy of the modern primitives—that he used shamanistic magic in locating his prey, that he used natural powers of 'dowsing' to locate water, that he possessed the same powers of 'homing' as birds and animals, that he could 'tune in' to the weather and the seasons in a way that would nowadays be regarded a 'supernatural' (when, in fact, it is profoundly natural), and that he knew how to use the 'force' residing in standing stones and 'blind springs' for healing purposes.

It was in the 1960's that modern science stumbled upon what is almost certainly the true explanation of this paradox of 'lunar' and 'solar' knowledge. It happened when an American psychologist named Roger Sperry realized that man literally has *two* brains in his skull—or rather, that the human brain consists of two identical halves that can operate independently. These two halves are joined by a knot of nerves called the commissure. If this commissure is severed—as it sometimes is to cure epileptics—Sperry discovered that his patients began to act literally like two people. A split brain patient might try to zip up his flies with one hand and unzip them with the other, or try to hit his wife with one hand while the other held it back. Information fed to one half of the brain would not reach the other. For some odd reason, the left side of our bodies is connected to the right side of our brains, and vice versa, and the same thing applies to our eyes.* If a split brain patient was shown an apple with his left eye and an orange with his right, and asked what he had just seen, he would reply: 'Orange.' But if asked to write with his left hand what he had seen he would write 'Apple.' Asked what he had just written he would reply 'Orange.' A split brain patient who was shown an indecent picture with her right brain blushed; asked why she was blushing, she replied: 'I don't know.' The person you call 'I' lives in the left brain; the person who lives a few centimetres away is virtually a stranger.

It has been known for a long time that the left brain deals with language and logic, while the right deals with intuition and pattern-recognition—the left is a scientist, the right an artist or mystic. The 'you' is a scientist. Which explains why 'solar' (or scientific) knowledge comes naturally to us, while 'lunar' (or mystical) knowledge comes only in brief flashes. According to Robert Graves, our 'matriarchal' ancestors were 'right brainers.'

Sperry conducted an experiment that throws even more light on this problem. If a red (or green) light is flashed into the left eye of a split-brain patient, and he is asked what colour he has just seen, he will reply 'I don't know.' Asked to make a guess, he naturally gets it wrong about half the time. But if the patient was allowed a second guess, he invariably got it right because

---

* It actually applies to the left and right visual fields of both eyes, but this is a technicality that need not concern us.

the right brain had overheard the wrong guess, and tipped off the patient by making him jump, just as if it had kicked him under the table. It did this by *making his muscles convulse*. And scientific tests have shown that this is how 'dowsing' works; when the dowser goes over an underground stream, his muscles convulse so as to make the dowsing rod twist in his hands. It looks very much as if the right brain is able to detect water, but can only inform the left brain (the 'you') by making the muscles convulse. So here again, we seem to have proof that the right brain has access to a kind of 'lunar' knowledge to which the left is blind. Of course, it ought to be perfectly easy to pass on this knowledge to 'the other half', since the two halves are joined by the commissure. And in fact, this *does* happen in primitive people—aborigines can detect underground water without the aid of a 'twig'. But modern man has become virtually a 'split brain patient.'

I apologize to readers to whom all this is familiar, but it can be seen that it forms a vital step in our argument—John Michell's and Paul Broadhurst's as well as mine. It demonstrates that civilized man has suppressed his 'intuitive' side until it is little more than a very faint voice on the telephone, instead of coming across loud and clear, as it did to our ancestors.

What *would* the world be like if we could somehow 'amplify' that lost faculty? Most of us glimpse the answer to that question in deep states of relaxation, when the centre of gravity of consciousness seems to move to the 'right'. These are the states described, for example, by Wordsworth in *The Prelude*, when he tells how he rowed into the middle of lake Windermere at night, and how, looking at the vast shapes of the hills, he experienced a sense of 'unknown modes of being.' In these mystical states, Wordsworth felt as if nature is *alive*. We take this to be merely a 'manner of speaking'—for, after all, a mountain is just a lot of dead rock—but if Graves (and Sperry) are correct, it could be far more than that.

There are still, in fact, many people who see the world as Wordsworth—or Graves' 'matriarchal primitives'—saw it. They are known as psychics or clairvoyants, and although the majority of scientists refuse to take them seriously, there has, in fact, been a great deal of scientific investigation of their powers. (See, for example, Lawrence LeShan's *The Medium, the Mystic and the Physicist*.) One of the most remarkable of these was a commonsense and down-to-earth lady called Rosalind Heywood, who was one of the most staunchly 'rationalistic' members of the Society for Psychical Research (until her recent death.) Ever since childhood, Rosalind Heywood had been aware of 'presences' in nature, as well as of a 'presence' in her bedroom—she only learned later that two people in her family had seen the apparition of an old woman in there. As a nurse during the first world war, she became accustomed to curious intuitive promptings that enabled her to save lives, as well as to curious precognitions. Her autobiography *The Infinite Hive* is an immensely impressive book, because of its intelligence and honesty. And again and again, she describes sudden powerful impressions of certain 'forces' in nature. There is, for example, the phenomenon she calls 'the Singing', 'a kind of continuous vibrant inner *quasi*-sound, to which the nearest analogy is the noise induced by pressing a seashell against the ear', and which she was able to hear most strongly in lonely places such as open moorland—although she was aware of it to a lesser degree most of the time. Significantly enough, she also heard 'the Singing' in churches and libraries—anywhere where intense thought or worship had taken place. One day, she mentioned 'the Singing' to a young engineer, assuming he would pooh-pooh it; she was startled when he replied placidly: 'Yes, I hear it too.' (And only a few days ago, I received a letter from a correspondent named Peggy Brittain, who had read my account of Rosalind Heywood in my book *Afterlife*, and who wrote: 'Rosalind Heywood's words (about 'the Singing') made me gasp with pleasure because this is something which I've experienced all my life, and haven't been able to find anyone else who seems to know what I'm talking about.')

What is so interesting is that Rosalind Heywood was able to hear it so clearly in old churches and libraries—as if these places had somehow *recorded* the feelings and thoughts that had taken place there over generations. It is also worth bearing in mind that—as Paul Broadhurst points out—many churches are built on the sites of 'pagan' temples or sites of worship, and these sites, in turn, were apparently chosen because of some powerful quality in the ground. It seems a logical inference that such places were chosen because the 'earth force' there was so strong, and could therefore record and store up the religious emotion of worshippers, until the site had absorbed a certain sacred essence.

Guy Underwood, a remarkable dowser—who is quoted several times in this book—concluded that ancient monuments such as Stonehenge are built above 'blind springs' or aquastats, so that the 'earth force' associated with them may be merely the 'magnetic' field of water. I mention this to emphasise that we are not now speaking of 'the occult' or supernatural, but simply about natural forces to which our ancestors were undoubtedly sensitive. The dowser (and retired Cambridge don) T. C. Lethbridge was convince that so-called 'ghosts' are merely 'recordings' of powerful (often tragic) human emotions on the electrical field of water.

Having said that, it is necessary to admit that Rosalind Heywood herself finally became convinced—in spite of a fundamental tendency to scepticism—that not all 'psychic phenomena' can be explained by these more-or-less scientific terms. She describes, for example, how she and her husband arrived at Okehampton (in Devon) and went out to watch the sunset on the moor. 'Suddenly, without warning, the incredible beauty swept me through a barrier. I was no longer looking at Nature. Nature was looking at me.' And she did not like what she saw. 'It was a strange and humbling sensation, as if numberless unoffending creatures were shrinking back offended by our invasion. . . .' She found herself thinking 'of the old days when simple souls linked themselves to wild nature by the ancient magic of oak and ash and thorn.' They decided to stand still, and try explaining that they came as friends, with humility, only wanting permission to walk quietly on the moor.

And almost immediately, both felt a sense of relief, as if they had been accepted.

Such an experience could have been totally subjective. But she was convinced that an experience two mornings later was not imagination. ' . . . I was alone by a window, facing the moor . . . Then I . . . suffered an invasion, a delightful one. It was as if, like ebullient children, a covey of little invisibles floated in at the window to say 'Hullo!' and coax me to play with them. For a moment their visit seemed perfectly natural, but then my analytical mind got going, and at once, for me, they ceased to exist. . . .'

Did the 'covey of little invisibles' exist in any objective sense? Rosalind Heywood insists that she keeps an open mind on the subject. But I personally have no doubt whatever that, in a relaxed 'right brain' state, she *perceived* 'unknown modes of being' just as Wordsworth perceived them.

It seems to me that there is an important lesson to be learnt from all this. In our ancestors, 'lunar' perception was as strong as—perhaps stronger than—'solar' perception. In the course of creating civilization, we have suppressed these 'right brain' perceptions. Yet I would suggest that, in a sense, we still have an important advantage over our ancestors. Our left-brains have developed an analytical power and force that would have struck them as rather repellent, just as most schoolchildren find the idea of quantum physics or symbolic logic repellent. Yet although we have suppressed our 'lunar' perceptions, we have not destroyed them; we can recover them by *learning* to 'relax into the right brain.' And this, in a fundamental sense, is what this present book is about. Paul Broadhurst is arguing that the 'healing power' that Matthew Arnold found in the poetry of Wordsworth also resides in the 'secret shrines' that so fascinate him, and that if a man of the 20th century should wish to learn about these deep forces of the human psyche and the natural world—and about the link between them—then he might find that the 'elementals' of such places make admirable tutors.

I have reason to believe him correct. It was just over thirty years ago—in 1957—that I began to find myself depressed and confused by my life as a writer in London, and by the exhausting persistance of journalists who had discovered that the so-called 'Angry Young Men' made good copy. After a preposterous scandal involving my girlfriend's parents—who arrived at my flat with a horsewhip, and were soon followed by hordes of reporters and photographers—I took the advice of my publisher, and decided to leave London. It so happened that a poet who lived in the next room had a cottage in Cornwall, which he offered to let to us for an absurdly low rent. We moved there in the spring of 1957, and have been here ever since.

I realize now what an incredible piece of good luck it was that my friend happened to have a cottage in Cornwall—and not, say, Durham, which I would have accepted just as readily. Even now, Cornwall has not quite emerged from the 19th century, and the majority of its small villages have hardly changed since the time of Shakespeare. But the real magic of Cornwall resides in those places that never change—in the moors and the cliffs and the rocky inlets. Every afternoon, I work until 3 o'clock, until my brain seems to have lost its power to make intuitive leaps, then drive a mile to the clifftop, and walk along a footpath that has an almost continuous view of the coast from Plymouth to the Fal estuary and the Lizard. And as I walk, I allow the empty sea and the unchanging landscape to soothe me into a state of quiescence. When this happens, it is as if some invisible wall dissolves away, and I catch a glimpse of a mode of existence that is completely foreign to flesh and blood, yet which seems to possess its own alien form of awareness. Words and images can never capture this mode of existence, but they can acknowledge its reality. The words and images that follow are an acknowledgement of this magical reality.

PART ONE

1

OLD BOOKS
AND ANCIENT WAYS

alf-hidden in the natural seclusion of the Cornish landscape, there still exists a diverse, and somewhat mysterious, array of old Nature temples which connect us with the remotest past, back far beyond the age of written records to times when Mankind lived for forgotten thousands of years in mutual harmony with the Earth. Many of them are far older than the enigmatic monoliths of our obscure ancestors which have made such a vivid impression on the popular imagination, and which now begin to reveal some of their secrets to modern research. Yet the natural springs that bubble from beneath the surface of the planet have been held sacred from the very dawn of human evolution, and despite the ravages of millennia, they still flow on as the ebb of time carries us further away from our dark origins.

In deep, wooded valleys, narrow green lanes and tranquil country churchyards, distant memories of a strange past echo around the countryside, infusing the atmosphere with an almost hypnotic fascination. By curious, quaint villages and isolated farms, on bare, bleak hills and dripping from stalactitic caves, the waters that flow through the veins and arteries of the planet were revered by our precursors as the Elixir of the Earth, responsible not only for life itself, but essential for the fertility and health of the people and the land which they inhabited. As well as the more practical and obvious benefits of such places, and the intrinsic curative properties of the natural springs, the people of old saw the wells as gateways to the Otherworld, where the vital flow of Life-force could be used to penetrate the veils of matter to experience a more formative reality. And so they were used to contact the unseen realms where communication could take place with the gods and spirits of their Nature religions, a purpose which has come down the ages to very recent times and still persists in certain Celtic regions.

So these springs have always been thought of as holy wells, despite the changes wrought by new gods and new religions, which have always had to recognize the central importance of the old wells in the collective human psyche, and adapt them accordingly. Yet their very existence today gives us a direct link with a time when Mankind lived in intuitive sympathy with the natural forces of the planet, which were acknowledged and celebrated by the priests, shamans and ordinary people of the past for aeons before the recent events of the last couple of thousand years.

The eccentric edifices that are often built over the old springs possess a strange aura of agelessness. Viewed from the perspective of human history, which may well go back far beyond any current scientific approximation, it may seem a little surprising that they still exist at all. But what these solitary shrines may lack in rigidity of structure has been more than made up for by their simple maintenance by countless generations of evolving humanity. The time-worn stones of these often crumbling monuments, dripping with moss and ferns and penetrated by the gnarled roots of twisted trees, sometimes seem to be protected by the very forces of Nature that ordinarily erode such man-made structures with slow but remorseless purpose.

The early people who venerated these hidden shrines were not, however, quite as uncivilized and barbarous as some archaeologists would have us believe. With their capacity for technology as yet unevolved, their view of the Universe was of an essentially mystical nature, a world where everything that existed was interdependent. There was no feeling of Man's separateness from Nature that is the hallmark of our modern society, no concept of the countryside fulfilling the role of a food factory or pleasant rural landscape preserved for the purposes of relaxation. The inhabitants of the land; human, plant and animal; the rivers, springs and rocks, as well as unseen entities, the Nature spirits and Gods, were all parts of the whole, dependent on each other for the harmonious continuity of the Earth, and, by their interaction, their own individual evolution. Nature was tamed for mutual benefit, not profaned to satiate human greed and profit.

Fortunately there is a great shift of consciousness back towards the ancient view, as we realize the folly of purely mechanistic theories of Creation. The Spirit of the Age is one of a vast and powerful memory, stirred into activity by the potentially devastating consequences of such a superficial World-view. Perhaps as the seed of this realization grows, we will learn to utilize the enormous benefits of technology within the context of age-old wisdom; for the parts of the mind which we have deliberately suppressed in our quest for control over the Earth's resources were, in our ancestors, alive with an intuition which showed them a deeper reality. A world filled with the flux and flow of unseen forces which manifest in the human condition as well as Nature itself. As a stimulus to the understanding of our own inner selves, dwelling on the past and the old shrines, whether stone or spring, opens up the channels through which these archetypal forces flow. To sit silently in a rarely-visited wooded hollow, to touch the old, worn stones of an ancient mossy shrine above a sacred spring is to rediscover that subtle sphere of the mind which we all still possess, but which is all but eclipsed by the frenetic activity of modern man.

This book has been an intriguing adventure spanning just a few years,

4

season through season. Yet the very act of sifting through the centuries has a peculiar effect upon the mind as the modern perspective increasingly diminishes, and the past comes alive. You begin to realize that if you imagine human history as just a single day, the last couple of thousand years from which we tend to judge our current civilization are equivalent to the time spent in putting the cat out before climbing the stairs and sinking into slumber. The weird dreams that follow are no less vivid, perhaps even more, than the often hazy recollections we have of the everyday world. Often, in dwelling upon the distant past it is as if we are somehow remembering old dreams that become clearer as we focus upon them.

The dreamscape for this nocturnal search, a gentle groping about in the dark of the unwritten past, is set in the antique land of Cornwall, a place of increasing rarity where the remnants of our long sojourn on this planet are not as yet overtly vandalized by the Machine Age. Much is yet to be re-discovered about those people who inhabited this wild landscape for millennia, leaving behind them an enigmatic network of monuments whose purposes are lost in obscurity. However, the old holy wells complement the stone circles and monoliths as temples to a Natural philosophy that transcended the inward-looking, tribal and superstitious images of popular archaeology. And yet, if anything, the old wells are even more obscure than the megaliths, for the infant science of astro-archaeology shows us that the mind of 'primitive' man was far more complex than we can grasp. Sun, Moon and stars were for them a pervasive, intimate experience of which we can only catch the haziest glimmer of a distant reflection.

The sporadic search for the wells has often led to lonely, isolated spots at times of the year when only a mad dog, an Englishman or an incurable well-addict would steel himself against the onslaught of the Cornish weather. Fortunately or otherwise, I qualify under at least two of the foregoing headings, and the search was conducted with the full blessing of the elements. Invigorating, some might call it, but scrambling across cliffs in the teeth of an Atlantic gale or trudging knee-deep in mud across remote fields is often much more enjoyable when remembered from the depths of a comfortable armchair. But the sheer, stark contact with the raw elements has the effect of stripping away the invisible veneer of our modern world, and this always intensifies the exhilaration of discovering the crumbling ruin of an old well.

It sometimes seems that the cliffs and countryside of Cornwall are not quite themselves on a glorious summer's day, as if some lazy indolent mood of inertia suppresses the vital activity of the elemental forces. Though this is fascinating to the student collecting material for a degree in soporifics, or even to those who actively seek the famous enervating aspect of this inertia, cannot be denied. But the essential character of the county reveals its true self when the flecks of white foam are torn tempestuously from the crashing breakers, and a brooding, dramatic sky adds a new depth to the primeval landscape below.

Often during the search, the old holy wells seemed to assume a cloak of

Well Chapel, Menacuddle, St. Austell

invisibility, a veil was drawn over the senses, casting a spell to obfuscate the mind. It was almost as if they possessed some innate magical power, a strange gift of melting into their natural surroundings. The quest for a particular well sometimes seemed like a sort of initiation, a curious species of ordeal involving a pagan baptism of the elements. Some steadfastly refused to be discovered even after many visits, the elusive Nature temples revealing themselves only after the price had been paid with due diligence. I began, dimly at first, to realize that each old well struck some lost chord, like becoming aware that somehow, you already know the person you have just been introduced to. Each well was a distinct personality in itself, with its own peculiar history and past purpose, and as in the case of meeting fellow humans, they have a specific effect upon the psyche which echoes some aspect of their essential nature.

The way the book came about still strikes me as oddly intriguing. Like many other thousands of people, I have always been overwhelmed by a consuming fascination for ancient objects and buildings, drawn by the magnetic pull of old ruins like a moth to the beacon of a candle flame. I have spent years fluttering between the monuments of past ages, soaking myself in their strange ambience, but find it essential to visit them when there is little likelihood of bumping into others of a similar disposition. The presence of others seems to stultify that productive brooding that is akin to meditation, that mood of reverie that cuts through the intellect to some primitive instinct. I recall one time when I visited the bewildering stone alignments at Carnac in Brittany, but was so revolted by the litter, exhaust fumes and squalling children that I had to leave almost immediately. You could hardly see the serried ranks of thousands of standing stones for the milling mass of humanity! Because of this antisocial aversion to my fellow creatures, I harboured a secret fantasy. Somewhere, down in the hidden depths of what I like to think of as my subconscious, I had a clandestine ambition to explore ancient sites that were rarely trodden by the foot of man. My conscious mind, however, registered this secret urge as entirely unrealistic, transforming it into a whimsical source of amusement. I was left under no illusion that such an adventure was about as likely as discovering remote and uncharted regions of the planet on a discount package tour abroad.

Over the years, my attraction to the artefacts of the past had led me to haunt the local auctions, and a box of old books bought for a few pounds were always guaranteed to provide hours of amusement as I leafed through the musty pages. It was to such a saleroom bargain that I owe my adventures in the search for the almost-forgotten holy wells. A collection of cheap novels, dog-eared schoolbooks and religious tracts bought at a sale in Lostwithiel revealed a rare copy of 'Ancient and Holy Wells of Cornwall' by M. & L. Quiller Couch, published in 1894.

This book had been initiated by a bundle of notes discovered amongst various papers after the death of Thomas Quiller Couch, a 'desultory antiquary' in his words, a doctor from Bodmin, and father of the notable Sir Arthur Quiller Couch, known throughout the world as 'Q'. During his lifetime, the old wells had exerted a powerful fascination over him, and he had spent much of his spare time wandering the lanes of Cornwall in search of the neglected ruins. These sacred wells, he commented, were fast disappearing, and he felt it important that such knowledge as he could glean should be set down before the decaying structures vanished completely. And so, armed with 'wallet, pen and pencil', he proceeded to make many a pleasant pilgrimage to these ancient sites, 'Sweet journeys through lanes of flower and fern and moss, the air as redolent of health as the waters I was in search of'. The interest in such matters was obviously a family trait, for upon the discovery of these notes, the Misses M. & L. Quiller Couch decided to continue the researches started by Thomas, and eventually publish them as a book.

At first, it seemed little more than one of those delightful old volumes that evoke the somnolent charm of Victorian England. The comments on the state of the wells before the turn of the century suggested that there would be precious little to see after three-quarters of the twentieth century had done its best to change the countryside with modern farming methods and road improvements. But the ancient holy wells that had stood for so long were not so easily disposed of. On my travels as a photographer, I began idly to seek out some of the wells mentioned to see just what the last hundred years or so had brought, whether it be destruction or desuetude.

It was then that I realized that these old stone antiquities were alive as they had been for thousands of years, despite being almost entirely forgotten. Many were now dry, due to mining, the cutting of railway embankments, the draining of fields or natural causes, and the spirits that had once been venerated were no more. But they often lived on in the minds of the local people, although perhaps unconsciously. Many wells had been restored, which often destroyed any atmosphere of antiquity, but was certainly preferable to total destruction. It would seem a strange paradox that the natural sympathy of the trees and plants that swarm over old masonry often has little place in the minds of those who would preserve these monuments for posterity.

But a large number astounded me by their state of natural preservation, very similar to the descriptions in the Quiller Couch book. Gnarled and twisted trees grew out of the timeless masonry, moss and dripping ferns lined the interiors where a pellucid pool of pure water bubbled forth. Those wells which lay in the more secluded sanctuaries were always half-forgotten by the local people, who often had no idea whether they were still standing or had been torn down for use in farm buildings, a fate which befell many of the old stones.

The discovery that so many of these sphinx-like springs still existed after uncounted centuries spurred me to follow in Thomas Quiller Couch's footsteps, over a hundred years later. A mere twinkling in the eye of those spirits of the wells that were of such great age! As he armed himself with pad and pencil to record them for posterity, so I took advantage of modern technology and set off with cameras and tripod, maps and wellington boots. As I set off in search of these old shrines, they seemed little more than a collection of interesting, if obscure, antiquities. This attitude did not last for long, however. I soon became captivated by the magical atmosphere that seemed to hang like a cloud around some of the old remains, strange thoughts began to filter into the mind and I started to dwell on the meaning of these places. Slowly, I began to 'tune in' to the wells until some sort of sympathetic interchange seemed to take place. I would become lost in wondering about the vast ages of time that they had witnessed, and their intimate connections with countless generations of humanity. Some had watched our stone-age ancestors change from nomadic hunters to establish the foundations of a more settled society, others had stood implacably as the current of evolution caused great upheavals and change. Some had been founded, or re-discovered, by early Christian mystics in the most recent phase of the Earth's spiritual metamorphosis. But all had been closely bound up with human development down the ages, and their very obscurity is a refreshing change from our usual view of history, coloured as it is by centuries of politics and preconceptions.

So I became, as it were, immersed in wells! On closer inspection, they appear to have struck such a chord in the evolving human psyche that they have become a true archetype in our collective imagination. We habitually refer to the symbolism of the well in the metaphors of our everyday thought and speech, the very word 'well' in the sense of 'well-being', whilst seeming to have no connection with a watery hole in the ground, nevertheless implies good fortune, abundance, prosperity and a whole host of other connected ideas that can be traced back to the associations of our ancestors with such places. And who can resist to toss a coin into a well or fountain and make a wish? The very act connects you with a primitive urge, not understood by the conscious mind, but which is so deep in the sub-conscious that people do it automatically, without pausing to ask where the impulse springs from. The mesmeric medium of the rippling waters snaps its fingers at our psychic centres like some stage hypnotist, forcing us to react in some pre-ordained way.

And in my mind, the wells became a focus of history and prehistory that in some ways was apparently more valid than other such similar places. The megaliths possess a potent power from those early times. Ancient churches concentrate the mind on the cult of Christianity. The old wells, used by the ancient folk of the former and adapted by the followers of the latter, provide the missing link which connects us with our past.

This is no exhaustive survey. To tabulate each and every well was not my intention, which was just as well, for as I discovered when I had almost finished my adventure with the wells, two excellent little books have been produced by the Rev. A. Lane-Davies, one time vicar of St. Cleer, and later, J. Meyrick, listing most of the known wells and many that have long gone. Nevertheless, the remains of many old wells still lie awaiting rediscovery by the ardent well-hunter. And it is amazing to discover the extent of the proliferation of old wells in the county, whether they were places of ancient worship or of more mundane character being impossible to determine. But persistant enquiries in almost every town or village will lead to some obscure well, dimly remembered by the countryfolk or preserved in a place-name, often simply a roadside spring or boggy corner of a field, its presence and purposes long-lost. There is much interesting work to be done by someone who is drawn to searching out and listing the remaining wells, humble remains with no legend or story attached to them, but interesting in their own right. (The incurable well-seeker will find at the end of the book a short list of some of the lesser remains worth visiting).

There are also the more famous wells, well-kept and signposted, and much visited by modern pilgrims in the summer. Usually, more is known about these, their fame having come down the centuries and their embroidered myths surviving intact, with a little extra needlework around the fringes supplied by imaginative countryfolk. My approach was that of a rambling adventure, full of serious intent and sometimes paradoxical humour, accompanied by those passing anecdotes that may, in some strange way reflect the diverse images that rise to the surface of such an enterprise, a journey back through the ages, and the mind, of Man.

The quest was to seek the spirit of the wells, to observe impressions which were personal and subjective, yet which may give a feeling of the magical nature of these half-hidden places. And to photograph them in a sympathetic manner which may give a glimpse into the mysterious qualities of these sacred springs, once worshipped by our remote ancestors, and now only haunted by their ghosts.

A TIME-WORN GARGOYLE peers out from the side of a busy Bodmin street, bringing the waters of St. Guron's Well from the churchyard above. Because of the position of the ancient spring, rising amongst the gravestones below St. Petroc's Church, the waters have fallen out of favour in the past, when it was written 'It breedeth therefore little cause of marvaile that every general infection is here first admitted and last excluded'.

2

MAN, MEGALITHS
AND MAGIC

PRACTICALLY all the written records from which we draw our view of history are lessons in the art of early propaganda. Official scholars and commentators, invariably employed by the ruling elite, were commissioned to paint glowing images of the heroic deeds and aspirations of the current heirarchy, whilst exaggerating the barbarism and decadence of their enemies. Such ruthless censorship can be seen throughout history, from Roman accounts of Druidism, the destruction of Celtic records by Athelstan and the wholesale eradication of the 'Glory of Britain', the vast medieval libraries pillaged by Henry VIII, through to the book-burning of the Third Reich.

Consequently, it is a labyrinthine task to find the thread that leads back to a time when knowledge was passed on by word of mouth or obscure secret cipher. The days before official reports, when laws and customs were not dictated by edicts from a centralized source, were organized according to different principles. The time-hallowed oral teachings of a largely stable society may well have been a conscious decision by the Ancients not to commit the Wisdom to stone or parchment, and an effective attempt to prevent the manipulation of the minds of the masses by those who may be unworthy.

However, we live in a very different world today, and we see Reality, the one dream that we all share, through the eyes of scientists and academics who often have a vested interest in maintaining a rigid attitude. All too often, the prophets of such a world-view would have us believe that Magic, which has been the energizing core of society throughout its evolving religions, is no more than some ephemeral paranormal effect that may possibly be verified in some sterile laboratory on a good day. They view the enlightened approach of mystics and the societies they nurtured as no more than victims of their own self-delusion. It hardly needs to be pointed out that this is something of an unscientific attitude, where certain evidence is rejected because it does not fit neatly into current theories.

The antidote to this peculiarly modern disease is an understanding of the magical nature of the Universe, a subtle invocation of the Ancient Mysteries. This is not to resurrect images of barbarous and ignorant people of the past, still a widely-held view based on centuries of misconception. It is more an attempt to see that their world was alive with forces which they comprehended in a direct manner, without philosophizing or trying to fit them into a pre-ordained intellectual pattern. There is a danger here, though, of falling in love with any wild speculative fancy simply because of its imaginative appeal. A taut tightrope has to be walked, strung between those professional sceptics who refuse to believe anything and the credulous mystery-mongers who will believe everything.

The surrealist artist Salvador Dali, penetrating the mysterious workings of the human mind, wrote 'Objectivity is but a snare, a delusion', thereby touching the perennial problem that so far has separated scientists and mystics. One thing, though, must be accepted as we become more enlightened about our ancestors. The myth of ignorant savages behaving more like demons of the pit than human beings must be dumped in the dustbin of history along with the cranium of Piltdown Man. I recall bellowing with laughter at an artist's impression of how the Neolithic natives brought the giant bluestones to Stonehenge, illustrated on the cover of the guidebook for the elucidation of visitors to that noble edifice. Dirty, ragged savages clung desperately to a crude raft in the teeth of a gale, a vast stone tied to a rough collection of logs that were, no doubt, lashed together by the stone-age equivalent of baler twine. The whole image was ridiculous in the extreme.

Fortunately, we are now beginning to accept that whilst savagery existed then as it exists now, the heirarchy of these early cultures were men and women of deep learning and sophistication, an image that, with all our conditioning to the contrary, is one that we can comprehend only with extreme difficulty.

The science of astro-archaeology is yet young, even though it is almost a century since the real groundwork was laid by the pioneering research of Sir Norman Lockyer. Since then, the inertia of orthodox science has slowly and painfully given way to a grudging acceptance of the importance of this work, and the meticulous examination of the old standing stones by such figures as Alexander Thom and Gerald Hawkins. Professor Thom, the undisputed expert in his field, has shown that the people of the early cultures responsible for the stone circles and monoliths were of somewhat baffling sophistication, capable of creating exceedingly intricate structures of stone and earth that demonstrate their deep understanding of geometry, mathematics and astronomy. Professor Hawkins has shown that Stonehenge is, amongst other things, a vast astronomical computer using a base of 19 years (the system used by the Druids) to bring solar and lunar cycles into synchronization, besides other more esoteric purposes. And John Michell, in 'The Old Stones of Land's End' proves that the standing stones of West Cornwall are all that remains of a complex network of structures that are aligned with 'rifle-barrel accuracy'. The image of

ON THE BLEAK SLOPES OF ROUGHTOR, on the edge of Bodmin Moor, there is little to show that this place was once a highly-populated centre of Neolithic culture. Scattered remains of hut-circles and stone enclosures are scant testimony to the habitation of our ancestors, and a stone circle and holy well are all that remain of their Earth shrines.

the crude, uncomprehending ape-man is demonstrably absurd.

It seems that a synthesis of science, skill, superb craftsmanship and magical knowledge gave rise to the enigmas of the past which we cannot understand because we are ignorant of some of the basic elements, notably those pertaining to the magic and mysticism of the old religions. Yet there are many mysteries which are acknowledged, even if we cannot comprehend their purpose. The existence of ley lines, or alignments of ancient sacred sites, after years of research, cannot now be in doubt. It is their function that is currently in question. Those who may scoff at the phenomenon of dowsing, or divining hidden objects, underground water and subtle energies, might be intrigued to know that the British Army have a Sappers division who are trained to dowse for mines, and that the Thames Water Board send their staff to night-school to help develop the faculty of this very mysterious, but awesomely practical, innate power of the human mind. Scientists around the world daily take measurements of the fluctuating magnetic field of the Earth as it is affected by sunspots, the phases of the moon and other planets and stars as well as various other factors. Yet the orthodox standpoint is to denigrate pioneer researchers who put forward the idea that this vortex of energy which cascades over the surface of the planet may well have a more subtle and potent effect on the Earth and its inhabitants. It seems increasingly likely, they claim, that such effects were understood by the Ancients, who manipulated the invisible forces for both practical and esoteric purposes with their vast structures of earth and stone.

And the myths that enshrine the archetypal images that come down to us across the abyss of the ages have been shown to have crucial significance for us by fearless searchers such as Carl Jung. The symbols that arise from the hidden depths of the mind are invariably all pervasive, their psychological power untarnished by great epochs of time. This is the stuff of Magic, the systematized remnants of a once Universal understanding that still inspires those whose minds quest for enlightenment. Many of the first true scientists such as Sir Isaac Newton or Nicolaus Copernicus, or even more recently such figures as Nikola Tesla, made their concept-shattering discoveries through revelation pondering the magical nature of the Universe.

This rejection of the 'occult' or 'hidden' aspect of existence, from which the conditions of our being arise, is now acknowledged by leading physicists as an unscientific approach. Matter and energy are part of the same spectrum, and basic forces behave as wave energies or particles depending on how they are observed, taking us right back to the claims of traditional mysticism. But such is the slow growth of understanding in this area that many of those spawned by orthodox academia will never admit it until they have devised a machine to measure all the unseen forces, and can register the hidden power of the mind on an encephalogram. Even then, they may cloak it all in incomprehensible jargon to make it inaccessible to ordinary people. The real test of the age is to acknowledge that science is only that part of mysticism which is measureable, or the imbalance may be too much for this old planet to bear.

St. Dominick Well in the last century

In looking at the remote past, it is necessary to also take account of archaic traditions, the most pervasive of which is the constantly-referred to legend of a long-lost Golden Age. This idea crops up again and again in all the diverse records of antiquity, as if they were all fragments of the same forgotten folk-memory. Throughout history, writers have referred to the widely-held belief that in some distant aeon, Mankind was possessed of a profound wisdom, lost secrets that were eradicated by some great cataclysm, eroded by progressive barbarianism, or a combination of the two. Is it possible that the remains of the megaliths and the Nature temples are the last visible remnants of our lost heritage? As we learn more about our ancestors, we may be somewhat surprised at the sheer efficacy of their beliefs and their view of the Universe, a paradigm that created a sympathetic balance between Nature and themselves that continued for millennia, something which the modern world cannot boast after a few mere centuries.

On something of a lighter note, the reader of this strange tome might occasionally experience the feeling of floating in a bottomless sea of purple prose, with great waves of colourful verbiage lapping like the swell of the

Cornish sea, distantly booming in the depths of some great sea-cavern. This is partly pure self-indulgence. Yet in describing the atmosphere of these haunting places, poetic imagery is the only literary approach that works, somehow describing intangible elements not through the words themselves, but by some misty infusion of meaning which may just trigger off the desired reaction. Hopefully, the reader will be caught up in the mood sufficiently to seek out the ancient sites in person, and experience the phenomenon of their strange ambience at first hand. If this is so, I most stridently urge the well-hunter to approach the countryside with humility and the respect due to the already much-abused landscape. It is, after all, the sympathetic rapport between humanity and the Earth that we are investigating, and with the devastating encroachment of building development and the destructive farming policy formulated by people who are obviously entirely ignorant of the individuality of local regions, we must preserve and protect the little that is left. Fortunately, much of Cornwall has escaped the worst ravages of twentieth-century greed (1988), but there is little room for complacency as the bulldozers and earth-movers grind away in the background.

At every twist and turn of the narrow Cornish lanes, new housing, holiday homes and the annihilation of trees and hedgerows are changing the face of this archaic land. In a spiral of bureaucratic lunacy, the traditional landscape is being irrevocably destroyed, whilst at the same time it is acknowledged that it is also the one timeless asset of the county and virtually the only hope for future prosperity. The intensely sad thing is that our modern civilization is suffocating exactly those raw elements that bring people to stand in awe of the wild beauty of it all. If allowed to continue unabated, we will certainly leave a despoiled landscape as our legacy to those who come after, who will surely be appalled at our baffling desecration.

The old Nature temples, in order to achieve any degree of sympathetic rapport, need to be approached with an attitude of almost child-like reverence, and this is necessarily bound up with country manners. Many of the wells are on private land, and although it often appears to the casual visitor that some countryside is 'open' or 'common', a simple enquiry at a nearby house will always inform whether this is the case, or where the owner can be found. Farmers are invariably helpful, and usually show a keen interest. When approached in a courteous manner, they often seem delighted that someone is asking about a well that they have sometimes played about when they were children, and despite the bad press that farmers sometimes get, which would be better directed at the politicians, they are often very much aware of the power of these places. But it is essential that they are left with the feeling that visitors to the wells are in sympathy with the countryside. It only takes one collection of raucous litter-louts to convince an otherwise co-operative farmer that he must be mistaken about the wisdom of encouraging visitors to his well. He wonders how they would feel if he acted antisocially in their back garden. And as one farmer told me, 'Tiz allus best to axe fust, as 'e offin keep a bull in that there field!'

3

IN THE
BEGINNING

HROUGHOUT the ages, the places that men have held Holy
have been bound up with the current of human evolution in a
sometimes subtle but potent manner. As with cities and
centres of learning, they are subject to the tide of events which
may carry them away altogether, or may merely veil them from
the mortal mind until they resurface with renewed purpose,
and the more important sacred sites of old still to this day draw countless
thousands of people seeking to wonder at their mysterious presence. It is
almost as if these places are charged with a subconscious magnetism that
appeals directly to the imaginative, magical level of the mind, attracting huge
numbers of people who may be only dimly aware of the real depth of the
gravitational pull. The old wells have seen many such changes of emphasis, all
linked in the chains of history with the continuing development of Homo
Sapiens. As it says in the 'I Ching'; 'Towns may come and towns may go, but
the well remains'.

The age of Man's appearance on the Earth is still a matter of wild speculation,
with archaeologists adapting their viewpoint with the increase of discoverable
data. Nobody knows when, or even if, apes took a great leap in the dark to
emerge transformed as Pithecanthropus Erectus. But something of great
significance caused Man to be singled out as the subject of some vast Celestial
experiment of bewildering complexity. As Ovid put it in his *Metamorphoses*;

> *All other creatures look down towards the Earth,*
> *But Man was given a face so that he might turn*
> *His eyes towards the stars and his gaze upon the sky.*

It is almost impossible for us today to have the slightest idea of how the
primitive mind viewed the environment, but the nature of the human mind is
such that the diverse phenomena of existence are inevitably seen as subject to
some great plan or purpose. This eternal quest to comprehend the underlying
order of the Cosmos is what distinguishes humans from animals, as we lurch

18

from one religious system to the next with an unslaked thirst. What is certain, then, is that the people whose hands skilfully fashioned barbed arrowheads and polished hammer-axes also possessed this outlook that is such an essential part of Man's make-up, that collection of ideas and beliefs which we commonly put under the heading of Religion. Not that our modern understanding of this word has any relevance to an all-encompassing concept where every single thing, both seen and unseen, were interdependent parts of an incomprehensible whole. In such a system, mountains and valleys, rivers, springs, trees and rocks were seen as specialized aspects of the Earth-force which gave rise to the existence of Man himself, and were each viewed as unique entities of a different order who had access to secrets of which Men were kept ignorant. The way to understanding, leading to increased power and knowledge, was to form a special rapport with these Nature-entities which not only strengthened the ties between the world of Nature and the primitive people, but also increased their awareness and development.

The worship of wells was one of the most potent forces in the primitive pantheon of tree, rock and spring; and the importance of water as the essence of life and the only naturally-occurring liquid was paramount in both material and spiritual terms.

Water had been the cradle of the earliest forms of life, and without it, no existence as we know it is possible. It created the oceans, the seas, the rains and the rivers and springs, the primary fluid that coursed through the veins of the Earth as it flows through the human body, eroding, decomposing, rejuvenating and stimulating new life in all its different aspects. As it cleanses the body so it continually refreshes the surface and depths of the planet, balancing the extremes of the other elemental forces. And to the mind of early man, it possessed other properties that were truly magical. It instantly took the shape of whatever receptacle held it, it could control the powerful destructive nature of Fire, and any small pool would reflect back a weird image of primitive features, in some way partaking of a usually unseen side of the early inhabitants of the primeval landscape. This reflective power must have seemed particularly significant to people who otherwise would have no idea how they appeared to the outside world, a powerful symbol of the godlike qualities inherent in the magic fluid.

That some of these wells, discovered by the early wandering peoples of the world, should stretch back into the remotest antiquity, then, is not difficult to understand. In a nomadic society as in the more settled civilizations to follow, where life changed exceedingly slowly for thousands of years, it must have occurred to later generations that these sites had already existed for an immense amount of time. We have little to evoke this great age of human evolution other than a few domestic and ritual implements and our imaginations. Perhaps the closest we can get to glimpsing how the mind of Man approached his world is by contemplating the moving cave paintings such as those at Lascaux in France, where early shamans would dress themselves in animal skins and recite primitive invocations in smoky caves, drawing symbolic effigies on the walls and projecting the mind into an Otherworld trance or spirit flight.

This primitive scenario would seem to have changed little for many thousands of years until a new and more advanced stone age society appeared through one of those evolutionary leaps that seem to surface throughout history. Whether these enigmatic people were the remains of some previous epoch that is so far away from us that only scraps of mythology remain is a matter of speculation. Many formative legends throughout the world tell of how the Gods lived amongst men and instructed them in the arts of existence. Even in later ages, it was commonly believed that these supernormal beings were responsible for the tuition of humanity, teaching them the control of the four elements and guiding Mankind positively along a chosen path. These divine beings have become deified in the religious mythologies of all races, and many of the great sages of antiquity refer to them directly, like Pythagoras' intriguing statement that it was '341 generations' since the Gods had dwelt among men. An amazingly concise comment from the great mathematician! Whatever the basis for these widely-held beliefs that permeate the psyche of Mankind, the Neolithic people approached their Cosmos with a new insight.

These pioneers appear to have arrived on these shores from Europe, although they may originally have come from lands far distant. Their approach was to subdue Nature, not in a tyrranical sense but with an empathy based on the essential animism of the Paleolithic experience. It was an evolutionary jump that introduced a new efficiency in the making of stone implements, resulting in their ability to clear large areas of forest where they could till the land and graze animals. Wild creatures were domesticated, crops were sown and reaped, and the people lived in the same place, giving a new focus for their more sophisticated traditions. The magic of their shamans moved away from the pursuit of animals to become increasingly bound up with the cycle of the seasons, strengthening that essential bond between the Human race and the Earth. The dictates of an annual calender immersed them in the rhythms of the Cosmos, the nodes of this endless round being Summer and Winter, Spring and Harvest. They set about building temples to the heavenly bodies, where they could venerate and observe the celestial movements, all the time expanding their consciousness of Creation.

With the arrival of the more settled, New Stone Age society, the land must have assumed a different character. No longer was it a wild landscape through which tribal man wandered in his annual pilgrimage to the places visited by his forefathers. The abodes of the Neolithic folk were permanent places, the foundations of their civilization and the fulcrum of their religious outlook. The veneration of trees, rocks and springs likewise assumed a central importance, providing a continuity that spans all ages, except perhaps the most recent.

Fortunately, we are now leaving behind the simplistic images of primitive savages that have been foisted upon us for generations. There was a time when you only had to mention the Stone Age to conjure up mental images of grubby, stinking, loathsome creatures clad in filthy animal skins, trudging through black bogs or huddled around some smoky fire in a thatched hovel. The reality, we are now beginning to realize, was very different. These people possessed a dignity in their way of life which is totally remote from our modern urban culture. Their religious festivals, synchronized to the crucial natural cycles, were high points of the year, involving the entire surrounding countryside, when people joined together in common purpose to venerate the Gods and Goddesses of Nature. Some of the most bewildering monuments that exist are from these times, from the Stripple Stones on the slopes of Hawk's Tor, one of the oldest structures in Cornwall, to the awesome grandeur of Silbury Hill and the Avebury complex.

The vibrant landscape in which these people lived would have struck us as almost a different world. Their temples and shrines which served as meeting-places as well as focal points for their sacred magic would not be the crumbling ruins that stir our imaginations today, but would have been kept immaculately in accordance with their divine purposes. The great stone circles would have possessed an electric atmosphere, terrestrial power points regularly charged by the powerful rituals organized by the priesthood in synchrony with the natural cycles of the Cosmos. These sacred sites, whether they be circles, monoliths or wells, would continue to pour out their potent beneficial influences into the surrounding countryside, stimulating fertility by the essential harmonisation of underlying Universal energies. By this conscious interaction with the forces of the Earth, a subtle and beautiful symbiosis was achieved, resulting in what would appear to us as an almost dream-like state of exquisite harmony.

In a few rare corners of the world even today, usually islands or places remote from civilization, it is possible to experience that strange intimacy of the land, where every tiny corner exudes an atmosphere of being lived in and lovingly tended by its inhabitants. This is certainly the case in the valleys of the Land's End peninsula and the Isles of Scilly where this feeling which must have once been universal still persists, as it does at many holy wells. The dwelling-places must have been hallowed by time, with small huddles of thatched huts surrounded by patchwork meadows and enclosures. Dotted about the landscape were the barrows, mounds and burial places of ancestors, timeless mounds with a guardian power over the fertility of this green land, enshrined in the myths and fables of their tribal cultures. Perhaps someone tending a sacred well would have heard the bubbling laughter of children carried on the breeze, and watched a distant thin spiral of woodsmoke thread its way past a crystalline moon towards the stars.

This must have been the scenario for much of the vast amount of time that we have inhabited the planet. The evolutionary changes wrought by technology such as metal-working, and its consequences of tribal warfare and new tools and machinery, are but a glimmer in an almost endless stretch of time. But change did come, slowly but surely, affecting the traditional ways of existence in a way that would have only been noticeable by succeeding generations rather than particular family groups, such was the slow stealth of evolutionary progress.

When the Beaker Folk arrived with their knowledge of a new magic, employing the power of Fire to forge the mystical art of metalworking, they heralded an increasing sophistication and constructed complex stone arrangements in what is known as the great Age of the Megaliths. The technological breakthrough into the era of metal-working introduced a period of change on the Earth and its inhabitants that still moves restlessly on. The Bronze Age traders from the cultural centres in the Mediterranean travelled widely in search of tin, copper and gold, galvanized by the latent nomadic instinct. The world was growing smaller, the cultures were subject to an intermingling of influences, and the basic animism that had developed from early times was becoming increasingly absorbed into an ethos of cosmopolitan complexity. And moving in, slowly at first, were a new breed of settlers called the Celts.

Then the relatively quiet evolution of the Bronze Age seems to have erupted in a cauldron of conflict as a flood of these new warriors descended on the inhabitants, wielding fearsome weapons made from a new, stronger metal. Warlike and quarrelsome, the Iron Age Celts conquered most of western Europe, settling in the West Country and building a comprehensive network of hill-forts, invariably on previous old sites, to protect their domain.

The artistic flair and dynamism of these invaders somehow produced a new momentum in the culture into which they were assimilated which remains to this day, preserved in the fierce independence of the Cornish and other Celtic descendents. But they did not eradicate the structure of belief of the original inhabitants, for their vision of the World was based on the same precepts, a pagan worship of the Earth Mother and her forces. And the more cataclysmic disturbances of invasion and war that play such a part in human life were always, not least for purely practical reasons, to take account of local customs. Despite the inevitable murder, looting and pillage that makes up the drama of history, the strangers who conquered the land knew that to successfully exercise dominion over the natives, it was essential to preserve the fabric of their society. They may seek to impose their own gods and cults on the local people, but the old sacred places, the shrines and temples that have been hallowed by time, remained as always. The character of the old gods may be moulded and shaped to reflect the attributes of the new, but the vast body of tradition remains essentially intact, drawing in the invaders themselves until they are absorbed in a subtle blend of the two.

Tribal warfare was common among the early Celts, some of whom collected the heads of their enemies and devoured their essential organs to imbue themselves with the vitality of the slain. The primitive barbarity of these people may appear to our eyes as the very essence of bloody savagery, but this is only one aspect of what was a complex and noble civilization, whose influence has come down to us despite the attempts made to stamp out the remnants of this age-old culture. Such is the potency of this phase of history that it impresses itself deeply into the human psyche and lives on in a myriad of ways, crystallizing in some of our everyday attitudes and superstitions. The word 'fortnight' reminds us that they reckoned their calendar by nights, not days, and the throwing of salt over the shoulder and the making of Corn Dollies all date back to these times, and still exert the Celtic influence.

The name of Cornwall (Kernow) itself may be derived, through the Celtic root CRN, from Cernunnos, the great Horned God of such power that the Christians later equated him with Satan, and this is the fearsome image that comes down to us today as the Horned God of the witches. His power must surely be immense to still be worshipped after two thousand years of the cruel persecution   of his followers. Other Celtic memories still linger on, with November the fifth marking one of the great Celtic fire festivals that has defied the centuries. November the first was the ancient festival of the dead, Samhain, symbolized by the burning of a human effigy. The night before, Hallowe'en, was marked by the lighting of enormous bonfires on the tops of tumuli and burial mounds, for tradition has it that the shades of the dead were intent on luring the living in to join them.

The old Midwinter Solstice celebrations are still with us as Christmas, with its yule log and mistletoe taking us back to the old days. The May-day feast of Beltane was a potent ritual across the face of the Earth as the inhabitants of the countryside welcomed the return of the Sun. The derivations of these powerful festivals are still alive in Cornwall, with the Padstow 'Obby 'Oss and the more sedate Helston Flora Dance attracting huge crowds of people, who must surely feel something strangely primitive stirring within their subconscious. All this and more testifies to the extraordinary tenacity of a system of belief in which the sacred wells were viewed by the Celtic priesthood as doors to the Otherworld. The old shrines were woven into the warp and weft of daily life, and were focal points for the Gods and Goddesses and the rites that invoked them, for the rise of the warlike Celts did not endanger the continuity of the old Nature-temples, although no doubt the magical properties associated with them were of a particularly dynamic type, reflecting their own aggressive stance.

Besides the curative, prophetic and magical properties of the waters, inherent as a gift from the Gods, the wells offered a connection between the living and the dead, for as far as the Celts were concerned, the dead were very much alive. They would burn letters to the deceased in the sure knowledge that they would be read by the spirit of the lost one, and could enter into direct communication through the medium of the trance state. Even debts were held to be payable in the next life, showing that the old adage 'Live now, pay later' may be far older than we normally suppose.

The early tribal cultures of the Celts, with their own brand of aggressive dynamism, laid the foundations of a society that provided fertile soil for the growth of an evolving phenomenon, a fresh impetus that incorporated the most enduring qualities of their civilization. At the same time as the warlike tribes began to merge with the landscape as if they had always been there, a corresponding merger took place between the Celtic heirarchy and the native priesthood. A new sense of purpose seems to have gripped the elite of their formidable society, burgeoning like a great oak that grows from a tiny acorn. The tribal traditions that had been passed down by word of mouth for countless centuries were to become the cornerstone of a more organized and cohesive Nature religion, the essence of the old ways distilled into a more potent formula. The mystical knowledge of early Celtic culture seems to have been absorbed in a manifestly practical manner by a powerful heirarchy of priest-magicians, inspired with great talent for leadership and organization, who we have come to know as the Druids.

PREHISTORIC PLACE. . . . The potent, primeval atmosphere of the subterranean shrine of Sancreed Holy Well exudes an air of extreme antiquity. The ruins of an old chapel stand above the well, at a spot that impresses the mind with a poignant mood of ancient sanctity, drawing us back to distant times.

4

THE DRUIDS

'Uplifted by searching into secret and sublime things'

HE Druidic priesthood were the guides, prophets and spiritual leaders of the heroic Celtic society, a fusion of the unique Celtic character with those traditions that seem to have originated in the more stable atmosphere of Neolithic times. In Cornwall, their formidable powers of organization had overruled the tribal differences to a great extent, for they were able to continue the use of the great network of stone circles, monoliths, mounds and cairns that stretch out across the moors in much the same way as successive previous generations, inheritors of a comprehensive body of magical lore. As we know from all the classical sources, their observations of the movements of the heavens were meticulous, the old circles and stones being amongst other things observation points for the crucial movements of the spheres which provided a natural rhythmic interchange between that which is above and that which is below, the famous Hermetic axiom that has pervaded magical thought throughout the ages. The imposing cairns found on the peak of practically every moorland tor must have given the landscape a unique quality, the stone mounds perhaps reminding the people of the great Pan-God Cernunnos, and so, through the Celtic derivation of the modern Cornish word carn (a rock-pile), giving the county its name.

Although it is necessary to sift through the propaganda of early observers, it is nevertheless remarkable to acknowledge the esteem in which they were held, and they were recognized by other cultures as possessing great wisdom and power. Various interpretations of the word 'Druid' include 'Wise man of the Oak', 'The Invoker', and 'Holy One'. That they were magicians, natural philosophers, masters of the elements and overseers of the Sun, Moon, Stars and the seasonal tides, has become apparent from every observer who had contact with them. As Lewis Spence comments in 'The Mysteries of Britain'; 'The probability is that they were at least the equals in scientific ability and general scholarship with the Egyptian priesthood of the closing centuries of the last pre-Christian millennium.' And the two civilizations had much more in common, for they were both centred on the cult of the Dead. The one great difference was that the priesthood of Ancient Egypt was largely bureaucratic, which is of great value to us as we decode their heiroglyphics recording all the minutiae of everyday life. The Druids, with their strictly oral tradition, supplemented occasionally with runes and sparse Ogham script, left us no such record of their mystical practices.

The magical wisdom which flowered during the heyday of the Druids, like that of their Egyptian counterparts, could well be the basis and root of what we revere today as science. Their knowledge of numerology, astrology, herbalism and alchemy was the seed which spawned our modern concepts of scientific enquiry, although to them these arts were not distinct classifications of physical phenomena, but interrelated aspects of the Universal Life-force. It looks increasingly likely today, with the modern physicists coming to exactly the same conclusions about the workings of the Universe as mystics have always maintained, that the magical arts which gave birth to mathematics, astronomy, medicine and chemistry, will eventually be re-united with them.

The classical writers who recorded their impressions of the Druids seem to have been somewhat perplexed by their unique nature. Both the Greeks and the Romans had highly structured, if effete, systems of religion, and from their extensive travels had first-hand experience of the religions of many lands. It would seem strange, then, that nowhere do they refer to the Druids as priests. Although they were obviously an elite priesthood, mediating between men and Gods, they were largely outside the experience of foreigners, whose priests were looked upon more as scribes and clerics. The Druids seem to have impressed observers as a dramatically different caste of magico-religious heirarchs, described by Ammianus Marcellinus as 'uplifted by searching into secret and sublime things', and by Caesar as 'occupied about things divine'.

Caesar also records a succinct description of their general Cosmology in 'De Bello Gallico', Book VI;

> 'As one of their leading dogmas, they inculcate this; that souls are not annihilated, but pass after death from one body to another, and they hold that by this teaching men are much encouraged to valour, through disregarding fear of death. They also discuss and impart to the young many things concerning the heavenly bodies and their movements, the size of the World and of our Earth, natural science, and of the influence and power of the immortal Gods.'

Their unique character seems in some ways to fire some imaginative recess of our collective mind, peopling our dreams with white-robed figures performing their divine rituals amongst the monoliths and sacred groves. Such visions have obsessed many of those who have immersed themselves in contemplation of this period of civilization, from the famous arch-Druids such as the Rev. William Stukeley and Iolo Morganwg through to the fanciful images of the romantic poets such as Alfred Tennyson and W. B. Yeats. Unfortunately, the theatrical nature of these images has blighted the popular image of the Druids, appearing to many less romantic types as a faintly ridiculous collection of perambulating pedagogues, bloated with self-importance, a mockery of the wise men of old. It is indeed unfortunate that such people, feeling the inner call to continue the ancient traditions that connect us with our unique heritage, should be seen as strangely quaint eccentrics out of touch with twentieth-century reality whilst their minds try to grasp the depth and scope of the Druid experience.

Caesar also noted that Britain was the birthplace and true home of the Druids, and perhaps partly due to geographic position, they were famous for their hospitality and genuine interest in travellers from foreign lands. Britain, and especially the West Country, was the crossroads of many various races, including those as far afield as Africa and the Mediterranean, and must have provided much trading in ideas and philosophy as well as goods.

They performed their rituals in the open, under the canopy of the stars. The Celtic buildings known as temples are invariably from Roman times, for the only appropriate place for worshipping Nature for the Druids was in the midst of it. Their sacred places were the circles and enclosures which had been venerated by countless generations of their ancestors, often on the banks of a river presided over by the Goddess of the waters, or at holy wells, openings in the body of the Earth Mother where the waters came bubbling up like the subconscious powers that they invoked.

Being priests of the trees, rocks and waters, a natural spring in a grove of oak or rowan would draw together the potent forces of the earthly and watery elements in a cauldron of primal power that could be harnessed in a rite of known efficacy. They were famous as diviners and prophets, hydromancy being one of their most powerful techniques. The foretelling of future events was honed to a fine art with the aid of the Nature gods and spirits, and even the very flow of water was looked upon as divine activity. Apart from the wells and the rivers, the standing stones, circles and sacred enclosures also had their connection with water, for these structures are almost invariably erected on top of, or around, a confluence of underground streams which can be detected by dowsers, often referred to by the strangely Druidic-sounding term of 'water-diviners', as if harbouring some distant memory of hydromancy. And it seems significant that the old tools of the dowser were always recommended as branches of hazel or willow, trees sacred to the Druids.

The Druid priests especially revered the weird piles of rock that guard the landscape from moorland tor and craggy cliff, impressing the shape of the surrounding countryside with their strange silhouettes. Such massive granite slabs, stacked irregularly and seemingly sculpted by Nature into the most startling forms, are frequently found throughout Cornwall protected by what appear to be fortifications and cliff-castles. Often thought to be purely defensive, it may well be that these walled enclosures were in fact originally constructed to protect the great stones themselves from the attentions of the common people in much the same way as the Egyptian temples restricted entry only to initiates. In later times, it is likely that such places of spiritual power were seized by invading forces as symbols of their command over the countryside, giving rise to the idea that they were no more than fortifications. But practically all of these enclosures are in such inaccessible places that the small number of men who could be contained in them would have been starved out rapidly, with no hope of escape.

Yet the great piles of rock that stand poised on the horizon possess other features that indicate the great reverence in which they were held. It is well-known that the Druids held in particular veneration those stones which were capable of rocking to and fro, the delicately poised logan stones which were said to pass judgement and indicate prophecies in true oracular fashion. But these awesome rocks frequently possess a remarkable feature that brings us right back to the ancient worship of water. The Cornish antiquary Dr. Borlase noticed the great profusion of what he called 'rock-basons' in the eighteenth century. All over the landscape of Cornwall, and particularly on the Isles of Scilly, the great rock-piles that defy wind and weather seem to be shaped by Nature with a great many of these shallow receptacles, some of which seem to be deliberately joined by channels chiselled into the rock so that the waters may flow from one to the other. Some are certainly not so shallow, and it is impossible to look at them, brimming with water from the heavens, without thinking that certain of these 'basons' have been deliberately widened and hollowed out. Such rock-chalices are particularly impressive at that most evocative of such structures, the Cheesewring. Cut into the great rock that overhangs from the largest pile inside the remarkable hill-top enclosure known as Stowes' Pound, a large hollow 'bason' flashes in the sunlight as the pure water brims over the stone. Slightly lower, other shallower receptacles are joined together with cut channels so that the water may flow freely from one to the other.

It seems that the Druids had a special place in their religious practices for those manifestations which were defiled as little as possible by contact with the Earth. This would explain the special significance attached to logan stones, which are only in contact with a tiny area of ground, the great rock-piles themselves, (the Cheesewring, for instance, is balanced on small slabs at the bottom which get progressively larger towards the top) and these very special 'heavenly holy wells', the Druids' fonts, where they could collect the pure waters from the heavens, undefiled by earthly contact, for their sacred and secret purposes.

The Celts had always associated flowing water and rivers with powerful feminine deities, and the names of most rivers today are derived from the ancient Goddesses who bestowed harmony and abundance on the countryside through which they passed. Along with the more specific tribal deities, they also worshipped those primal Gods whose origins reach back into the deepest levels of early Celtic history, perhaps deriving from the mixed influences of African, Indian and European prehistory. These included Belenos, Teutatis, Taranis, Esus, Epona and Cernunnos, the Gods of the old days. These often have correspondences with the gods of other cultures, as if they were all drawn from the same archetypal spectrum. Yet Cernunnos, the Pan-God of Nature, seems to have been central to Druidism. Traces of his worship were expunged first by the Romans and then by the Christians, who seized upon him as the very personification of their religion. They both projected upon him the image of Satan, seeking to extirpate the great God by aligning him with wickedness and evil, and to a large extent succeeded in only driving his worship underground. The witches, those descendents of the old religion who still share the remnants of the Druid wisdom in their knowledge of herbal medicine, occult power and second sight, still venerate this image as a potent symbol of the masculine, fertilizing force in Nature which balances the feminine energies of springs and rivers.

The power of the Druids as leaders of their people was based on practically every aspect of life, a testimony of their custodianship of the accumulated wisdom of the ages. As well as functioning as priests, they were the lawyers, doctors, artists and poets of their day. Strabo called them 'the most just of men', and from Caesar's descriptions we know they judged murderers and arbitrated in civil disputes, the punishments ranging from the banning of attendance at the rituals to being condemned to death, roasted alive in a huge wicker colossus. It would seem that the ritual killing of criminals was inextricably bound up with the concept of sacrifice, although at the peak of Druidic influence, there is no doubt that the victims, specially chosen for the rites of divine invocation, went proudly to the altar, fully aware of their fate.

It may well strike us today as barbaric in the extreme, but the reports of the blood-soaked altars were no doubt much exaggerated by Caesar's accounts of a culture that he deliberately portrayed as bloodthirsty and cruel in order to magnify as well as justify his own achievements. And, in the context of the ancient world, the Druids never wasted life. Every sacrifice was devoted to religious ritual with a specific purpose, and was a part of their high magic of rebirth and transmigration of the soul, the very essence of their beliefs. As Ward Rutherford succinctly points out in his book 'The Druids; Magicians of the West', it was typical of the Romans that Tacitus threw up his hands in horror at the tales of human sacrifice, whilst at the same time consigning the early Christians to be torn apart by starving lions in the name of entertainment.

Their obsession with the severing of heads is also abhorrent to the modern mind. The Celts had always cut off the heads of their victims, often mounting them on tall staves, as Herodotus tells us, above the chimney where they became guardians of the house. This may well have given rise to the later practice of adorning the roofs of churches and cathedrals with grotesque gargoyles. They believed, along with the Egyptians, that the spirit could leave and re-enter the body through the head, and that the cranium was the pivotal point of earthly existence. In their royal tombs, the Egyptians painted 'false doors' and eyes at the head of the sarcophagus to allow the migration of the spirit. The Druids would saw off the cranium above the eyebrows, clean the interior and line it with leather or sometimes gold, for use as a cup.

There is some strange connection between this trait of using skulls as drinking vessels and the old wells, and skull-cups have been found in wells in other parts of the country. Some of the wells in the Outer Hebrides actually have the word 'head' in their names, and the use of cranial goblets at curative wells gives an interesting insight into the Celtic mind, which obviously associated the human head with protective and restorative influences, and perhaps with the very preservation of life itself.

Despite our assumptions derived from the remaining remnants of this obscure time, and the ideas drawn from writers whose perspective was coloured by vested interests, it is virtually impossible for us to comprehend the Druidic experience. It may be that the more romantic visions of the Druids have a part to play in our understanding of the esoteric side of Celtic society, for the magico-religious rites that gave them their power are naturally more amenable to the poetic and inspirational approach than to lines of scientific enquiry. Yet what does shine through the grey mists of this period is an attitude that we would normally find totally perplexing, were we not to take account of the impressive scope of their world-view. Despite the attempts by the Romans to portray them as bestial barbarians to excuse their own cruelty, the Druids often appear to us as moral and just in the extreme, a compassionate society bolstered by a deep understanding of the 'Nature red in tooth and claw' principle. The Druids did not even imprison their debtors, as did the Romans, who were jealous of the power of the priests and bitter about their ineffectual attempts to seize it for themselves.

The pervading atmosphere of the heyday of the Druids seems to have been peculiarly responsive to another influence that was to change the face of the Western world. There would appear to be a strange paradox here, for the fierce independence of the Celts seems largely to have given way to the active development of a new gnosis that was eventually to replace the old religion. From the East burst a new religious principle that we may have expected the indiginous Europeans to have been strongly hostile to. And yet, amazingly, the precepts of what was a new religion were openly accepted, and the basic system of a new set of beliefs seems to have even been welcomed as a spur to human development, destined to eventually become fused with the ancient ways.

The new ideas of this flowering eastern faith seem to have found their way to Britain in a surprisingly short time, becoming absorbed into a new code of Earthly conduct and thriving in the uniquely fertile ambience of the place. If we knew nothing at all about the Druids, we would still be able to grasp a little of the flexibility and universality of their vision in the way that they recognized and encouraged what was a totally new code of ethics and religious observance. Such was the co-operation of the priesthood in this great transformation that Britain became the first country in the world to openly acknowledge its adoption of the new faith, while the Romans were persecuting the followers of the old and the new religions alike.

5

THE CULT OF
THE CHRIST

HE advent of Christianity established a new aeon whose early years are shrouded in proverbial mist. The popular view of this great shift from Druidism to the establishment of the earliest Mother Church of Christianity, as recorded by all the notable writers of the succeeding centuries, is one of the Christians versus the Pagans in a vast battle for the hearts and minds of the peoples of the western world. The reality, when divested of its encrustations of religious hysteria preached by generations of Victorian vicars, is far more enigmatic and thought-provoking. The beginnings of the new religion which still exerts a powerful subconscious effect on the way western civilization looks at the Universe after almost two thousand years has many curious features relevent to the islands of Britain.

It is, for instance, rather curious that one of the major divinities worshipped by the Druids was called Esus, or Hesus, which various writers assert was regarded almost as a coming Messiah, destined to herald a new religious and mystical current. Perhaps it is somewhat enlightening about the scope of the Druid experience to realize that rather than struggle against what would have appeared to have been a foreign and radical concept, they seem to have anticipated such an event and even paved the way for the coming of the new faith. It seems that in those early and obscure days, the Druid colleges, famous as repositories for the ancient Wisdom, evolved smoothly into Celtic Christian monasteries, as if privy to the destiny of human evolution. While it was still some time before the scholars of the fifth and sixth centuries were to record their views, which we depend upon today for so much of what we believe happened around this time, the old ways of passing on knowledge by word of mouth were slowly superceded, giving way to a new era of writings compiled and preserved by the elite of Celtic Christianity. While as always, these must inevitably be viewed as coloured by historical propaganda, the records of these early chroniclers throw much light on the attitude of the people at the time.

One of the lingering popular misconceptions that still persists here and there is that Christianity was brought to Britain by the missionary Augustine in 597 AD, despite all the evidence that the Roman Catholicism introduced at this time overwhelmed the unique purity of the Celtic concept of Christianity, politicising and manipulating the new faith in an attempt to smother the potentially explosive mixture of traditional Druid lore and fresh mystical revelation. If we peer back to the years immediately after the birth of Christ, deftly steering clear of whether this was a historical or legendary occurrence, it becomes apparent that the early gospels reached these Western Isles right at the beginning of the new aeon, and were openly accepted by the priests who were the spiritual heirarchy of the time.

Meanwhile, the Roman Empire, pursuing its militaristic policies of domination and exploitation, was staunchly pagan, and was obsessed with stamping out Christianity in a brutal and barbaric manner, desperate to undermine the threat to its authority. Whether the new cult was brought to these islands by missionaries or by those intimately involved in the momentous events that surrounded the legendary life of Christ is somewhat speculative, but it does seem that the people of the day were convinced that the followers of Christ did indeed travel here from the Holy Land and founded the Mother Church of the new religion at Glastonbury. The early accounts leave us in no doubt.

The ecclesiastical historian Eusebius, who lived 300 years before Augustine came to Britain, writes in his *'Chronica'*; *'The apostles passed beyond the Ocean to the Isles called the Britannic Isles'*, and Gildas, a sixth century monk again writing before Augustine, says; *'Meanwhile, these islands . . . . received the beams of light, that is the Holy precepts of Christ, the true Sun . . . . at the latter part, as we know, of the reign of Tiberius Caesar.'* Tiberius, was, of course, the reigning Roman Emperor when Christ was crucified, and Gildas' reference to 'as we know' would seem to indicate that in his day this was common knowledge. Of more recent origin, Sebellius states; *'Christianity was privately confessed elsewhere, but the first nation that proclaimed it as their religion, was Britain'*, and Archbishop Ussher wrote *'The British National Church was founded in AD 36, 160 years before heathen Rome confessed Christianity.'* So it appears fairly conclusive, if we are to believe the old chroniclers, of whom these are just a tiny selection, that the new religion did come to these islands at a time not remote from the death of Christ, and was immediately adopted and assimilated into existing Celtic traditions.

The early Culdee church would also seem to echo such a memory of Britain playing host to the disciples of the Nazarene. Some authorities believe that the term 'Culdich' from which we derive 'Culdee' can be translated as 'certain strangers', a rather curious term when we remember that the Druids were famous for their hospitality and dealings with travellers from far and wide. And a tenacious tradition throughout the West Country remembers the arrival of certain 'Judean refugees' who appeared on these shores in these early years. Are these references to those who were persecuted following the Ascension who found asylum in the Druidic colleges under Caractacus, King of the West Britons? Certainly the historical record leaves us with the definite idea that something of the kind occurred, with even Augustine himself writing *'In the Western confines of Britain there is a certain royal island of large extent, surrounded by water, abounding in all the beauties of nature and necessaries of life. (Glastonbury?) . . . . God beforehand acquainting them, found a Church constructed by no human art, but divinely constructed.'* Even such an authority as the Domesday book refers to *'Glastinbury, called the Secret of the Lord'* and exempts it from paying all tax accordingly.

Without penetrating too far into the mysteries of Glastonbury, it is perhaps a good opportunity to mention the most famous holy well in the land, and one which still draws large numbers of people who have heard about its magical and mystical virtues. The Chalice well, at the foot of the Tor, is an anciently sacred place, with underground structures built in true megalithic style which are more like something from the days of the Bronze Age than early Christianity. Its chalybeate (iron-bearing) waters stain the stones red in the way appropriate to such symbolism as the sacred chalice of the Holy Grail. However, another book would be necessary to explore these mysteries.

All the diverse evidence points to the ancient Britons being the first race to recognize Christ as the focal point of a new religion, stimulating them to become energetic pioneers of missionary work. And we also know that in these dawning years of the new faith, a stream of Celtic-Christian converts roamed throughout the islands, spreading out to carry the Word to the continent and beyond. How deep a root it had taken in the British Isles in these early centuries may be judged by a short extract from Chrysostum, patriarch of Constantinople from AD 347-407;

> *'The British Isles which are beyond the sea and which lie in the Ocean (the Atlantic) have received the virtue of the Word . . . . Though thou shouldest go to the Ocean, to the British Isles, there thou shouldest hear all men everywhere discussing matters out of the scriptures with another voice indeed, but not with another faith. With a different tongue, but the same judgement'.*

To a great extent, the old and the new faiths co-existed in the more tribal regions, as the slow processes of transformation and integration moved gradually forward. At this time, before the Romans were themselves to carry the banner of the new beliefs, they were to persecute the practitioners of the ancient arts and the followers of the new faith with equal vigour, and yet they only succeeded in driving both underground. There is a corpus of circumstantial evidence to suggest that the Druids and the early Christians, drawn together in the fight against a common enemy, spent centuries assimilating certain facets of both viewpoints in a synthesis of Christian myth and Celtic magic that comes down to us today enshrined in the legendary tales of King Arthur, the once and future King. The heroic exploits of the great magician Merlin, surely the most powerful of Druidic sages, and the Christ-like figure of the solar King Arthur are the central core of a hidden wisdom that was added to by later, Medieval chroniclers in an attempt to align the stories even further. The twelve places at the round table with their associated personalities and the twelve apostles obviously share the same sympathetic symbolism, and the whole mythology is overlaid with concepts of Christian purity and Celtic chivalry in a cosmopolitan blend of unique magical lore that appeals directly to the remnants of that Celtic imagination that is hidden under the conscious mind.

It was in 410 AD that Rome finally gave notice that it could no longer support its forces in Britain, and after 360 years, a number that would have been strangely significant to the Druids, the Roman legions withdrew, much to the alarm of the inhabitants who were being subjected to the bloody and barbarous attacks of Saxon raiders.

History tells us that the Romans marked their final moves in subjugating the major Celtic territories by attacking the Druidic centre on the Holy Island of Anglesey, after which the Druids and their influence appears to have declined. But the new cult of the Christ was continually absorbing the remnants of the Wise Men of the Oak, and in its wake a fresh impetus of well-worship blossomed as the mystics and hermits of Christianity drew together the wisdom of the past and the inspiration of the present in what is commonly known as the Age of the Saints.

Caught up in the current of a great religious metamorphosis, the early Christian followers emulated the old precedent of their Celtic precursors by building their new temples and oratories on previously sacred spots, those special places on the surface of the Earth that had always been intuitively understood to possess some special, inspirational quality. Sometimes, a crude church or chapel, often constructed in the earliest days out of wattle and daub, was erected alongside a holy well, or in certain situations, directly on top. Many of our churches and cathedrals have holy wells still rising beneath the ancient flagstones, which serves to impress us with the timeless continuity of these old shrines. Dowsers, who possess the mysterious gift of being able to detect the flow of energy that surrounds these underground streams, often find that there is a conjunction of these springs under the building, sometimes directly beneath the altar. The first Christians combined in a particularly expedient manner their own doctrine of baptism with the more ancient ideas of cleansing and rejuvenation, and the extreme age of many church fonts demonstrates the practical side of this. The wells of old were brought inside these temples to the new religion, the holy water contained in a bowl hewn from a solid piece of rock.

Those shrines that did not attract a new church often gave rise to small chapels, hermitages or oratories which provided a more orthodox place of worship for the newly-converted pilgrims. But the arrival of the Cult of the Christ did nothing to reduce the time-honoured popularity of these places, for with the ensuing fervour of a new age, people were caught up in the emotions of a great revival. Attempts were made, however, to stamp out the old well-worship where the natives refused to admit the new faith, and stringent laws were passed by Athelstan and the Saxons forbidding their use in pagan rituals. These, though, were never really effective against the traditions of millennia, and although similar laws were in operation right up until 1242, such legal restrictions are a classic example that ultimately, legislation can never control the hearts and minds of humanity. That this did little to stem the tide of well-worship is seen by the number of Celtic saints who not only adopted existing springs but founded new wells with the inspiration of their fresh mystical insight. Even today, the sheer abundance of wells testifies to the durability of the old Nature religion and the lingering echo of it that lies buried deep within the human psyche.

The early centuries of Christianity saw a time of slow transformation as the rural inhabitants of the countryside found that their old animism was gradually absorbed into the new ideas, the tiny well-chapels, though often as crude and simple as the shrines of the old religion, becoming the focal point of the symbolic rebirth of old ways in the rite of baptism. Their lives continued much as before, with little change in the annual rhythm that ordered the lives of an agrarian people. The ancient rituals of celebration and festival that marked the passage of the Sun through the constellations and which provided the anchor-points of the Celtic year were somehow implanted in the very land itself, rooted in the collective make-up of an entire race. Perhaps the rites and reorientation of pure, early Christianity had a purifying effect on the degenerate attitudes of a superstitious paganism, a religion so ancient that the freshness of its youth was long lost in the mists of prehistory.

The practices associated with many of the wells and other ancient shrines may well have been corrupt in the eyes of the new order, but here history blinds us to the great unifying nature of the widespread beliefs, which penetrated into the very soul of the current civilization. The Romans, in their rejection of their own brand of paganism, sought to represent the idigenous priesthood as steeped in degenerate magical practices, encouraging lurid stories of rampant debaucheries and brutal blood-letting. Eager to consolidate their crumbling empire, they played their part in the vista of human development by a vast attempt to draw together the frayed threads of their world by the expedient introduction of the new faith. This affirmation of a new religious principle, the cult of Christ as the son of God, was enforced throughout the lands of their dominion.

The political impact of such a maneouvre was felt throughout the world. Opposition was routed and champions of the new faith were supported in the most enthusiastic manner. Holy writings were commissioned to appeal to the varying temperaments of their subjects, and such was the success of the campaign that the power over vast tracts of the Earth has remained centralized in Rome for practically two thousand years. But beneath the purely historical view of events, there is the feeling that the entire enterprise was merely a physical reflection of an evolutionary change taking place at a deeper level, the Christian saints and mystics sparking off a rejuvenation of the spiritual core of humanity, a rebirth of collective consciousness.

Yet Christianity also allowed overwhelming power to be wielded over the minds of millions of remote subjects. A succession of endless dictates from

Rome exercised uncompromising political power over the thought of the world, mental fetters that still shackle us to this day. But the immediate effect of this profound transformation was one of renewal. The old Nature religions were subject to an influx of new ideas, new values, and a gradual transition from pagan rites to Christian beliefs was set in motion that eventually affected the daily lives of practically all the inhabitants of the countryside.

Pope Gregory, in a letter of 601 AD, gives us an insight into the Roman attitude to the problem of converting the pagan masses just before he was to visit Britain;

> 'When (by God's help) you come to our most reverend brother, Bishop Augustine, I want you to tell him how earnestly I have been pondering over the affairs of the English; I have come to the conclusion that the temples of the idols in England should not on any account be destroyed. Augustine must smash the idols but the temples themselves should be sprinkled with holy water and altars set up in them in which relics are to be enclosed. For we ought to take advantage of well-built temples by purifying them from devil-worship and dedicating them to the service of the true God.'

And so the stimulus of the new faith combined with the older ideas that were firmly grounded in ancient tradition to form an amalgam of the different religions. The new Christian festivals and feasts were purposely made to fall on the old pagan Holy days, and the new churches were often built on or near the site of a sacred tree or rock, as well as over a revered natural spring. Echoes of these times are often to be found in the local legends of such places, such as Trelill Holy Well near Helston. The myth surrounding the building of the well tells how the people wished to build Wendron Church at the site of the well, but in the dead of night crows (sacred creatures of Celtic Deity Bran the Blessed, and formerly thought by the common people to possibly contain the soul of King Arthur) removed every stone with the exception of the porch, which now forms the covering of the well. A dim recollection, perhaps, of the opposing forces of pagan and Christian powers battling for supremacy.

Where circumstances dictated that it was impractical to build a church directly on the spot, small chapels sprang up, and in the sanctuaries of Nature, remote and often far from the centres of collective mankind, these were usually crude and primitive buildings of wattle, daub and thatch, constructed by itinerant holy men searching for the mystical contact of the hidden realms. The most successful of these invariably attracted disciples, as well as a sometimes formidable reputation amongst the local people, according to the success of their spiritual quests. It was these saints of old who performed such a unique function in welding the essence of the old ways to the cult of the Nazarene across the changing landscape, guided by the intuitive insight that heralded a new phase of evolution.

As the fame of their mystical operations spread across the country, in much the same way that holy men still permeate the lands of the East with their enlightened presence, aspirants to the quest for knowledge were drawn to the saints in the search for hidden wisdom. These followers were the ones who perpetuated the stories issuing from the first hermits, erecting buildings of stone to commemorate the lives of the saints, and perhaps indulging (as encouraged by Pope Gregory) in thinly-veiled ancestor worship as in the old days, appealing to the spirit of the dead mystic for enlightenment. Groups of disciples would gather at these sacred places, building chapels and churches across the land, and sometimes founding a small religious community devoted to the Great Work. The names of these early saints come down to us like an unbroken thread, woven into the fabric of the local culture, their names lingering about the places of their habitation by some magical process of their own initiation.

The continuity of these ancient sacred sites, then, was not only guaranteed, but revitalized, becoming revered centres of devotion, the focal points of spiritual activity for the inhabitants of the surrounding countryside. The decaying remains of some of these old chapels may still survive near the porch of a country church, places where the old Nature religion meets the scriptural traditions of Christianity on anciently hallowed ground. The aura of sanctity that pervades the cloistered calm of a country churchyard may well be due to more than the Christian aspirations of the last eighty or so generations.

So throughout the length and breadth of the land, the time-hallowed sites and sacred springs were re-dedicated to Christian saints, their latent spiritual properties transferred to the latest in a long line of mystical tenants. The celebrations, rites and spells that had developed over many millennia were adapted and clothed in Christian imagery, moulded into a new formula for the new aeon, which is a witch's cauldron of ingredients from many diverse systems of belief. Lingering superstitions and the survival of such ancient rituals as the Padstow 'Obby 'Oss, which may well be a rite to the Celtic horse-goddess Epona, show how difficult the later Christians found it to stamp out the essential paganism of the Cornish and other Celtic factions. In fact they never really succeeded.

PEERING OUT FROM THE PAST, an ancient, pre-Christian effigy guards the waters of St. Anne's Well at Whitstone, and may well take us back to the time of the Druids and the great Nature-religions. It is remarkable that it still exists at all, especially in a country churchyard where idolatry is normally despised, for most of the remains of the pagan cultures were destroyed by the followers of the new faith.

6

ANCIENT RITES

There was a time when meadow, grove and stream,
The earth, and every common sight,
To me did seem
Apparelled in celestial light.

William Wordsworth - Ode;
Intimations of Immortality from
Recollections of Early Childhood.

HE precise reasons for the powerful attraction of the Holy Wells over so many generations of tribal, Celtic and Christian people will always be obscure to our modern minds, for we see the world through dramatically different eyes. Even the records upon which we base our entire judgement of the past are non-existent, for the old religions had little place for the written word. The customs and innate habits that were the foundation of their lives were passed on as part of an all-encompassing experience, watched over by the spiritual heirarchy of the time, whether it be shaman or Druid, priest or priestess. Whatever the traditions of this elite group within the community, their common root was a knowledge and understanding of the causative forces behind physical phenomena, the basis of all mystical and religious systems, Natural Magic.

In the early days of human development there seems to have existed a totally different relationship between the mind of man and its environment. The differentiation that clearly marks out the individual from his surroundings today was not so pronounced in those early times, and Man could feel the power of the essential 'one-ness' of things. This phase of the evolving mind can be experienced by those who delve into the mysterious workings of the human consciousness, and is recorded by mystics throughout history as the classic trance-state where the 'subject' and 'object' become one. In this higher state of awareness, knowledge which is normally concealed from the workings of the brain is made directly available through intuitive rapport, not a state to be argued about by the rational mind but one to be experienced. Because of this, even if we were able to travel back through time to carefully observe the rites and traditions of the Ancients, we would be very little the wiser. The underlying meaning of the laws that guided their lives would be veiled from our minds, tuned as they are to a much more superficial view of Creation.

In order to probe the innermost realms of life thousands of years ago, we need look no further than ourselves. Rationality and logical deduction have little relation to that part of the mind where all the experiences of the evolving human race are stored deep within, ready to reveal themselves to those who follow the traditional techniques of meditation and self-knowledge. As the human foetus develops, on the physical level, from two cells, through distinct stages of fish, amphibian and mammal, so the evolutionary memory is imprinted with recollections of ancient days, which can be glimpsed in flashes of meditative insight. To cultures where such techniques were understood and used commonly by the priesthood, our world would seem very shallow, for the natural magicians of old perceived, through the tried and tested traditional techniques handed down to them, an order of reality that is very different from our modern viewpoint. All the arcane systems of the world in some way contain the remnants of this lost world of subtle perception, known by the elite of the world's religions to be the well-spring of knowledge and power.

The sensual world seems plain enough to our modern eyes, with its infinite array of mysterious wonders to delight the senses of man with the glorious sights, sounds and smells of the natural Earth. But the hidden, invisible forces that actually give rise to these manifestations and which we today only dimly perceive were seen by the Ancients to be far more real than anything a man could eat or touch. The awareness of the elemental powers brought the priests and shamans into intimate contact with the underlying causes of physical phenomena, powers which are symbolically referred to as Fire, the thrusting creative force, Air, the flowing, ethereal medium, Water, the crucial fount of surging Life-force, and Earth, where the three elements combine to ground themselves in the tangible world of the senses.

The current state of our understanding of the vast system of anciently sacred places that stretches across the surface of the planet, channeling the flow of unseen forces in a bewildering attempt to balance the primeval powers, is still somewhat speculative. But the great corpus of evidence that still accrues daily can no longer leave us in any doubt that the people of previous ages devised a universal system of Earth-magic that unlocks the mysteries of pyramid and prehistoric trackway, stone circle, sacred mound and holy well, leaving us their temples and shrines scattered throughout the countries of the world as testimony to the ancient manipulation of terrestrial energies. It seems likely that these forces are similar in nature to the energy meridians used in acupuncture, but of accordingly greater potency, and that the bio-magnetic field surrounding the Earth, which is affected greatly by the phases of the Moon and the cycles of Sun-spots, is capable of surges of energy at certain times, triggered off by the influence of other great stars or nearby planets.

Recent years have seen something of a revolution in our understanding of megalithic science, revealing a depth of sophistication that we ourselves find difficult to comprehend. These revelations, the result of dedicated commitment by a small band of fiercely-independent individuals, are currently scorned by a large section of orthodox academia, who prefer to snigger smugly in their ivory towers, dismissing the whole idea of some anciently-understood Universal principle now lost, but slowly being re-discovered, as the ravings of the lunatic fringe. A predictable reaction, perhaps, to a time-bomb placed under the very foundations of the already tottering edifice of materialistic science. But the evidence from all corners of the world testifies to an ordered system of structures moulded in earth and stone, a planetary network of baffling complexity that was apparently devised, built and used by the people of old for purposes that seem very obscure to our modern viewpoint. Yet to judge from the vast scale of the system, such principles were once universally understood. The monuments of the past and the almost-forgotten traditions of practically every land are all that is left of the tantalizing Cosmology of the Ancients.

The rationale behind the intricacies of such a lost system of knowledge is exceedingly difficult for us to grasp, mainly due to the vast scope of the concept, which overwhelms the analytical mode of our modern minds. But as we focus on certain parts of the whole, the great rapport which the geomantic civilizations had with their universe begins to unfold. Cornwall is particularly rich in the remnants of the much-misunderstood cultures that were guided by forgotten principles. In 'The Old Stones of Land's End', John Michell shows that the circles and stones of the tiny Penwith peninsula are the fragments of a comprehensive network which are somewhat startling in the accuracy of their alignments. It seems that at one time, much of the country was covered in similar patterns of stone structures, each area unique and individual due to its particular place on the surface of the Earth, and yet a mere part of a network that stretched out across the ancient landscape. At the time of writing, more research and investigation into the ancient sites is in progress, which promises to shed crucial light on the pattern and purpose behind the old stones, and perhaps ultimately the meaning behind the baffling system of the Ancients.

The amnesia that mankind suffers from in this respect is not too surprising when we look at the current exploitative attitude towards the Earth. The evidence indicates that at some time so remote that we have no recollection of it whatever, a universal culture built and operated the Megalithic network, perhaps achieving such a state of harmony between Man and his environment that it is only dimly remembered in the widely-held belief, alluded to in the classical and religious writings of the world, of an antique 'Golden Age'. Some crucial event or change in attitude disturbed the delicately-preserved balance of such a time, and successive ages eroded the original understanding as the aeons passed, the knowledge and power of the old system preserved by the elite priesthood, until it was lost altogether, only to be recalled by the traditional worship of stones, sacred springs and the implacable continuity of anciently hallowed sites.

The awe-inspiring heritage left to us by the geomancers of old, who ordered this system and were responsible for the siting of Stonehenge and all the lesser such monuments that abound across the countryside, has a poetic feel about it that often seems distasteful to the scientific enquirer. This is because the subtle qualities evoked by the study of the Earth Mysteries appeals directly to the imaginative, poetic part of the mind, the very part that is developed and fine-tuned by mystics and magicians, and held by them to be the fount of Creative power. The natural sensitivity that wells up in the hearts of those who ponder the mysteries invariably brings an intuitive appreciation of the poignant delicacy of landscape and earthly order. The trained eye can discern the way the Ancients moulded the land to achieve maximum harmony of the elements by stimulating or re-directing the telluric currents that course over and through the surface of the planet. Even today, the casual explorer can occasionally be caught up in an enchanted dream on glimpsing the prominent tower of a distant church, as if the countryside is being guarded by a site of almost unimagineable antiquity.

Despite the fact that we have entirely forgotten the reasons for the origins of these sacred sites, many of them still emanate a strange power over the human mind, a lost dream where stone circles and monoliths, mounds and barrows, hilltop shrines and holy wells were utilized to create an intimate contact with the secret rhythms of the Cosmos. Fortunately, though, there is a relic of this world-wide system that can throw much light on the theory and practice behind the ancient Cosmology, even if our own memory has faded with the ages. The ancient knowledge is preserved in a body of lore that comes from China, the details of which are enshrined in the archaic Chinese art of Feng-Shui, which means, literally, Wind and Water.

The practice of this art over millennia has resulted in the legendary beauty of the Chinese landscape, a supreme example of Man living harmoniously with Nature. The techniques of Feng-Shui show unseen powers at work across the face of the Earth, which can be modified or enhanced by various methods. The bio-magnetic currents that flow over the countryside are sometimes stimulated by artificial structures placed at precise spots which are the natural fusion points of these energies, preserving a Cosmic interchange and balance. Human architecture and dwellings as well as pagodas and temples, are all sited according to the traditional principles of the art, which are highly complex and take into account the astrological as well as the terrestrial influences. Palaces, tombs and whole cities were sited in this manner by the Chinese geomancers, who employed the techniques of topography, calculation and dowsing to balance the Yin and Yang energy flows. The male, creative current (Yang) was traditionally symbolized as a dragon, a pervasive image that also dominates Western culture, and the female, receptive current (Yin) was represented by the 'White Tiger'. The natural paths of the Dragon are the high places and hills of the countryside, with the meandering paths of the White Tiger following the lowland valleys as a watercourse winds its way towards the sea. The geomancers could create a delicate harmony between the two opposing forces, shaping the surface of the Earth into a reflection of the Cosmic patterns created by the unceasing movement of stars and planets. As above, so below.

Towards the end of the nineteenth century, the English missionary E. J. Eitel recorded the beliefs behind Feng-Shui, and his observations from his years in China provide a remarkable insight into the complex techniques employed by the geomancers. In his book 'Feng Shui: Natural Science in China' (Trubner & Co. 1873), Eitel interprets the system that gave rise to the exquisite landscape depicted in Chinese painting as a form of Natural Alchemy, a planned fusion of the Yin and Yang forces that were obviously understood by the Ancients to have a profound effect on earthly life. The intricate complexity of the art, divined by its practitioners who were also required to be expert astrologers as well as geographers, is based, like the Universe itself, on the basic building blocks of Creation, the male and female polarities that pervade all phenomena. In this respect, Feng-Shui in many ways resembles the Chinese divinatory technique known as the I Ching, where the two archetypal symbols for Yin and Yang combine to form all the differing aspects of the Life-force in its 64 hexagrams. The two systems are, in fact, based on the same paradigm, not only a view of creation that runs through the whole of Chinese culture, but one that seems to be responsible for the enigmas of prehistory, and our great difficulty in comprehending their meaning and purpose. As Eitel summed up the raison d'etre of the art; 'The influence of the natural configuration of the ground is very powerful in its influence upon the destiny of men, but man may alter the natural configurations, and improve the aspects of any unfavourable locality.'

This system appears to have been world-wide in its scope, and throughout Britain and every other country, the legends and remnants of its operation persists. Sacred hills are invariably dedicated to Christian dragon-slaying saints, a memory of the men who harmonized the potent power of the dragon with the balancing feminine opposite, creating a powerful equipoise that reverberated throughout the countryside, and which seems to a great extent to still operate in unspoilt areas. Many of the old hills, often now with churches perched on top, possess natural springs which are the physical embodiment of the female force that balances the dragon power. Impressive examples such as Brentor, looking out across the hills of Dartmoor, have so much natural water rising to the surface that it has often proved very difficult to use the churchyard for burial in the past, as the graves fill continually with spring water.

As we rediscover the meaning of the mysterious Earth-magic practised for aeons by the inhabitants of the ancient world, we may well be amazed at the sheer power of the forces involved, which may possess a potency far greater than science is presently capable of imagining. The whole concept of Geomancy, the lost art, would seem to be somewhat crucial to our continued existence, being as it is a system of 'invisible ecology' which not only affects the land and those who live on it, but represents the living expression of Man's attitude to his environment. For those who are drawn into this mystery of mysteries, this book offers but a glimpse of the successive cultures and religions that, to a diminishing degree, understood the power of the ancient sacred places. The burgeoning revolution that this crucial field of thought now nurtures can be followed in the works of John Michell and others (see bibliography), especially the classic, almost legendary book 'The View over Atlantis', and evocative 'The Earth Spirit'.

But before moving on from the noble art of Feng-Shui, which in essence appears to be the secret source of much of the world's traditional mystical lore, one apparent anachronism needs to be looked at, and one which seems to be greatly concerned with the phenomenon of holy wells. There is one great difference in the landscapes of China and Britain, and the way the Wise Ones of old moulded it into an earthly representation of Cosmic harmony. The Chinese always tried to avoid straight lines in their countryside, a fact that created many problems with the introduction of railways. And yet, as we now understand from the pioneering work of Alfred Watkins and those that followed his vision of the aligned sites that are demonstrable throughout the land, the whole of Britain is criss-crossed by a network of intersecting straight lines, or leylines, deliberately created by early man.

This diversity of approach appears to lie in the unique characteristics of the consciousness of the respective inhabitants of China and Britain. The former possess a natural tendency towards the receptive, Yin polarity which is seen in the Oriental disposition to introspection and the meditative nature of their culture, and in the collective group consciousness of the race. So the introduction of straight lines would disturb the serpentine meanderings of the female force that flowed across the land. Britain and the West are, however, very different. A strong masculine and individualistic attitude has been the predominent archetype in western society, and it was this potent dragon power that was marked out by the stones, hills and mounds that still remain as testimony to the vast scale of this terrestrial engineering. But the dragon must be kept tethered to its balancing opposite, and it seems that the holy wells were sources of the feminine energy which smoothes out the paths of the dragon, preserving a subtle state of equilibrium that is noticeable to those of a sensitive nature in their atmosphere of deep tranquillity. And one is reminded of the numerous legends of dragons that lie asleep in the wells, which, if aroused, can bring catastrophe to the surrounding countryside. This natural essence, or spirit, seems to be the peculiar property of such springs, sought after and utilized by mystics and magicians through the ages. The many traditional tales of Celtic saints striking the ground with their staff to give rise to a holy well are legends of the same order as that of St. Michael and St. George, who slayed the dragon with their lances. The stories overlay the ancient memory that these places are in some way receptacles of the Cosmic breath, the vessels of a strange, forgotten natural alchemy.

The Cosmology of our ancestors was founded on a rapport with the rhythms of the Universe. The cyclic ebb and flow of the great tides that pulse through the planet not only influenced the land itself, but exerted a powerful effect over the minds of the people. At the peak of activity, the surrounding population were drawn to the old shrines where, dimly remembered in the details of archaic rites, they performed certain ceremonies designed to 'earth' the power in the resultant orgasm that took place between heaven and Earth. Successful rituals based on tradition and the experience of millennia resulted in a beneficent and beautiful harmony throughout the land. The wells, mounds, the very Earth itself, were indeed holy.

On a strictly local level, the people of old saw each particular place on the surface of the planet as a singular part of the network of energy flow that energized the area surrounding it, distilling the raw elemental forces into an essence containing its own peculiar properties, reflecting the unique relationship of the site with the trees, streams, rocks and other natural features of the surrounding countryside. The precise location of a natural spring, its waters of a unique composition of both chemical and ethereal characteristics, was seen as a magical flow of vital energy, in which were dissolved the essence of the spiritual properties of that particular place.

Consequently, holy wells are rarely found where water would actually be needed for drinking and other mundane purposes. The great majority are situated on the sides of, or at the bottom of, verdant valleys where sparkling streams abound. Some are to be found on bleak hills and cliff-tops, places that impress the imagination with the powerful evocative qualities which surround such places where Earth meets Sky.Living as they did, in the midst of the untamed elements, the countryfolk of previous cultures perceived such matters by direct intuition, realizing the reality of the hidden forces behind physical phenomena with the natural understanding of their uncluttered minds. The Earth was always regarded, until very recently when industrialization spawned a veil of separation between humans and their environment, as a living, breathing organism. As all bodies are subject to the daily, monthly and yearly cycles that are governed by the celestial spheres, so the planet itself pulses with the rhythms that pervade all earthly life. The complete identification of the planet with all the lesser creatures that live on its surface is an attitude that is somewhat foreign to our modern mode of thought, but nevertheless, the total interdependence of all the myriad inhabitants and the living planet itself was the realization that provided the central hub around which the ancient world revolved. They knew with a knowledge beyond reason that the Earth was an immense body, whose veins and arteries coursed with the life-blood of the planet, renewing and rejuvenating as it flowed ever onwards. And they saw that the fertility and destiny of people and planet were inextricably bound up with each other, an endless drama played out against the regular rhythmic backdrop of the changing seasons.

The crucial monthly cycle of fertility was intuitively recognized as being ruled over by the powerful influence of our closest celestial neighbour. The intense rhythmic effect of our silver satellite has, since the earliest times, been understood to exert its power over all life on Earth, from the tiniest creature to the greatest ocean, and the ceaseless round of the changing phases of the Moon as directly responsible for the fertility of both living creatures and the planet, for the ebb and flow of earthly tides is echoed in the menstruation of humans and animals. It is hardly surprising, then, that the flow of water from a sacred spring personified this great fertility aspect to the followers of the old religions, who by a sympathetic communion with the natural forces flowing through it believed they could exert a strong influence on the fecundity of both planet and inhabitants.

The traditional wisdom handed down through the ages taught that the holy wells were vital centres of renewal and regeneration, sparkling fountains of the surging Life-force where human beings could, by various arcane methods, tap the very essence of Life itself. The tribal fables and mystic legends that preserved the old knowledge were woven into the basic fabric of earlier cultures, continuing as an unbroken thread for many thousands of years until relatively recent times, when the once-bright threads of a living raiment gradually became faded and eventually crumbled into barely-visible remnants. These ancient teachings, inextricably connected with the immediate shrines and sacred places, were in the nature of parables which functioned on many different levels, fascinating the ordinary folk and enlightening the elders with their concealed truths. The vista for the epic myths, recounted in the bardic poems by those whose memories were specially trained for such marathon recitals, was a Universe existing on many different planes, which interpenetrated and spoke of a pervading mystical contact between the people and the Elemental forces. The inhabitants of the spirit-worlds of Nature, the faery realms of the Otherworld, were once much more familiar to humans, and the stories of their existence still linger on in Celtic regions.

What are classed as folk-memories and superstitions today are the dim recall of a time when the contact between humanity and the unseen spiritual forces was considerably more common. Deep in the collective unconscious of all races are persistant memories of the elemental entities which inhabit the hidden realms. And in the mystical traditions of the World, the gnomes, sylphs, salamanders and undines populate the Astral plane, performing the tasks appropriate to their particular elemental domains of Earth, Air, Fire and Water respectively. This ancient understanding of the elemental forces is currently scorned by academic science, whose devotees have usurped the term to describe their classification of the building blocks of the physical plane. But the original concept, still alive in the occult traditions of East and West, is one that recognizes the four formative streams of Cosmic energy that pour through the condensing planes of existence, interacting to create Life in all its myraid forms.

The crude human senses are not refined enough to penetrate this subtle sphere. The sensory organs can only decode a certain small facet of such diversity, feeding it into the brain computer where it can be realized and stored if necessary. But we know that the mystical lore of the World teaches of special rites and magical techniques that result in the contact of humans with the individualized streams of Universal energies. Modern urban man is so far removed from the Natural World that he has no direct knowledge of such forces, but the primitive people of old possessed a natural creative power of the imagination that gave them a far greater awareness, a trait that is still strong in the Celtic temperament. In Cornwall, as in Ireland, Wales and Scotland and any other vestiges of the old way of life, the faery representatives of the elemental realms are still remembered in the folk traditions of the piskies, gnomes, fairies, naiads, dryads and all the other 'little people'.

During the course of the annual cycle the times of solstice and equinox were celebrated in a mystic recognition of the changing pattern of the heavens, which brought about the seasonal tides on which all life depends. These primeval nodes of existence are so basic to the functioning of the planet that they still persist in modern society, marking the high-points and nadirs of the Sun cycle, little changed after countless millennia. But similar crucial rhythms of the celestial bodies were also recognized as affecting the countryside in a more localized fashion, concentrating pulses of energy into the fusion points on the Earth's surface. At certain phases of the Moon, or when there arose some critical relationship between the heavenly bodies which directly affected the flow of Earth-energies, these forces were at their most potent. Waves of unseen elemental energy would course across the landscape as the magnetic flux of the Earth reacted to the changing influences of the planets and stars. Cascading currents generated by the invisible interaction of the great bodies would cause the sacred shrines to assume a special potency as this power was concentrated at the old sites, drawing in the local people who knowingly channelled the pulsing energies in a magical rapport with Nature. Today, the Saint's Day or day of dedication of a particular well is a direct memory of these localized rituals, a quite remarkable testimony to the way the Earth is bound up with these vital cycles of Life.

These particular times, when the old sites are alive with the Cosmic Breath, were specially revered as the times when the priest or priestess could summon up the Nature forces in a particularly potent manner. Versed since childhood in the Mysteries, and trained by the 'hoary-headed eld of old' in the magical techniques, the initiate would thus dip into the mystical cauldron of inspiration, communicating with the concealed regions. The well-spirits, or Naiads, were particularly venerated as beings of great wisdom and secret knowledge, for they existed independently on a plane beyond our visible world, unrestricted by our mundane concepts of space and time. Communication with these levels of being gave access to knowledge of past, present and future, and the wells became the focus for such activities, famous in the time of the Druids as centres of hydromancy.

The rituals employed to such ends were similar in nature to those tribal rites still important to primitive peoples today, and the basis of the more sophisticated ceremonies of modern covens and occult societies. The clairvoyant who was to be the focus of the ritual, (often a priestess, for women are naturally more receptive to the mystic arts), was surrounded by the workings of a magical rite concentrated on the sacred shrine, with the assembled people chanting and drumming to create a rhythmic vortex of psychic energy. Lost in a heady invocation of the well-spirit, the mind of the medium would soar to a great crescendo of energized enthusiasm, leaping at the crucial moment into the trance state of the Otherworld.

The state of mystical reality that exists in this sphere of manifestation is incomprehensible to the conscious mind. It is a formative plane of higher vibration than the physical level, where the inhabitants and natural formations are moulded from the Astral Light of magical tradition. The rate of refined vibration is outside the experience of our senses, a transcendental state which can only be entered into by those who increase their own rate of vibration to the necessary pitch, usually by potent ritual. Returning from this other-worldly dream state of higher awareness, total recall of the events of the operation would be preserved in the mind of the participant. Back in the realms of subjective time and space, the knowledge gleaned from such a rite could have enormous significance for the local populace, and was interpreted by the elders as the divine direction in which they should guide their people, in the world of mundane consciousness, imprisoned by the intellect. For the Wise Ones of old received their revelations and shaped their society not by the deductions and tactics of the rational mind, recognized as merely a tool of the spirit, but by the intuitive awareness created by their magical rites, centred about their Nature shrines, the sacred groves, the rivers, mounds, trees, rocks and wells of antiquity.

7

HEALING WATERS

N THE eighteenth century, Franz Anton Mesmer made certain discoveries which were to reverberate throughout Western society. Ahead of its time, and consequently viciously attacked and dismissed by the orthodox thinkers of the day, his revelation of an unseen force which emanated from the bodies of humans and animals is yet to be adequately assimilated into the philosophy of twentieth-century science. He found that this strange influence also radiated from magnets, which could be used to heal certain disorders and produce other remarkable effects on the body and mind. He called this force 'Animal Magnetism'.

In his healing experiments, Mesmer noticed that this force could be transferred from magnets or other more 'highly-charged' people to those whose personal level of Animal Magnetism was depleted, causing various ailments and disorders. It seems that this could well be the rationale behind the effects caused by 'the laying on of hands', as this effectively channels the flow of power from an area of strong charge to one of lesser, in Nature's attempt to bring about balance. One of Mesmer's pupils, the Marquis de Puységur, later discovered that this magnetic fluid, transferable by various little-understood techniques, possessed other peculiar properties and could be directed by will. He found that certain subjects, touched by hand or magnet, would fall into a trance-like state in which many remarkable things were observed to occur under the direction of the person in control. The new art of Hypnotism has shown us many astounding insights into the workings of the human mind, and the previously unknown (by modern science) powers of the subconscious.

It appears that living creatures, and any substance capable of being 'charged' possess properties which are capable of intriguing interactions with other beings and materials. We are practically forced into the recognition that the traditional magical properties of various stones and metals are based on an invisible reality, one which was well understood and used by the people of ages past and only preserved in folklore and fragments of arcane wisdom.

As we know, the Earth is, like the other heavenly bodies, a vast magnet, with its poles and continuously fluctuating terrestrial flux flowing over the surface of the planet. The sheer size and scale of the earthly sphere is such that the inductive effect on a human being, at a place where such a force is concentrated, would seem to reproduce the phenomena observed by Mesmer and his followers, but to an accordingly vaster extent. A later investigator of such profound mysteries was Wilhelm Reich, predictably vilified by the Establishment, and who died in prison when he could have been working on ideas that may well have had far-reaching consequences for civilization. Reich found that he could accumulate what he called 'orgone energy' by certain techniques, and that this 'primordial life energy' streamed in concentrated form from various natural structures on the Earth, notably stones, trees, and especially WATER. All of a sudden, we are back in the world of animism, where the ancients venerated the primitive pantheon of tree, rock and spring.

Yet perhaps the most tantalizing property of 'Animal Magnetism' was the ability to put sensitive subjects into hypnotic trance, when a new world of almost limitless possibilities opens up for the human mind. In 1808, an investigator of Mesmer's magnetism put forward his conviction that it could also cause an effect that is variously described as Astral Projection or out-of-the-body experience. Other mesmerists believed that spiritual vision was imparted to those whose psychic centres were stimulated by the unseen force. The healing and psychic properties of holy wells seem to parallel many of the effects of this mysterious energy, which has been called by others Odic force or Vril, and perhaps we are close to the essential reason why the sacred springs were the focus of magical rites for by far the greater amount of time that humanity has inhabited the planet. They appear to be places where this force is concentrated, and can be tapped by those who understand its secrets. The force itself seems to be what mystics and magicians have always described as the Astral Light, a fluid, invisible essence that can be manipulated by the human will and capable of whatever the focussed imagination directs. In religious terms, it is pure spirit. When it cascades from a natural spring, it is Earth Spirit.

In the midst of these revelations, it is not surprising that for many thousands of years medical science was a half-priestly, half-magical power possessed by those who were traditionally taught the secret significance of the old shrines. The sacred power of healing, born out of long experience and arcane knowledge, was passed on by oral teachings in much the same way that the local myths and legends were perpetuated, with the common people very much aware of the power of the ancient places, but only the initiated versed in the hidden workings of the potent spiritual forces. Through their mystical insight into the formative workings of Nature, they were the guardians of the archaic lore which empowered them to conduct rites which could effect miraculous cures and even avert pestilence. The universal veneration of such places, still remembered in the folk-legends of the world, is but a faint echo of the once formidable power of the old shrines.

In many ways the healing and protective rituals were closely bound up with prophecy and divination. Offerings of goats or lambs milk, oil and produce were made in time-honoured ceremonies that were guided by the priest or priestess from the inner levels of perception, perhaps by the spirit of the well itself. At certain stages of human evolution, there is no doubt that the 'magical links' of such sacrifices took on a more extreme character. Yet it seems that the ceremonies which were attended by the ordinary folk eventually became committed to our collective psyche, and still lie deep within us. Tossing a coin into a wishing-well is a dim memory of those offerings to the well-spirits of long ago. In Victorian times, nearly all the holy wells had their collection of pins and other shiny objects glistening beneath the crystal waters.

Wonderful cures were also claimed by the Christian priests who took over the tenancy of the wells from their Celtic predecessors, some wells assuming great fame in Medieval times when the sick and ailing would flock to them seeking health and rejuvenation. Doubtless in many cases the early saints understood the secrets of the Earth Spirit that issued from the waters, and together with the unquestioning faith of simple folk, continued the tradition of miracles into historical times. The seemingly credulous superstitions of the countryfolk may well have played an important part in this, for as we take more note of the part the mind plays in the health of the body, we may well conclude that the much-vaunted properties of some wells was not simply idle, superstitious nonsense based on what we would call today good business.

As the waters course through the different strata of the crust of the Earth, the minerals with which it comes into contact dissolve in a way which gives each particular well a distinctive physical quality of its own, over and above the spiritual properties. Perhaps it is this which led to certain wells being famous for curing the halt and the lame, or some which were especially recommended for clear sight (strange that the word clairvoyance means exactly this), or the cure of rickets and the whole gamut of diseases that affect miserable humanity. By virtue of its tortuous travels beneath the surface of the planet, each sacred spring could endow benefits both mystical and medical. The bathing of deformed limbs or the immersion of the entire body to guarantee robust good health was common, and the Romans exploited this philosophy to great effect at their spas, which came to resemble vast commercial holy wells which pilgrims flocked to in their thousands. The waters which bubble to the surface at the spa town of Bath have penetrated so deep into the planet that not only are they hot from contact with the interior of the Earth, but it is estimated that they are at least 10,000 years old. The great veneration for such water, with all its inherent properties, is hardly surprising when we dwell on the matter.

The pagan Romans particularly revered such springs, and votive gifts were cast into the waters continuing a tradition that has been with us since the dawn of Man. Recent excavations at Bath have revealed a great wealth of offerings thrown into the spring, as layer after layer of gold coins and precious objects have been uncovered, mostly small effigies of the Goddess Diana, who ruled over the Moon and earthly tides.

Another system of 'magical linking' found great favour at particular shrines, and was more appropriate for the rural folk whose wealth was bound up in the basic needs of everyday life. The custom of tying rags to the surrounding bushes and trees of the spring is still followed today as can be seen by visitors to Madron Well, near Penzance. These rags are not left as offerings, but after being touched by the body of the believer, it is hoped that the disorder might be communicated to the rag, where it is healed by the power of the well. As the rag decays, so the disease leaves the body in the best traditions of sympathetic magic as practised by witches and wise women throughout the ages.

The efficacy of such curative wells is considerably enhanced at certain times of the year, in accordance with the changing nature of the Earth cycle. The dipping of limbs or bodies should take place on a certain day, at a certain time as the local custom dictates. No doubt the essential core of such rites and practices has been overlaid down the centuries by much simple superstition, but perhaps it is as well to take note anyway, and make sure instructions concerning whether the ceremony should be held in silence or with certain words of invocation are followed closely! Three would appear to be the significant number in such operations; three dips in the water, three walks backwards round the well, prayers said thrice. And May seems to be the favourite month, with its potent position in the calender as a symbol of rejuvenation and fertility, although some waters dispense their particular virtues more freely on Midsummer Day, some on the last day of the year, many on Ascension day or at Easter, and still others on Holy Thursday or the day sacred to the saint to which they are dedicated.

Miraculous cures would seem to be more than embroidered superstition. At Madron Well in 1640, the Bishop of Exeter testified to an event that sent the infirm clamouring to the shrine in the fervent hope of a cure for their ills. He wrote that a certain John Trelille, who had been forced to crawl on all fours for sixteen years, bathed in the waters and slept over the stream after experiencing a prophetic dream. Some days later he gradually became stronger and finally was completely cured of the knotted sinews of his limbs, and soon after he enlisted as a soldier in the King's Army, where he showed great stoutness of mind and body until he was killed at Lyme in Dorset in 1644. Many other well-attested cases are on record.

Others in search of the health-giving properties of the sacred springs were not so lucky. In the dark times of the Middle Ages, witches were not the only ones to be persecuted by the zeal of the Christian Church. In the days of Edgar and Henry the first, the idolatrous adorations of fountains or their saints were carried to such excess and attended by such gross abuses that well-worship was classed with augury and necromancy and strictly forbidden, and many were punished for seeking to commune with the spirits. As late as 1628, several offenders were summoned before the magistrates in Scotland for going to Christ's Well, 'to seek their health', and were ordered to do penance, and threatened with fines and imprisonment. But the simple Cornish folk at the other end of Britain were much more remote from such magisterial

Holy Well, Laneast

interference, and even until the turn of the century, weakly children from the St. Austell area were carried to be bathed in the waters of Menacuddle Well, and starched Victorian matrons were advising their charges to drink of its salubrious fluid.

In many ways, the superstition surrounding the curative properties of the wells needs to be viewed through the perspectives of prehistory to be understood more clearly. A medieval mother bathing the limbs of her sickly child in the healing waters is an image that is but a pale shadow of the original rites of old, although the watered-down knowledge of their former power may well have effected a degree of healing, especially if the crucial days were observed. The Natural magicians of ancient times used the sacred springs to connect with that aspect of the Life-force symbolized by the element of Water, the element that is the very medium of life, fertility and regeneration. So a particular well, charged by thousands of years of use, possesses a facility where those that follow can take advantage of its inherent properties, and encourage the healing aspect of its flowing forces to stream through their own frail bodies by a sort of magnetic induction. And then there is the innate unconscious knowledge of the power of such places, irrevocably lodged in the depths of our psyche, and which can turn on a tap to pour forth the necessary power in exactly the same way that an ordinary mortal can be capable of superhuman feats in certain extreme conditions.

So the legends that come down to us are invariably dim recollections of a past power, but a power nevertheless that can still be efficacious, sometimes even miraculous. Yet the Cornish maids dropping bent pins into a well to see who they would marry is a far cry from the Wise Ones of old who channelled their powers of divination into other levels of reality, observing the formative phenomena that had not yet materialized, and taking action accordingly. Still, the threads of the original purpose persists in people's minds, that of restoring harmony. The Christian mystics who founded or re-discovered the holy wells must have been guided because of their quest for equilibrium, intuitively aware of this need for the body as well as the spirit to be in a state of equipoise, a more noticeable physical property of the force flowing through the sacred waters.

That indefatigable researcher of the Earth-force, Guy Underwood, sheds much light on the potency of the wells in his book 'The Pattern of the Past'. He found that animals are naturally aware of what he termed 'blind springs', centres where underground water converges to produce spirals of energy that are detectable by dowsing. There seems little doubt that our ancestors were also very much aware of these manifestations of the Earth-force, for all prehistoric monuments are found to be enclosed by the spirals produced by one or more springs, which appear not only to have universally been held sacred but also as having some powerful healing and fertility properties (hence the traditional associations of such places with the curing of all sorts of ills and the stimulation of fecundity). He pointed out that as all farmers know, animals kept in enclosed places frequently attempt to break out when they are about to give birth. Further researches led him to discover that as far as he could deduce, all animals naturally choose to bear their offspring on these 'blind springs', and that geese and hens, when free, find such places to build their nests. Owls have their favourite roosts at such places, and rookeries are always built over groups of these springs. Horses, especially old 'pensioners', always have their favourite places where they stand and meditate over them, which often wears bare patches in the grass. Wherever possible, cattle always sleep on them, and it is apparent to those who seek out old stones and wells that cows tend to congregate at such places, often standing dramatically against the skyline on the tops of ancient mounds and barrows.

As Underwood remarks, animals and birds would not behave like this unless it were in some way beneficial to them, perhaps easing the labour of producing offspring, making them more healthy, or both. Other creatures simply seem to prefer such spots for their habitation or daily tasks, and we are reminded of the old legends where a saint founded a church or oratory after observing a pig or cow give birth. It would appear that the animal kindom, along with ancient Man, instinctively recognizes some innate power in these places, often invisible to the senses but in some way potent with the spiral serpent-energy essential for life and health. Stories of old campaigners sleeping rough tell that they always chose a spot where a cow had lain to prevent rheumatism.

As further evidence of the sensitivity of creatures to these 'blind springs', he points out that gnats seem to swarm over such spots, performing their circular dances as if in recognition of the cyclic energies involved. He tells of the somewhat amusing incidents that seem to hang around the spire of Salisbury Cathedral, the centre of which 'is precisely over a blind spring of great importance'. On various occasions during the last two centuries, the fire alarm has been sounded when columns of smoke have been seen swirling around the towering spire. On the last recorded occasion in June 1952, firemen climbed to the top of the 400-foot spire to discover that the smoke was a swarm of flying ants!

As for the effect of blind springs on fertility, Underwood discovered that mistletoe, the sacred plant of the Druids, was always to be found growing on blind springs, and never elsewhere. Yew trees (often to be found in old churchyards) were similarly found to be growing on such springs or nodes, as were isolated hawthorn trees, including the famous Glastonbury Thorn supposedly planted by Joseph of Arimathea. Those that seek out the old wells will frequently be amazed at how thorn trees grow directly out of the well-buildings in some obvious natural sympathy. Other trees, such as the solitary standing oaks, often of great age, that lend the English landscape such a poignant charm, are often similarly located, and trees that grow near these springs are often notable for the writhing and twisted appearance of their branches and roots. Yet again, we seem to be penetrating to a memory of the rapport between tree, rock and spring that was held both holy and health-giving by our ancestors, and which was invariably based on some natural law of which orthodox science is presently unaware, but has always been recognized by traditional mysticism as a manifestation of the Earth Spirit.

IN A MYSTERIOUS SEA-CAVERN . . . weird shapes, normally sunk in continual darkness, are
formed by the mineral-rich waters which drip down in the tiny cave above the well at Holywell
Bay, near Newquay. In the Middle Ages, it is recorded, people frequented the well 'In incredible
numbers, from countries far distant' in search of a miraculous cure, often leaving their crutches in
the cave, which is just big enough for a man to crawl into.

AN ECHO OF THE HOLY WELLS. . . . A Victorian drinking fountain stands at the side of a town street in the clay capital of St. Austell, its situation below the church reminiscent of many of the old wells.

PART TWO

8

IN SEARCH
OF THE WELLS

FTER much peering into the past, it is now time to find ourselves firmly back in the present. As we wander the lanes of Cornwall finding out what has become of the old wells, we may find the narrow country roads seething in the summer or desolate in the depths of the winter, when the county returns to its primeval aspect despite the myopic folly of planning authorities. But in this county the past and the present live side by side in a strange Cornish experience, and minutes after leaving your weird mechanical contraption it is easy to find yourself standing on the edge of prehistory.

The antique land that juts out defiantly into the Atlantic is a land on its own. It may appear to be geographically connected to the rest of Britain, but with its own peculiar history, landscape and character, it is steeped in the feeling that in many ways it is an isle in isolation. The people who are born within the bounds of the county, or those that choose to soak themselves in its rarefied atmosphere, are always aware of this sense of isolation, and even the visitor experiences a subtle, but distinct change of consciousness when crossing the border. Its remoteness has preserved in elemental aspic the prehistory of the area, and it stands as a timeless granite outcrop from which to view a world spawned by industrial and technological revolution. A curious, uniquely Cornish experience like looking through the wrong end of a telescope, everything in focus but distant and made trivial by perspective.

The landscape itself is largely of granite, one of the most ancient of rocks and a byword for endurance, hardness and inflexibility. This stubborn rigidity is reflected in the rugged, primitive countryside which refuses to acknowledge the transience of mere centuries. Nowhere else in Britain do so many monoliths, holy wells and stone circles abound to impress the mind with their mystic ambience. History, superstition, legend and magic hang heavy in the air around them, for Cornwall has always been thought of as a holy land and has in all ages been a centre for the spiritual quests of those who wish to experience Natural laws by direct knowledge. The tradition of holy men and hermits is reflected today in a new breed of settlers who intuitively sense some secret in the landscape, as if the very ground itself guards some ancient memory from the thin veneer of modern civilization. So the sacred spirit of the far West echos previous ages, when thickly-wooded dells, mountainous cliffs, tiny islands and rocky crags harboured Druids, hermits and early Celtic saints who left their imprint and their names upon the land. As the old saying goes; 'There are more saints in Cornwall than in heaven'.

Despite the fact that industrialization has destroyed the relationship we once had with Nature, our minds can be magnetized by the potent archetypal images found in mythology. The old Gods and their ways are in no way daunted by the juggernaut of our technology, for they are in reality aspects of our own inner selves, hidden sides of our own nature that can be summoned by those who seek within. King Arthur or Christ, the myths embody ideas that communicate directly with the hidden part of the mind, setting off a chain reaction of inner events. It is a matter of idiosyncratic individuality which myths are preferred, and the recorded history of Mankind is a torrid tale of those who would inflict their own myths upon others.

With myths and legends, then, it is each to their own. Some may be fascinated by the potency of the old Gods of the Celts, others may find their innermost nature soaring free in the quest for the Grail or enlightened by the contemplation of the life of Christ. It does not matter which system is adopted, only that it is the right system, the one that strikes a sympathetic chord deep in the consciousness. In looking at the holy wells of old, the legends are often an amalgam of early Pagan, Norse, Celtic and Christian beliefs, overlaid by the romanticism of medieval days and surrounded by the supersitions of simple folk. This does not invalidate these legendary tales, rather it frees the mind to pluck the resonant notes that reverberate around the mind. Where there are no legends, we are all the more free to enter the realms of our personal mythology, to sit and wonder at the fleeting images that condense and dissolve before our eyes, connecting us with other ages, other minds.

9

THE WELLS
OF THE NORTH

Of coracles and Kings—The parson who 'called down the Moon'—Ghosts, ghouls and old legends—A face from the distant past—a moorland murder—lost wells and buried villages

HE NORTH coast of Cornwall still has a remoteness about it, an elemental dramatic quality that appeals to the romantic spirit. The sheer cliffs fall away precipitously to the crashing Atlantic below, its giant breakers mouthing and mumbling among the boulders and tearing at the very structure of the land, great stratified rock platforms knotted and twisted by some unimagineable upheaval. As gentle as a lamb on a soft summer's day, but with all the combined ferocity of a whole host of mythical beasts in the winter, when the forces that shape the strange sculpture of the land are at their height, with nothing but sea and sky between these grey cliffs and the coast of America.

This most deadly stretch of the Cornish coast, where the ribs of fearsome granite teeth which strike out under the sea can reduce a large wooden ship to splinters in half-an-hour, did not seem to deter the missionary zeal of the early saints, who were greatly possessed by the idea of setting off for unknown lands, so legend relates, in their coracles. Guided perhaps by some celestial navigator, these frail figures in their tiny leather boats set off across the same seas that wrecked many commercial trading vessels, and it is likely that many were lost, never reaching these shores to immortalize themselves in fable.

The naked grandeur of this land was the setting for the arrival of a certain Morwenna, complete with coracle and a burning desire to devote herself to the contemplative religious life. She was the daughter of Brychan, King of Wales, who had the reputation of being the proud father of no less than twenty-three other children who forsook their homeland to become wandering ascetics in search of enlightenment. Tradition tells us that Morwenna settled in a cell on the cliffs at Morwenstow, the most northerly point in the county, from where she could glimpse the shape of her homeland on a clear day, and no doubt visit the other numerous members of her family who similarly inhabited the West Country. It was here, half-way down the bracken and gorse-covered cliff, that Morwenna tapped a natural spring issuing from the slate and founded *St.*

Morwenna's Well. Here she found inspiration amongst the turbulent tides of life, and as she lay dying in her brother Nectan's arms, she asked to be raised up so that her eyes might rest for the last time on her native Wales. And so, we are told, she died on Morwenstow cliff, looking out across the Severn Sea to the faint blue line of the Welsh mountains.

The legend of this early saint, with its poignant romanticism typical of medieval times, was flourishing in the twelfth century long after the supposed death of Morwenna in the fifth or sixth. And as it is inherent in the human condition that legends are often invented or adapted for a variety or reasons, it is likely that this version was tailored to fit in with the prevailing fashion of religious myth. Morwenna may well once have been an historically credible figure, a saint or hermetic priestess stretching back into Celtic culture, who was later attached to the story of King Brychan to conform to the current trend of the time. That there was originally a holy woman connected with this place who comes down to us with the name of Morwenna, though, cannot be in doubt. All of these old traditions have some basis in reality, for it is impossible to imagine that the local population would swallow a manufactured legend, cooked up with foreign ingredients for their unhesitating consumption.

Over a thousand years after Morwenna looked across the sea to her homeland, this wild part of the county attracted another visionary, the eccentric figure of Robert Stephen Hawker, who was similarly drawn to gazing out across the ocean lost in mystic meditation. The unorthodox cleric, who devoted more than forty years to the service of this remote parish, was a remarkable character who communicated freely with the literary giants of his day, and even infected Tennyson with his passionate enthusiasm for Celtic legend, which led to the Poet Laureate's 'Idylls of the King' and a revival of interest in the atmospheric north coast of Cornwall. John Michell casts a ray of sunlight onto the man's rare genius as he notes that 'His famous eccentricities were not just whimsical but expressions of his true character which was that of an old Celtic saint, one of the legendary fathers of Celtic Christianity as a reformation of the former Druid religion.' Hawker's life was no rural idyll, though, amongst the area's notorious tradition of smuggling, wrecking, violence and non-conformity. His natural wit and flair for poetry which led him to become world-famous as 'the Vicar of Morwenstow' was part of a complex character that recognized other orders of reality in Qabalistic symbols and the legendary associations of the past. It was he, clad beneath his formal attire in seaman's jersey and seaboots, who repaired the crumbling well and echoed the spirit of St. Morwenna by building 'Hawker's Hut' nearby from old ship's timbers, a place for poetry and meditation looking out towards the distant land of Wales.

The story of this curious folly gives a sharp insight into the character of Hawker, and his preoccupation with matters mystical. He very much respected the wisdom and lore of local witches, and he cultivated their friendship. One such old wise woman lived nearby and was called 'Old Cherry', and it was she who introduced Hawker to the antique art of 'calling down the moon'. She

LOOKING OUT OVER THE ATLANTIC is the small stone building of St. Morwenna's Well, half-way down a gorse-strewn cliff and looking like the entrance to some network of labyrinthine passages in the rock behind. Legend tells us that it was here that Morwenna died, gazing out across the Severn Sea to the thin blue line of the Welsh mountains.

chose the special spot, no doubt invoking various arcane or intuitive techniques, where the old Druid erected his hut from timbers washed ashore from the great number of wrecks that abounded in this part of North Cornwall. According to Cecil Williamson, who runs the fascinating 'Witches' Museum' a little further down the coast at Boscastle, 'calling down the moon' is a form of self-hypnosis or mesmerism long practiced by the witches of the West Country. The instructions are thus, for anyone who is inclined to try their luck along with Old Cherry, Parson Hawker or even, perhaps, St. Morwenna herself; When the moon is full, select a vantage point high upon a cliff top with a clear view of the moonlit sea and the moonbeams' path. Sit down, gaze at the moon intently and lower the gaze from the moon's face to the path of the moonlit sea. Trace it to the point where it goes out of sight under the sheer cliff, and as it goes out of view, the moon will come right up to you. After practice, the moon will appear to roll right up before you, when you can ask questions of it and enter into conversation.

To start with St. Morwenna's Well is to set the scene for some of the more remote wells, hidden as they are from the haunts of men. Half-way down the tangled gorse-strewn precipice of Vicarage cliff, it crouches in a small, open hollow that invites the full fury of the Atlantic weather. Standing beneath a great oak in the churchyard, an elderly resident of the parish leans on his rake and casts his mind back to his childhood. He had last seen the well when he was about six, he tells, but it is impossible to explain how to get to it for lack of distinguishing features. For many years it has been completely inaccessible, but recently the National Trust have cleared the tangle of thorns and thick undergrowth leading down to it. Crisp autumnal leaves flutter down to land at his feet as he describes the tortuous route with exaggerated gesticulations.

To find the well, you take the track that leads from the church through a kissing-gate and over a stile to the edge of the cliff face, treading in the footsteps of countless generations of people who have previously trod what a document of 1296 calls 'the ancient way'. A final stile is thoughtfully provided where you can lean against it and take in the breathtaking view, but instead of climbing the stile towards Hawker's Hut, you turn right and take the cliff edge for about fifty yards. Peering over the spiky gorse, a narrow and barely discernable path leads away down the cliff, recommended only for those who possess a firm foot. Elderly grandparents should be left at the top waiting for the wonders of St. Morwenna's Well to be related by the fearless explorer on his return.

Picking your way carefully among the sharp thorns, and gratefully resting against huge spongy cushions of sea pink, no sign of the old shrine presents itself to the mountaineer until the descent is complete, and the path comes to an abrupt end. There, peering out to a hazy horizon, is the small, slate-built well, looking like the tiny entrance to a network of mysterious labyrinthine passages in the cliff behind. The stonework encloses a pyramid-shaped triangular stone above the slate lintel, but sadly, the interior is now as dry and dusty as a saint's relics. The opening is just big enough to put your head in and examine the slate fragments that line the bed of the well, the reverberations of the Atlantic rollers below being concentrated by the acoustics of the tiny stone chamber. Water, water, everywhere, and never a drop to drink! Evidently about a hundred years ago the spring that fed the well worked itself through another stratum of slate, and sprang out of the sheer cliff some way down, to fall in a miniature cascade, a silver thread of lustrous water, into the sea below.

Hawker believed that on a green spot in the side of the valley stood a chapel to the old saint, visited by those who sought her sacred well. Somehow you can feel the presence of the Vicar himself as you immerse yourself in romantic reverie, here on the cliffs that were his regular haunt and the inspiration for his writings. And the mind is magnetized by the thought of the pilgrims through the ages that have sat at this spot, their backs against the cold stone of the well, looking towards Wales and thinking of the legend of St. Morwenna.

Resting on a spongy tuft of grass back at the top of the cliff, you can drink deep of the sharp sea air before striding off on level ground again, back in the direction of the church. Returning along 'the ancient way', the eye is drawn to the staring windows of Hawker's Victorian vicarage, with its curious Gothic chimney pots, and then to the tower of Morwenstow's Norman church, echoing the words of the Vicar's 'Morwennae Statio';

> *'Still points the tower, and pleads the bell;*
> *The solemn arches breathe in stone;*
> *Window and wall have lips to tell*
> *The mighty faith of days unknown.'*

There is reason to believe that as early as the sixth century, a Celtic oratory made of wattle and daub and thatched with reeds stood on this secluded site. Before that, perhaps a pagan shrine and holy well dating from an era when the land was densely forested, with lions, bears, wolves and reindeer roaming across the region, for crude Paleolithic implements have been dug up on this land. After that, the Neolithic people arrived from the continent, with their distinctive religion of the Great Goddess and their impressive array of megalithic monuments. And then the Celtic tribes of the Dumnonii and the Cornovii (literally, 'the people of the Horn'), driven westwards by the Britons, and left to inhabit a land that was to maintain a great degree of regional autonomy from both the Romans and the Saxons as a collection of tribal areas known as the Dumnonia. This is when the northernmost parish in the county becomes historically recognizable, for the Saxons reached the Devon-Cornwall border about 680 AD, already Christianized, and gave it the name of Morwenstow (the dwelling-place of Morwenna). Inside the imposing structure of the church, a Saxon font, oval and irregular and one of only three in Cornwall, is still used to contain the water from the parish's other holy well, appropriately dedicated to St. John the baptist.

Standing in the churchyard, amongst archaic Celtic crosses and the graves of shipwrecked sailors, you can just see the sturdy, small stone building over *St. John's Well*, tucked away in the corner of the old vicarage garden, now a private house with no public access. Hawker was a man of many moods, remembered for his lusty love of life, his devout works and also his intriguing idiosyncracies. In tending his flock, building a vicarage and school and undertaking that most thankless of tasks, 'the effort to do good against their will to our fellow men', he was relentless. And with his rumbustious sense of humour, it is not surprising that he is also remembered for taking his black pig for a walk, or lying on a rock, draped in seaweed and singing hymns to the bemused townsfolk of Bude as he tried to persuade them that he was, in fact, a mermaid.

He had his own superstitions and beliefs that permeated his approach to the past and armed him with a stubborn intransigence against those who would disrespectfully tread on the toes of our ancestors. He believed that he had once met a demon, and that Satan's autograph was to be found in the library of All Souls, Oxford. He also believed that there was a remarkable continuity about places with sacred associations, and that these spots were possessed of a strange life of their own. So, besides restoring the crumbling ruin of St. Morwenna's Well, he also fought to protect the virtue of St. John's well when Sir John Buller laid claim to its ownership, thereby giving the old well a place in legal history at Bodmin Assizes in 1843. Hawker invoked a clear reference to the well as far back as 1296, won the case, and thereafter made much play of the difference between Sir John's well and St. John's well.*

His interest in the well was more than purely that of historical precedence, though. All through the forty years or so of Hawker's incumbency, he would drink no other water than the pure, sparkling liquid from the natural spring at the bottom of his garden, and continued the tradition of using its water for baptisms, a rite which connected him with the remote past, and still persists to this day. He certainly knew a rare vintage when he tasted it, for the water is remarkably cool and pure, and he was moved to include the well in his flamboyant ecclesiastical poetry;

> 'They dream'd not in old Hebron, when the sound
> Went through the city, that the promised Son
> Was born to Zachary, and his name was John—
> They little thought that here, in this far ground,
> Beside the Severn Sea, that Hebrew child
> Would be a cherish'd memory of the Wild!
> Here, where the pulses of the Ocean bound
> Whole centuries away, while one meek cell,
> Built by the Fathers o'er a lonely well,
> Still breathes the Baptist's sweet remembrance round!
> A spring of silent waters, with his name
> That from the Angel's voice the music came,
> Here in the wilderness so faithful found,
> It freshens to this day the Levite's grassy mound.'

---

* It seems, though, that all the hot air during the court proceedings was a little too much for him, for during the case, he promptly fainted! He never went to court again.

THE WELL THAT WENT TO LAW. . . . . St. John's Well in Hawker's Vicarage garden at
Morwenstow. During his life, the Vicar, once described as having the true character of an old Celtic
saint, would drink no other water than from this well. At Bodmin Assizes in 1843, he fought off an
ownership claim by Sir John Buller, proving the Church's rightful claim to it, and thereafter
delighting in pointing out the difference between Sir John's Well and St. John's Well.

THE VICAR AND THE WELL. . . . Blight's sketch of St. John's Well with Hawker, at the time when the vicar and the artist were good friends.

Standing just by the main gate, the well gives an impression of stubborn solidity much like the Parson himself, surrounded by an air of great age, its dark stones dripping with lichen and moss. An old sketch made by the tragic Cornish artist and antiquary J. T. Blight, shows the well with the peripatetic parson himself, together with his walking-staff and dog. But it was often Blight's way to diminish the size of the figures in his sketches, thus making the monuments appear more impressive than in reality. The diminutive figure in the hat and clerical garb is at variance with what we know of Hawker, who was assuredly not one of Nature's 'little people', for we know that Robert Stephen Hawker was as stout in body as he was in spirit. But this sketch marks a poignant time in the life of Blight, whose star was in the ascendent at the time he visited the reclusive parson. The man who was to do so much in recording the antiquities of Cornwall for future generations was flattered by the overpowering enthusiasm of his eccentric friend, but later the two were to quarrel over a triviality that in those of a less sensitive nature would have been forgotten over a glass of good claret. They parted with Blight regarding him with a mixture of respect and admiration, until Hawker was pestered by a series of unfathomable letters from Bodmin Asylum, where the poor mad Blight raved incoherently for almost forty years until his death behind the grey, looming walls in January, 1911.

Further down the coast, beyond the town of Bude that is beloved of latter-day Sun worshippers and Limerick writers alike, lies the peaceful inland haven of Poundstock. At least the church and Medieval Gildhouse, both situated in a romantic dell that cries out for the description 'picturesque', is peaceful. Less than a mile away, cliffs up to four hundred feet tower above the rumbling ocean, and all around, wind-sculpted trees are bent like ancient figures, frozen by the howling wind. And yet, deep, sheltered valleys bordered by hilly pastureland provide a sudden contrast in sympathetic echo with the weather, which can change notoriously from day to day. Tennyson captured the mood of the moment in his 'Guinevere';

> *'But after tempest, when the long wave broke,*
> *All down the thundering shores of Bude and Bos,*
> *There came a day as still as heaven. . . .'*

There in a hollow, protected by rookery-laden trees, the leaning gravestones stare blankly at the cob and stone walls of the old Gildhouse, which itself stares back through blackened oak-mullioned windows and medieval doorways. Since the fourteenth century, this long, low building with an exquisite air of age about it has been used for many things. Built to house the masons working on the church, it later became a day-school, a library, a club-room and a poor-house, where rooms were to let to paupers at 'four to six shillings a year. Three males, five females.'

But the old walls have witnessed much revelry over the years when the parish guilds met there for their festivities. Nowadays the functions that are held there are a little more sedate, and the traditional fair day is still kept as it must have been for many centuries, perhaps stretching back unbroken into early Celtic times, a memory of the power of the annual rhythms over generations of countryfolk.

The place has a magic about it that is reminiscent of other spots associated with Celtic monks, the earliest tenants within our recall of a site that by its atmosphere is far, far older. The trickling waters of a stream flow under a tiny bridge, and the stone seat and cobbled floor of the lych-gate are worn smooth by time. Across the lane, an old well stands, its wooden door shut tight against this haunting scene. A few years ago, it possessed a rare charm, a mood of poignant decay that was totally in keeping with its surroundings. Sadly, now it has been rebuilt in a peculiar rustic style by a mason suffering from the delusion that if you throw a load of old stones and some cement into a concrete mixer, you, too, can restore an old well. A neat, slate roof aggravates the situation, with a lintel from some old granite arch, purloined from its original purpose, scowling at the indignity of it all.

There appears to be no legend attached to the well, but it is interesting to the well-hunter because of its superb setting, the aura of antiquity that surrounds the place, and its connection, along with Poundstock's more renowned holy well standing half-a-mile away, with the Celtic saint Neot. Famous for his holy well on the other side of Bodmin Moor, the dwarf-like figure of St. Neot could often be found deep in meditation at his favourite well, immersed up to the neck in its miraculous waters, sometime around the fifth or sixth century. Recently, however, it has been discovered that there was an ancient dedication of the church to St. Winwaloe, one of the most eminent Celtic saints of Brittany, who was accustomed to reciting the scriptures daily with his arms in the form of a cross, dressing in clothes made from goat hair, sleeping on bare boards with a stone pillow, and drinking only water or cider made of crab-apples.

It seems such a peaceful spot, yet in the Middle Ages the area was wild with pirates, wreckers, robbers and thieves, mostly drawn from the families of the surrounding nobility who made a profession out of lawlessness. And in opening the creaking church door to examine the holy water stoup near the font, you may just catch a glimpse of a wispy figure walking down the aisle. This would be Poundstock's resident ghost, the ethereal remains of William Penfound, clerk of the parish, who was hacked to death before the altar by the swords and cudgels of 'certain accomplices of Satan' in December 1357, and still continues, unwittingly, to perform his earthly tasks.

But up the hill from the church, beyond the ghostly outline of the tall treetops with their cackling rookery, a rough track leads away towards Widemouth Bay, indicated by a signpost pointing to the sea. The ancient trackway undulates away from the pinnacles of Poundstock church along a gentle ridge, looking out over a land that rolls and swells, until cliffs and sea appear to hang on the horizon. The hedgerows are a wild profusion of glistening greenery, the Sun scuds across the countryside, and a brooding calmness descends as the weather rests between spring rains.

Walking through the second gate on the right, and down the side of the valley takes you to the edge of a rough wood that borders a stream. Here, in cloistered seclusion, is *St. Neot's Well*, standing looking down into the trees, and walled around to protect it from cattle. Unfortunately, there is no gate, and this is good news for the cows who like to take a good look at the well from time to time. An interesting building stands in the noisy silence, filled with the sound of the wind in the trees, the chatter of birds and the cool trickling of water into the well. Latin mottoes are carved into the granite roof arch, surmounted by a stone cross. One of the carvings on the front is of a fish, that pervading symbol of the Age of Pisces, inaugurated two thousand years ago by the Nazarene who called himself 'the fisher of Men'. Or so the legend goes. But in this case the fish may owe its presence more than a little to the legend of St. Neot, who, the tale relates, was told by an angel that as long as he took only

WITHIN THE SOUND OF THE SEA. . . . St. Neot's Well at Poundstock, peaceful and secluded in an area of North Cornwall that was once wild with pirates, wreckers, robbers and thieves. The nearby church is still said to be haunted by the ghost of William Penfound, viciously murdered at the altar by 'certain accomplices of Satan' in 1357.

one fish at a time from his well, there would always be one there for the next time. This lesson in archaic ecology was, however, flouted by Neot's servant, who was fortunately allowed to restore the balance by miraculous means. A timeless, archetypal lesson that is related in detail in the story told of the well at St. Neot's village on Bodmin Moor.

However, unlike the more famous well on the moor, this one has been restored with a certain style. An old cross-hatched oak door leads to the water, a round, clear, gurgling pool built loosely behind with rounded stones that must have been brought from a nearby beach. The restoration, near the turn of the century, is just far enough away for the Cornish elements to have weathered and worn the masonry into a mood of natural empathy. The stone seats on either side of the well exhibit a cushion of greenery, growing from the earth that has washed down from the bank above. A young thorn tree grows stubbornly out from between two stones in the wall, and under it, a stone bench has been sympathetically place to look down into the woodland, dark with thin shafts of sunlight penetrating the twilight of the trees. In a recess in the well, an old metal cup hangs on the end of a rusty chain, having been used by many who would sip the cool and crisp waters. The pellucid tang of the draught I had supped from my cupped hands was still there as I wandered back along the old lane towards the pinnacles of the haunted church.

A few miles westwards, *St. Genny's Well* can be found half-submerged in a sloping green bank in front of the church. St. Genesius, whose abbreviated name is given to this place, was reputedly a Roman soldier who became sickened by war and violence and took up the supposedly less stressful life of a holy man, attracting widespread fame both here and on the continent. The well is a crude, stone-roofed building, its stones growing out of the Earth, and its waters brimming over three feet deep in winter. The level drops in the summer months, but in this respect it is a thousand times more efficient than the curious edifice which masquerades as the real Holy Well, found at the back of the church. The laws of misrepresentation and forgery were not so stringent when this peculiar monument was built. Down in the sunless gorge between the carved cliff and the church, rests, for posterity, a building of singular disposition. It bears the legend, despite the laws of libel; 'The Holy Well of St. Genny's. Circa 6th century. Restored 1927'. It was built, I was told by the present father of the parish, by the Vicar of the time, in the hope of attracting visitors to the church, who may like to sip the sacred waters in return for a small donation to the church organ fund or some such worthy cause. It is a monument either to his sense of humour or his canny nature. It stands, solid in well-built stone blocks, defying the scorn of onlookers. But it is dry for most months of the year.

ST. GENNY'S 'HOLY WELL'. built in 1927, and which, despite the laws of libel, masquerades as the original 6th century well, which actually stands in front of the church.

Inland from the chasms and cliffs of the North Cornish coast is a most beautiful well, sensitively restored and superb in its setting. *St. Anne's Well* at Whitstone has a delicate felicity about it and an aura of sanctity that seems to be due to more than its position below the churchyard, looking out across rolling acres of forestry and farmland. The impressively carved but worn stones that are the basis of its structure would appear to be far older than the fairly recent restoration at the latter part of the nineteenth century, and may, like the fluted cross on the top, have been brought from neighbouring churches or chapels, and erected by some sympathetic soul of unusually fine taste. The roof of the well is sunk into the bank behind and covered with grass and a profusion of wild flowers, and the whole building is framed by an old thorn tree growing in harmony with the ancient spring. Above the doorway, beneath a niche for an effigy, is carved 'Sancta Anna' in Gothic script, and inside, another niche is below a rough piece of carved slate that would appear to be unique amongst

Cornish wells, and which may connect us with a time before Christianity came to these parts.

This crude carving has about it a feeling of extreme age, and while it is tiny and roughly made, these attributes enhance the aura of such a strange effigy, looking out as it does above the sparkling waters of the well. It is unlike anything else encountered during the rambling search for the wells, an ancient face with two holes drilled for the eyes, a rectangular nose and a rough slit for the primitive mouth that breathes great antiquity. Could this be a rare pre-Christian idol from pagan times, a relic that escaped destruction at the hands of the early Christians? Could it in fact be an effigy of the spirit of the well itself, taking us back to the time of the legendary Tuatha De Danaan, or the People of Ana, after whom the place was perhaps originally named before the followers of Christ changed the name to St. Anna? We may never know. But here, the link with prehistory is tangible as the ancient face peers out at us, from the time, perhaps, of the Neolithic religion of the Great Goddess Ana. But the fact that it is there, an affront to any self-respecting Christian who despises idolatry, is a powerful enigma in itself. There are tales of miraculous cures in this churchyard which adds to the mystery.

Tasting the waters, they are superbly sweet, with emerald green weed growing profusely under a variety of ferns. Down in the valley, a buzzard hovers with its hawk eyes fixed far below, and as the church door creaks shut, the arresting sight of a huge monolithic bowl of granite which serves as the church font makes you stop and stare. Vast by any standards, it is carved around with the twisting vine and leaf motif reminiscent of Celtic and Druidic art with their writhing patterns drawn from Nature. Tradition has it that the name of the place is derived from a huge white stone, now serving as a foundation stone for the church. Walking back past the dead generations of villagers, there is a certain sharp poignancy about this secluded place that strikes to the very root of some forgotten recess of the mind, evoking a primitive harmony that is more rare than jewels.

Launceston, the ancient capital of Cornwall, is presided over by the towering but tiny silhouette of 'Castle Terrible'. Whichever way you approach it, as long as it is not from the modern bypass, it assumes a fairy-tale aspect that jumps straight out of some distant childhood memory like a pop-up picture book. Of course, the mind might well be attuned to more earthly matters if you have had to dice with the juggernauts and summer traffic on the new dual carriageway, but if you happen down that way during the winter, along the road used by pilgrims to and from the West for thousands of years, you will be lucky to see a rusty and ramshackle old farm truck, complete with mud-encrusted dog, bleating sheep and bits of trailing baler twine, rattling uncertainly from lane to lane.

The castle was one of the most feared in the Middle Ages, and it was here that the Quaker George Fox was imprisoned in 'Doomsdale' in the castle grounds. Cuthbert Mayne, a young Jesuit priest of 33, also tasted the horrors of 'Castle Terrible', before he was dragged from the darkness of the dungeon to face a jostling, jeering market day crowd who spat obscene abuse at the blinking, wraith-like figure of the faithful priest, who was then hauled off to the square to face the gibbet, the butcher's knives and the cauldron. As the crowd roared, his severed head was impaled on a spike for all to behold, and parts of his torso were taken to other West Country towns as a grim warning to all who would not acknowledge the 'True Faith'. Such was the fate of those whose consciences dictated that they followed the religion founded by the 'Prince of Peace' down the bloody centuries. But the hangman suffered from some meagre sort of Divine retribution when he went mad a month later.

The pleasant greens below the castle, the general hubbub of country folk meeting in the town on market day and standing around in small groups, are a long way away from these grisly memories. But being the ancient capital, the town has known many such notorious events. It was only in the 13th century that the name Launceston was applied to the town of Dunheved. Before, it was the name given to St. Stephens, itself at the top of a steep hill to the North-West, a place that had a flourishing monastery long before the Norman conquest and which even had its own mint in the time of Ethelred II. The only remnant of a holy well in the modern town is preserved on the Ordnance Survey map as the 'site of Maiden's well', a dim memory of Cornish maids looking for prophecy with their bent pins tossed into the now lost spring.

But there still exists a large well at *St. Stephens*. It stands down a country lane not far from the church, past a crossroads called 'Gallow's Hill', conjuring up visions of Cuthbert Mayne and creaking gibbets swinging in the wind. It is a heavy, ponderous building in a relaxing country setting, besides being just a few minutes walk from St. Stephens Hill, where the sound of the traffic battling up its steep slope sounds as if it is flowing across from another world. The background noise and distant bustling acitivity of Launceston is given an even greater distance by the sound of the birdsong and the overflowing well. The granite doorway appears to be much older than the rest of the building, made of a curious mixture of grey granite and local brown slate. Above and behind the building is a strange reservoir, an ancient cave excavated in the side of the bank, its roof held up by the slate equivalent of pit-props. With a shaft of golden sunlight piercing the Stygian gloom, it seems to stretch back for some feet under the field above. The site of the well must obviously in past times have had some connection with the ancient monastery, although now we know nothing about it other than the fact that it stands here, in a lane that has the atmosphere of having been one of the old trackways from the one-time capital of Cornwall out into the surrounding countryside.

Trethevy is a small hamlet on the edge of King Arthur country. A mile or so along the coast road, the remains of a once-pretty Cornish village called Tintagel stand, jostling for their rightful position with the bow-fronted windows of cafes and tourist traps that all seem to offer the same somewhat tawdry merchandise. Luckily, this disturbing sight is rescued from its depravity by the existence of 'King Arthur's' castle, or rather the rocky headland where a castle and Celtic monastery once stood, a place of wild romance and invigorating atmosphere. On this old Holy Island are three wells, sunk in the solid rock, one of which has a delicious air of intimacy as the waters form a pool amongst fern and weed, not far from a prehistoric fogou or underground passage. This weird serpentine tunnel, deliberately cut snake-like in the rock, collects a pool of its own at the lower end as if by design, and one is reminded of William Stukeley's visions of the Druidic cult of the serpent power, impressed upon the landscape at such places as Avebury.* Whatever the true history of this mysterious island, there can be no doubt that at one time it was an important religious centre, for recent fires on the island have revealed the foundations of a large and previously unknown settlement capable of housing 1,000 people. Other than these few factual scraps, the enigmas of Tintagel are at the moment completely hidden from us. We are at the mercy of our imaginations.

King Arthur, historically speaking, never had anything whatever to do with Tintagel. This does not matter in the least, though, for countless thousands of visitors come every year to immerse themselves in the chivalric charisma of the legendary King, and an eccentric millionaire even built a vast Hall of Chivalry to perpetuate the myth, a superb edifice, all white marble and stained glass, complete with a huge round table. Most of the visitors have little idea that the Round Table is but a glyph of the celestial zodiac, that Merlin the magician can be equated with the Egyptian God Thoth, the Greek Hermes and the Roman Mercury, and that King Arthur is the central, solar figure of a tradition that has all the attributes of a mystic cult around the central theme of what J. G. Frazer called 'the sacrificed Gods', such as Jesus, Osiris and Baldur. Not that Arthur was ever actually killed, for although he sacrificed himself for his country he did not quite die, being carried off to Avalon until such time as he is needed again. But he gathered around himself a circle of men who imposed a new and exalted ethic upon the nation, symbolized by the quest for the Holy Grail. He was the product of a miraculous conception and mysterious upbringing, and will return when the time is ripe in his own version of the second coming, the priest-king returned to save the World.

It is into this rarefied atmosphere of mystery and legend, and other such phraseology beloved of guidebooks and holiday brochures, that the visitor steps tentatively, restraining any disbelief as to the magical properties of the place. It can be felt quite tangibly by anyone who escapes from the visible excesses of Tintagel's main street. Trethevy has more than its fair share of

---

*This pool has now been drained by English Heritage

magic, sometimes of a distinctly disturbing kind. *St. Piran's Well* stands at the side of an ancient lane that runs beside the Rocky Valley Hotel, its old slate stones looking like an early, somewhat unsuccessful attempt at pyramid construction. A rusty iron cross embedded in a piece of round granite watches from the summit, the whole building giving an impression of peculiarly pleasing proportions, lightly upholstered with yellow lichen. An iron gate bars the entrance to the interior, where a modern water pipe leads the waters of the sacred spring off for more sacrilegious purposes than quenching the thirst of weary pilgrims.*

The area around the well, the lane leading up to the superb spectacle of St. Nectan's Kieve, and the whole valley that leads down to the sea must be one of the most haunted as well as the most strangely beautiful places in Cornwall. The breezes that whisper through the hedgerows and around the tree tops are laden with a mysterious quality that defies description. But first the legend.

The story of St. Nectan associated with this place must serve as a background for this old well, for there can be little doubt that there was an intimate connection between the anciently-revered spring and the other magical spots in this haunting valley. In medieval times, pilgrims on their way to visit the hermitage at the head of the glen would have invariably stopped at the well to drink its pure water, and to worship at the long, low chapel that stood opposite, and which much later was to serve as a pigsty, surely a most blasphemous contrast. Whether this was the same St. Nectan that held his sister Morwenna as she died looking out across the sea to Wales is confused by the mists of time, for an entirely different legend relates the life and death of another St. Nectan over the border in Hartland, Devon, that is permeated with Celtic symbolism.

However, our St. Nectan appears to have settled beside the Trevillett river, building his sanctuary above a mystic waterfall and kieve (Cornish for 'basin') in this most secluded spot, in about the sixth century. The waters tumble in a spray of silver mist through an arch of stone into the kieve, shaped like an immense sugar bowl twenty feet deep, before flowing away down through the densely wooded valley, past a ruined mill and mysterious, ancient rock carvings to find its meandering way to the sea. Tradition has it that Nectan's chapel over the waterfall had a tower in which hung a silver bell, which would ring out to summon help from the castle at Tintagel in times of storm and shipwreck, for from this tower, Nectan could see both castle and coast.

After a lifetime of contemplation, he approached his end when the country was bitterly divided by the differences between the older Celtic faith and the newer Roman doctrines. (A Roman milestone—very rare in Cornwall—stands near St. Piran's Well). He prophesied that the older, simpler faith would eventually return, and vowing that his silver bell should never ring for unbelievers, he dropped it into the kieve. It is said that at certain times, the

---

* At the time of going to press, it appears that this unique monument is about to be lost due to utter neglect.

muffled sound of his submerged bell may still be heard, a sure sign of ill omen.

After Nectan's death, two strange ladies (probably his sisters, yet more of King Brychan's numerous progeny), took possession of the chapel, and following the wishes of the hermit, buried him and his sacramental vessels and treasures in an oak chest under the waterfall. There are curious Druidic overtones to this old story which seem to bear the mark of genuine Celtic fable stamped on a hotch-potch of ancient memories. However, diverting the plummeting stream, they dug a grave below the kieve, buried the saint, and once again the river resumed its normal course, tumbling over the earthly remains of Saint Nectan towards the Atlantic. The sisters took up residence at the site of the hermitage, living a remote and frugal existence on a diet of wild berries, fruit, roots and fish, exciting the curiosity and vindictiveness of the local people. Suspicion and fear grew amongst the superstitious folk of the district, and in the time-honoured tradition, they accused them of being devils and responsible for every calamity that afflicted cattle, sheep or crops. One of the sisters died, and the curious peeped through the window to see the other old lady mourning, herself close to meeting the dark spectre of death. Common humanity overcame fear, however, and the sisters were buried under a large flat stone in the glen, their spirits haunting the lane that leads down to the well.

For many years I used to visit friends who lived on the way to the waterfall, and who had once lived in the hermitage on St. Nectan's original site. Many were the stories of hooded figures gliding effortlessly through tangles of undergrowth and trees, and of their Siamese cats hissing and lashing out at invisible foes. One night, my friend's wife was sauntering up the lane in late summer. In the gathering dusk, she saw two figures approaching, and thinking them to be a couple of the numerous visitors to the waterfall, bade them good evening. A bit miffed at their lack of acknowledgement, her mild annoyance turned to a cold, spine-tingling chill as the two figures walked right through her and disappeared into the evening air! It is only by listening to the baffled bewilderment of someone relating such an experience that one can touch on the strange incomprehension that accompanies such phenomena. Unless you experience them yourself, that is. . . .

Fortunately, perhaps, I never came across such ghosts or ghouls in my nocturnal ramblings up and down the lane, although the mind was often magnetized by the wealth of tales about the 'grey ladies', monks in the glen, and the stories of unearthly sounds wafted about by the wind, of invisible sobbing, the chanting of monks, inexplicable laughter and even beautiful organ music coming from an empty building. But one warm summer's evening, I was just about to open the garden gate when my friend's dog appeared with enthusiastic canine ebullience, only to change suddenly into a seemingly vicious beast, howling and alarmingly fierce. It was not to me that he had taken such a dislike, though. He seemed terrified of something that was coming along behind me, which passed in front as I stopped in amazement, and carried on further down the lane. You could see his eyes following it as he

ST. PIRAN'S WELL at Trethevy, near Tintagel, stands at the side of an ancient pilgrim's way that leads to the magical valley of St. Nectan's Glen. Near the old site of the hermitage, a waterfall threads its way through a hollow rock and so legend tells us, over the earthly remains of the saint himself.

snarled until it apparently disappeared from view, and he slowly returned to normal. For the rest of the evening he would suddenly bark fitfully, remembering the alarming presence of the unseen wanderer. I have to admit to a distinct feeling of unease as I walked back along the lane in the moonlight.

The landscape around Camelford is dominated by the distinctive shape of Roughtor. Whichever way you enter the town, the distant moorland crags of this rocky fastness glower on the horizon, partly obscuring Brown Willy, the closest thing that you can get to a mountain in Cornwall. Out there, close to the top of the world, any minor flight of fancy assumes an almost believable solidity, the definition between reality and romantic imagination becoming faint and indistinct. Up among the granite crevices, the cascades of tumbled rocks look exactly like the ruins of an ancient city, some vast edifice shaken to the ground by an Earth-shattering cataclysm. Here, below the ruined foundations of a chapel dedicated in Christian times to St. Michael, is *Roughtor Holy Well*, covered by slabs and chunks of grey granite, plain unhewn moorstone over a bleak spring that must go back to the very beginnings of Man's habitation of this wild area. Lower down the slopes, the legacy of our ancestors leaves its imprint on the windswept moor. A stone-age village, with hut-circles, animal enclosures, thoroughfares and a perfect stone circle, with an outlying stone aligned to the rising of the Sun. A landscape that sets the mood when travelling through this area of remote antiquity, providing a certain perspective against which to view the transient nature of our existence.

Such thoughts may well slink off into some secret recess of the brain in travelling through the old market town of Camelford, in search of an old well with a name of paradoxical modernity. But *Jetwells Holy Well*, in between Camelford and Lanteglos, is in fact an ancient title, derived down the centuries from St. Julitta's Well Parks, and as if to drag us screaming into the twentieth century, is now located below Juliot's Well caravan park. There must be some connection here, it would seem, with St. Juliot's Church near Boscastle, famous as 'Hardy's Church', where the young Thomas Hardy met and fell in love with the Rector's sister-in-law, Emma Gifford. Dedicated to a saint who was said to have suffered a violent death, there used to be a well near the church which was visited by pilgrims, and by those who wished to avail themselves of the water's reputation for the cure of skin diseases. In the last century, however, the well was filled in with the curiously carved stones that stood around it, one supposedly of the Virgin Mary, as it was considered to be dangerous to cattle! Later, when the surrounding marsh was being drained, one of the labourers found a gold circlet, said to have been worn on the head, and lost, or left behind as an offering, by one of the visiting pilgrims. Evidently, this interesting treasure was sold to a local antiquarian for its weight in sovereigns, who later sold it to the editor of a well-known daily newspaper, who, so the story goes, eventually presented it to the British Museum.

Sir John Maclean, in his 'History of Trigg Minor' tells us about this place, once one of the county's great Deer Parks: 'Jetwells contains about eighteen acres of rich meadow land. It derives its name from a holy well which formerly existed on the premises, and which has been ruthlessly torn down, and the place desecrated. . . . The two stones which formed the ancient equilateral arch still lie on the spot, as do other stones which formed the building. In 1569 it is mentioned under the name of St. Gitwell Park.'

However, the old well was to be re-incarnated, thanks to a certain Colonel Bake, who, in the last century, had the stones collected from their temporary resting place in the walls of an outbuilding, and restored them to their rightful place near the bottom of a field, in a leafy hollow sunk in shade. The new owners of Juliot's Well caravan park were intrigued to learn these facts about their holy well the day I turned up and asked if they could direct me to it. As I promised them a copy of the photograph, they pointed the way down a muddy lane and past a tiny, ruined cottage. At the bottom of a sloping meadow, a shadowy depression beckoned, and I crunched my way over a carpet of crisp leaves to the ancient site. A century ago, it was described as 'a quaint, picturesque little structure, with a weather-beaten thorn growing on the ledge above it, and luxurient ferns lining the interior. The roof, which slopes back to the level of the field, is rounded, and composed of rough masonry; the doorway is arched, the stone evidently being the original one; there is an old stone step at the entrance, slightly guttered in the middle, but the copious spring no longer runs over it, overflowing the building and the surrounding field as in former times, for the superfluous water is now drained off in a channel underground, and flows into a miniature lake . . .'.

The round roof had long since disappeared, the remains of the tiny building just a shadow of its former self. Ivy and dark green moss clung tenaciously to the remnants of old masonry, the granite arch balanced precariously on top, rocking like a logan stone as I touched it gingerly. Stones lay about, the interior of the well now dry and lined with mouldering leaves. A faintly sad sight, but with a piquant flavour of the remote past. And there, growing out above the well, a curiously misshapen thorn tree. Was this a remnant of the thorn described in that visit of 1891? I suddenly experienced a sense of the continuity of the place, somewhere that had once almost ceased to exist, and yet stands to this day despite the vicissitudes and vagaries of the past.

A sharp, chill winter breeze brought a flurry of thin snowflakes whirling around the old graveyard. The air had a crystalline quality as I looked up to see the sombre tower of Davidstow Church, looming in its grey solitude as a horse plodding along the muffled roadside verge took its rider home. On the road from Camelford, a few miles to the west, the eye had been mesmerised by the ever-present shape of Roughtor, its boulder-strewn slopes covered by a diaphanous film of icy whiteness.

LOST AND FOUND. . . . Jetwells Holy Well near Camelford, once 'ruthlessly torn down, and the place desecrated'. A certain Colonel Bake, however, rescued some of the stones from their more humble use in the walls of outbuildings, and the remains now stand, as dry as a saint's relics, in a secluded shady hollow.

In this churchyard lie the mortal remains of Charlotte Dymond, brutally murdered by her jealous and lame lover Matthew Weeks, although some still maintain that he was the victim of vindictive public outrage, and that the unknown killer went free and undetected. Charlotte, a maid at a nearby house, used to walk across the lower slopes of Roughtor to her home, until one day she was found face down in a stream bed, her throat cut and her blood staining the clear moorland water. It was said that she taunted the crippled Matthew Weeks about his disability, tantalizing him with tales of other lovers, and paying dearly for her moment of cruel amusement. Whatever the truth of the story, the unfortunate Weeks was hung at Bodmin Jail in 1844, and special trains were laid on to transport the 20,000 enthusiastic onlookers to the site of the gallows. The public also raised the money to erect a monument to the ill-starred lover, to stand near the stream where her lifeless body was found. Strangely, though, her grave was never marked by a stone, and the only thing that indicates where the bones of the young Cornish maid lie is part of an old, worn cross, lying forlorn amongst the memorials of others who met their end more peacefully.

The churchyard lies at the bottom of a fairly steep hill, the road leading off to Camelford in one direction, and to the old Cornish capital of Launceston in the other. Below it, a slate stile leads to a boggy meadow where you can see *Davidstow Holy Well* directly ahead, a twisted thorn growing from its roof. That winter's day, I was glad the ground was frozen solid and powdery snow blew about, for I could walk straight to the well without disappearing into the quagmire that normally surrounds the old spring, much trampled by cattle. It is an unusual well, and large. Built around in herringbone slate fashion similar to some Cornish hedgerows, the front is made up of granite lintel and supports, with grass and gorse growing over the roof below the stark thorn. The door is of heavy, old weather-worn oak, studded with iron nails and blacksmith-beaten hinges, and presents a picture of delightful desuetude. Carved roughly in the granite above it are the initials M. W. and the worn remains of a now illegible date.

The initials are of a certain Michael Williams, who restored the well in the last century, some of the stones being brought from an ancient chapel in the adjoining parish of Lesnewth. The old door squeaks as the hinges move against their will, and there, inside, is a watery chamber of damp and darkness. The well is copiously brimming with a pool of lustrous liquid, but looking up to the roof, a most unusual feature presents itself.

Built into the roof is a huge granite stone, hollow and hoary with age, at least a foot thick and with a squarish hole cut into it. It is reminiscent of a square version of the Men-an-Tol, down at Morvah, a holed stone supposed to cure rickets and other such diseases when afflicted children crawl through it. Could this be some remnant of such a primeval monument, or merely an old granite well-top? We can only speculate about its origins, but one thing grips the imagination. What a potent symbol to place above a holy well, with all its associations with fertility and the Earth Goddess!

DAVIDSTOW WELL IN WINTER. Nearby, a vast underground cavern feeds water at the rate of thousands of gallons a day to a cheese factory on the edge of the moor.

It was as I peered into the gloom that I heard a voice. A blue boiler-suited fellow was approaching as if he knew me. He thought I was the farmer, and he told me he had come to fix the water-pump, pointing up to the field above with its collection of rusting Victorian pipework and old plumbing sticking out of the ground. He told me that the water was so acidic that every few years the water-pumps had to be replaced, the metal of the pipes being eaten into by the minerals dissolved in it. Sure enough, there, at the top of the field, stood a whole succession of water-pumps, lined up like a museum display of pumps down the ages.

But he knew what he was talking about. Pointing to the old building that looks like a barn, just near the stile, he explained that it was a pumping-house for the cheese factory a short distance away on the edge of the moor. During the war, he went on, indicating some area beyond a row of trees, a vast underground cavern was excavated near the well. You could see the concrete entrance, raised above the meadow. From those subterranean depths, thousands of gallons of water a day are pumped up to the factory to be used to make tons of cheese, a most practical use for the sacred waters of old. As would be expected, the well is noted for its unfailing supply, as well as its unstinting and faithful service to Man both ancient and modern.

THE OLD OAK DOOR OF DAVIDSTOW WELL, studded with rusting iron nails and blacksmith-beaten hinges. Behind the door a large pool of water is built around and roofed over with a strange hollow stone.

It happened to be a sparkling November day as I turned the corner into St. Clether, on the trail of the largest well-chapel in Cornwall. As I crunched to a halt on the gravel outside the church, a collection of weather-beaten faces looked up, assuming the collective expression of a clandestine group of poked owls. A farmer was hanging a new gate, with one to do the deed, and the others to offer encouragement and background conversation. It must have been the most exciting thing to happen in St. Clether for months. I waved and walked over to them.

"Oyez, we get an offal lot o'vizters in't summer, but ye don't zee a body this time o'year. Oyez, we allus bring the water up from the chapel for they christenins". I felt like someone who had interrupted the annual general meeting of some insidious secret society. "Keep down below they rocks . . ." the words trailed off as the old church gate clicked shut, and I followed the path past the church to the gate beyond, to the wildness of a furzy moorland valley.

The remote setting of this place has a rugged romanticism that makes the spirits soar, the path winding below rocky outcrops through countryside that has changed little down the ages. Below, the mellifluous sound of a stream, bright with the luminous clarity of the crystal moorland water. A buzzard hovered high above the stunted trees, and, drinking down a gulp of air as if it contained the very essence of the place, I felt supremely at one with the world. Leafing through my trusty Quiller Couch book, its once bright blue cover now stained by the splashes of many holy waters, I found the page, with just a short piece about the old *Holy well of St. Clether*. A hundred years ago, the place was in ruins, the altar desecrated and the well almost unapproachable. It finished with the words 'One wonders how the possessor of such an interesting antiquity can be so indifferent'.

The original well was built by St. Clether himself, yet another of the numerous saintly children of King Brychan of Wales, long before the Norman conquests. Some sort of building has stood where the chapel is for over a thousand years, serving as the original parish church. Fortunately, it was rescued from oblivion by the Rev. Sabine Baring-Gould and his onward Christian soldiers at the turn of the century, during the Victorian revival of interest in such places. Guided, who knows, by the spirit of St. Clether himself, Baring-Gould made a far better job of restoration than did many of his colleagues, who often destroyed the atmospheric ambience of old buildings to conform to their own narrow ideas. The well, a solid, stone-roofed building that has had its original domed roof replaced, is sunk in the side of the hill beside the chapel.

The water cascades through a stone channel into the chapel, behind the altar and into a sunken basin for those who would bathe in the healing waters. It has a reputation of never drying up, but on a recent visit, at the end of a drought-stricken summer, no water flowed and the life of the place had drained away also. Perhaps it is fed by some underground cavern that was starved of its supply for the first time in many generations. But in more normal times, the

DEEP INTO NORTH CORNWALL is the largest well-chapel in the county. Along a furzy moorland valley the path leads to the chapel and well at St. Clether, where there has been some sort of building for over a thousand years. Inside, a thick, heavy silence pervades the atmosphere as the light from the east cascades over the great slab of granite that is the altar.

ST. CLETHER WELL CHAPEL during restoration in the last century, showing the monolithic granite altar that 'has never been moved'.

water flows copiously through the basin to another small well in the outside wall of the chapel, where it drips down to bring life to a clump of ferns and moss.

Near the monolithic granite altar resting on four crude pillars which Sabine Baring-Gould claims has never been disturbed, is a recess for the relics of the saint, so that the miraculous power of the bones may be transferred to the passing waters. The impression of the altar is one of great antiquity. It is carved with five equal-armed crosses, an elemental symbol sacred for aeons before being adopted and adapted by Christianity. The recess above the second, smaller well has a stone shelf, used for offerings left by pilgrims for the saint or his followers, who may well have lived solely upon such rewards. And a small wooden door opens on to the recess, combining efficient retrieval of the holy offerings with the maximum of comfort.

You could almost hear the silence in the chapel, a thick, heavy quietude that struck right to the core of some timeless level of the mind. The great slab of granite was bathed in a thin light from the east window that flowed reluctantly over a damp and decaying bible and gave a subtle clarity to the flowers in an earthenware pitcher. The stones breathed a peaceful tranquillity, and somewhere, a long way away, or maybe it was just outside, seagulls noisily made their way to the coast. A painted sign, dated Easter, 1913, rested on a worn stone bracket, asking visitors to place 3d in the box for the upkeep of the chapel. I made my offering to St. Clether and walked outside into the garish daylight. Shafts of sunlight struck points of pale yellow and green fire in the valley below, highlighting the texture of a tapestry of rare natural beauty.

Lost in reverie, I wandered back along the path musing about the magic of the place. In such a place as this, I thought, the great magician Merlin could slumber peacefully awaiting the call from Arthur. And I thought of Merlin in his old age, a hermit like St. Clether and the other saints of old, travelling widely without going anywhere. As Lao Tzu wrote;

> *The further one goes, the less one knows.*
> *Therefore the sage knows without going about,*
> *Understands without seeing,*
> *And accomplishes without any action.*

A stone's throw from St. Clether, but a meandering drive through the Cornish lanes, the interesting old well at *Laneast* sits solidly half-way down a marshy field below the church. When Thomas Quiller Couch visited it, the field was a 'secluded glen', and he found that the locals called it 'the wishing well' and 'the Jordan', the water being used for the church rites. He quotes an anonymous writer in a local newspaper, which gives a good idea of the condition of the building:

'If the attention of the Penzance Antiquarian Society were directed to the state of the holy well at Laneast, and the remains of the old Chapel Park, St. Clether, they might perhaps induce the proprietors of these remnants of antiquity to bestow a little care on the same, and arrest their further ruin and destruction.'

He feared that his brief note and a drawing by his friend J. T. Blight would soon be all that remained of it. Nearer the turn of the century, the building was still intact, the villagers going there to make their butter, but with no recollection of its use as a wishing well. Quiller Couch must have come across this place just as the old traditions were about to disappear forever, that time of change when what was common knowledge to previous generations held no mystery or attraction for a more modern breed of countryfolk.

It is a little surprising, then, considering the description of its decrepit state in the last century, to find the building in a very fair state of preservation, despite the fact that little maintainance seems to be lavished upon it. Built from chunky stone, with ivy and the roots of Pennywort creeping through the crevices, perhaps the members of the Penzance Antiquarian Society did eventually take notice, and restored the ruin. A formidable granite doorway leads to a pool of pellucid water, where one can imagine children of a bygone age playing noisily and young pinafored Cornish maids tossing in a bent pin to wish for the lover of their dreams.

LANEAST WELL photographed in 1891, when the superstition surrounding the well was just about forgotten, and the villagers used it to make their butter.

LANEAST WELL, as it is today, half-way down a field below the church. Despite the fears of antiquarians in the last century, the curious building still stands above the spring that drains away to a marsh below.

The roof presents a strange spectacle. It looks just as if the ridge has been sliced off by some giant wielding a devilish implement of cyclopean proportions, a crude and hasty repair being made by laying slates to keep the unholy water from the heavens from polluting the sacred spring below. The well drains into a small marsh, profuse with reedy growth and crystal rivulets of water running away towards a solitary tree, the legends and stories eroded into nothingness by the weathering of time.

For those who are drawn into pondering the mysteries of ancient landscapes, the image of St. Michael seems to hold particular significance. In Cornwall, there are over thirty churches and chapels dedicated to the great dragon-slayer, guardian of hills and high places and, before the arrival of St. Piran, the patron saint of the county. Some say that, like the slumbering King Arthur, St. Michael has a special role to play in the destiny of Cornwall, and that he guards and protects the sacred landscape and those that travel through it. As a Christian saint, he certainly is the great protector, vanquishing Satan and his fallen angels, although Michael the light-bringer would appear to be a much later version of the Celtic Sun-God Belenos the Brilliant, and the Apollo of the Greeks.

Amongst the dramatic hilltop St. Michael shrines, perhaps the most romantic is St. Michael's Mount, which seems, like the saint himself, to hold some profound significance. A legendary place of spiritual power where a vision of St. Michael once appeared to local fishermen, it is one of the shrines associated with perhaps the most famous ley, or leyline, in Britain. This remarkable alignment of anciently sacred sites stretches for over 300 miles, passing through such notable places as the Cheesewring, St Michael's Chapel on Glastonbury Tor, the great Henge at Avebury and the once illustrious abbey of Bury St Edmunds. In its course it has attracted a whole host of almost forgotten prehistoric ritual centres, as well as Christian churches dedicated to the dragon-slaying saint and his fellow knight St George. But the most intriguing property of this alignment is that it coincides with the direction of the rising Sun on Mayday, the first day of the ancient summer and the hub of the annual cycle. At this time, the power centre of our solar system aligns with a string of sacred sites once the abode of earlier Sun-Gods, seemingly created or adapted by our ancestors to conform in some forgotten way with the natural forces of the landscape.

Since the first publication of this book in 1988, the present writer and dowser Hamish Miller have spent some years investigating this phenomenon. The results of this work are published in THE SUN AND THE SERPENT, and demonstrate that there was an ancient understanding of the energies of the Earth and Sun, particularly at special places in the countryside where these forces manifest in a psychic or spiritual 'atmosphere' which affects human minds. These spots have always been considered 'holy', often attracting churches, but have their root in former times when the earth and its environment were thought to be alive and intelligent, and all life a sacred expression of divinity.

It is difficult to ponder the mystery of leylines without catching an imaginative glimpse of the revelation that took place when Alfred Watkins, in the early 1920's, peered down from a prominent position to the Herefordshire landscape below. There, before him in a flash of intuitive insight, he saw a vast network of glowing lines spreading out over the surface of the countryside, intersecting the sites of old churches, standing stones, holy wells and other places of traditional sanctity. He had rediscovered the ancient ley system of prehistory, forgotten for millennia, but still preserved in the secret traditions of occult societies. Dowsers find that these leylines seem to mark the flow of some invisible energy, but they can also be investigated in a simple and straightforward manner without recourse to arcane theories or obscure paraphenalia.

For example, you can hardly help noticing that a ruler placed on an Ordnance Survey map of the area around Roughtor reveals some interesting results. The long, dramatically straight road that leads to the Cornish mountain always impresses the mind of those travelling along it as if they sense some mystery. And this mystery deepens as you discover that the ruler aligned on this road connects perhaps the two most significant ancient sites in this part of the county. A dead straight line joins that most impressive of prehistoric remains, the Cheesewring, with the island sanctuary at Tintagel, famous for its legendary associations and as a Celtic monastery. What exactly this means is at the moment open to speculation. Were the ancients tapping the power of the St. Michael Line and channelling it to Tintagel island? Only further research will begin to reveal such tantalizing mysteries.

However, yet another alignment appears to connect *Michaelstow Holy Well* with the former chapel on the rocky summit of Roughtor dedicated to St. Michael. It appears to pass over a prehistoric fogou, a stone circle and various tumuli to skirt the tops of nearby tors Buttern Hill and Bray Down, passing very close to Laneast holy well. In the opposite direction, the line appears to travel through St. Kew, where there is also a holy well.

The well in Michaelstow churchyard is to be found near the south porch, sunk in gloom beneath the tracery of old trees. A hundred years ago, stones lay about giving the impression of one-time importance, and one chronicler wrote 'There are also the ruins of an ancient baptistry, the restoration of which is intended.' The path to the well, however, whilst being once paved with good intentions, is now nothing more than a short inclined way leading down to a plain walled well, betraying little of its forgotten glory. Neglected and seemingly forgotten, only its position in this isolated country churchyard tells us that it may once have been greatly venerated by those whose culture was rooted in another age.

Just a few miles from Michaelstow, and connected to it by the unseen line that skirts the top of Roughtor, is the quaint hamlet of St. Kew. The history of the saint who gave his name to the parish is hidden in obscurity, when and from where he came unrecorded and lost. *St. Kew Holy Well*, though, is situated next to the road in the private garden of the old vicarage, brimming with deliciously sparkling water. Early in the nineteenth century, the old house was pulled down, the road diverted and the well lost sight of forever, it seemed. However, like many of the old springs, that was not the end of the matter. Disgusted and angry on discovering the facts of this sorry tale, the Vicar of St. Kew in the 1890's set to work to unearth the well, and at length found it, restoring it with a brick-built arch and placing a cross on top. He planted it around with trees and shrubs, and fetched all his drinking water from it, the quality of the liquid being highly regarded by the local people, who came purposely to drink at the well that was lost and resurrected.

The bleak, bare downland of St. Minver is used to the changes wrought by the shifting sands of time. Looking out towards the sea over Daymer Bay, if you could transport yourself back into prehistoric times, you would be gazing into a forest where wild beasts roamed. We know this because in 1857 a great gale shifted the sand and twelve feet below high water mark the stumps and roots of oak, yew and hazel trees could be seen, and the teeth and horns of deer were found. Coming closer to our own times, the remains of an ancient village have been found, the furniture still in the houses, and left hurriedly as it was overwhelmed by a sandstorm like some primitive Pompeii. The church of St. Enodoc, peering over the dunes with its leaning spire, has also spent much of its time buried in the shifting sands. One vicar, noting that the foundations were hewn out of solid rock, felt sure that this must have been the cave occupied by the hermit St. Enodoc, and later, when the flagstones were dug up, a small spring was found under them. Could this have been his hermitage, a lonely cave over a sacred spring? Nowadays the church is famous as the final resting place of another who was captivated by this stretch of wild coast, Sir John Betjeman.

Close by, on what is now a golf course, is a small walled enclosure containing *Jesus Well*, which also used to become half-buried by the sand piled up by the storms which devastate this exposed region. The legend of the well tells how some pilgrim saint travelled over these dusty dunes, weary and thirsty from his wanderings. Possibly having heard about Moses, who smote a rock to produce a spring, he struck the arid soil with his staff, whereupon water flowed forth with great abundance. Thus, Jesus Well came into being, and later a small chapel was built nearby, pieces of a Gothic window being seen on the spot in 1812.

This spring, enclosed by a well-kept building of some antiquity containing a niche for a saint's effigy, has been famous for centuries for its miraculous healing qualities. People travelled for long distances to take advantage of its curative waters, which were celebrated for a variety of complaints, and also for

Jesus' Well, St. Minver

the evils which befell scoffing unbelievers. One story tells of Mary Cranwell, wife of a boatman, who suffered severely from erysipelas, or St. Anthony's Fire, and could obtain no relief from orthodox medical treatment. In 1867, believing the reputation of the well, she knelt beside it, recited the 'Litany to the Holy Name of Jesus', and bathed the diseased parts in the waters. Evidently, she received relief straight away, and after repeating the process the necessary three times, became completely cured and never suffered the malady again. Whether this remarkable cure, which was fully verified at the time, was due to the magical properties of the healing waters, or was the result of unquestioning faith, we can never know. But the fact that it actually worked was enough proof for Mary Cranwell. Some time after, the farmer on whose land it stood intercepted the flow of water, throwing caution to the winds in view of the stories about those who would scoff at the old shrine. We have no way of knowing if some terrible omen was visited on him, or whether his drainage system was faulty, but not too much later, the well had a plentiful supply of water once again, and it became much used by children suffering from whooping cough. Some drank the revered liquid, some were dipped in it, and pins and money were thrown into the well for the telling of fortunes. One elderly resident told of how he had seen as much as sixteen shillings taken out by unbelievers on one Sunday alone, refusing to heed the curse of the well and reaping substantial profit from the supersitions of others.

The legend of *St. Constantine's Holy Well* is related in Hunt's 'Popular Romances of the West of England' and provides a classic cautionary tale of well-lore;

'In the parish of St. Merran, or Meryn, near Padstow, are the remains of the church of St. Constantine, and the holy well of that saint. It had been an unusually hot summer, and all the crops were perishing through want of water. The people inhabiting the parish had grown irreligious, and many of them sadly profane. The drought was a curse upon them for their wickedness. Their church was falling into ruin, their well was foul, and the arches over it were decayed and broken. In their distress, the wicked people, who had reviled the word of God, went to the priest for aid.

'There is no help for thee unless thou cleanest out the holy well'.

They laughed him to scorn. The drought continued, and they suffered want. To the priest they went again.

'Cleanse the well, 'was his command, 'and see the power of the blessing of the first Christian emperor'.

That cleansing a dirty well should bring them rain, they did not believe. The drought continued, the rivers were dry, the people suffered thirst.

'Cleanse the well, wash, and drink,' said the priest, when they went to him again. Hunger and thirst made the people obedient. they went to their task. Mosses and weeds were removed, and the filth cleansed. To the surprise of all, beautifully clear water welled forth. They drank the water and prayed, and then washed themselves and were refreshed. As they bathed their bodies, parched with heat, in the cool stream which flowed from the well, the heavens clouded over, and presently rain fell, turning all hearts to the true faith.'

St. Constantine who was the founder of the well, was also King Constantine, son of Padarn of Cornwall. He reigned just after the time when Cerdic the Saxon was founding the kingdom of Wessex, but seems to have been involved in some political crime, probably in an attempt to secure the crown, and killed two children of the royal family. After his murderous deeds, misfortune followed him and he was struck by repentance, wearying of his sovereignty and retiring to a monastery, dying in penitence and sanctity.

The story of the re-discovery of this interesting well gives a glimpse of how these old places take such a hold on the imagination. A few years before the First World War, Dr. Penrose Williams was wandering over some marshland known as the Fowling Pool just by the ruins of Constantine Church. Evidently he sensed that the well was situated beneath his feet, and upon digging with some friends, unearthed tell-tale springs of water. On digging deeper, they found that the excavations rapidly filled with water, and it was necessary to station a man overhead ready to pull out the amateur archaeologists should they be in danger of drowning. As the well and chapel were gradually revealed, the eyes of the men were continually looking for a golden figure of the Virgin which they fancied should have been in a niche at the end. Unfortunately it was never found, if it existed at all.

The local population became very excited about the discovery, but when the news reached the owner of the land, a certain lady who lived outside the area, she was exceedingly angry and wanted nothing to do with these 'Roman affairs', ordering that the site be covered in at once. Reluctantly, this was done, but the good doctor, and his friend Charles Mott wrote a message and put it in a beer bottle, which was buried along with the newly-revealed ruins.

After serving his King and country in the trenches, the doctor returned to find the farm (including the well) on the market, and gathered his resources to buy it. And so he was able to drain the marshland and uncover the ancient well once and for all, and allow local historian Charles Henderson to pronounce it approximately from the third century.

This rather strange well shares at least two of the attributes of Jesus Well at St. Minver. Firstly, its position is very similar, exposed to the Atlantic gales that sweep across the bleak hills, and second, it is to be found in the middle of a golf course! The ruins of an ancient chapel stand, stark and desolate, against the setting sun in the West, the hollow shape of a worn doorway framing the alizarin reflection of a bloody sea. Birds that inhabit the cracks and crevices of the ruins sing out in a tangle of undergrowth, concealing the decaying remains of earth and stone from distant ages. Nearby, small streams wind and trickle their way under tiny bridges and down below, the remains of the well, dug from what was in the last century, nothing more than a damp mound, grown over by rushes and weeds. Now, the old building made of substantial walls of slate layers is open to the gaze of humanity after being buried for centuries. Stone seats run either side of the building, where weary pilgrims would rest and bathe their feet as recorded in the Domesday book. When uncovered, the central gully was made from a hollowed-out tree trunk.

The remnants of this once fairly large mud and masonry structure are now roofed over as protection from the wind, weather and shifting landscape, and while it is unique among the Cornish wells in the formation of the building, it is tramped about by thousands of holidaymakers in the summer, giving it an air of slightly squalid curiosity, the slate roof and cut stone walls of its enclosure exhibiting no sympathy with the antiquity of the place. As with many of these spots that attract so many visitors, it is necessary to let those lashing storms wash away the taint of modern civilization before you can appreciate the naked grandeur, the elemental spirit of this wild site.

Gazing out from the ruins of the chapel, remembering the submerged settlement and the petrified forest of St. Minver, this primeval place has a way of stripping away the pretence and narrowness of our modern vision. The airy realms, endlessly darkening as the evening star hangs tinsel-bright over the horizon, make you feel very small indeed.

10

THE WELLS
OF MID-CORNWALL

*Illness and death foretold—Travelling wells?—Moody,
monkish places and a dark sea cave—old seekers of hidden
treasure—And did those feet?*

HERE are some intriguing wells near the modern holiday resort of Newquay. The town itself is gross and completely uncharacteristic of Cornwall; it could have been plucked at the whim of some powerful God from almost anywhere in Britain. It is, however, studded with the opulent architecture of Victorian hotels, and has become the centre of an area that was thriving for ages before bed-and-breakfast became big business. Now, an eye-searing spread of architectural shrapnel has exploded over the area, engulfing its rustic environs with a fragmented array of modern human habitation. B & B signs stand in regimented rows along the side of the road, bungaloid growths and turn-of-the-century terraces compete for breathing space in a town swarming in the summer, and deserted in its death-posture in the dark months. It is a comprehensive collection of the crimes of town planning, sprawled across the stately cliffs of an ancient area.

Around this one-time tiny fishing village, many monastic settlements and hermits pursued their holy vocations, with a constant stream of pilgrims instead of holidaymakers treading the paths and trackways that criss-crossed the countryside. Of the wells that once existed in this area, many have disappeared completely through neglect and the ravages of time. One of them, now an overgrown hole opposite the church lych-gate, was *Lady Nant's Well* at Colan, referred to by the Cornish historian Carew, and gives and insight into the superstitions of the countryfolk of his time, dim, atavistic echoes of a past age;

> *'Little Colan hath lesse worth the observation, unlesse you will deride or pity their simplicity who sought at our Lady Nant's Well there to foreknowe what fortune should betide them, which was in this manner;*
>
> *'Upon Palm Sunday, these idle-headed seekers resorted thither with a palme crosse in one hand, and an offring in the other; the offring fell to the priest's share, the crosse they threw into the well; which if it swamme the party should outlive that yeere; if it sunk, a short ensuing death was boded, and not*

altogether untruely, while a foolish conceyt of this halsening might sooner help it onwards'.

It would seem that for a considerable time, this well was the most notable thing in the parish, its waters being used for healing and baptisms in the last century, and then for the more utilitarian purposes of the villagers, its supernatural qualities unknown and uninvoked. No lingering trace of its original structure now exists for the observer to muse about, for in summer it is an invisible watery hole choked with nettles. Nevertheless a large draught of this liquid should be imbibed by any passing person who happens to suffer from sore eyes.

Wells, on the whole, do not travel about much. By their very nature, you might say, they are of necessity immoveable and stationary. This would certainly apply to the sacred springs themselves, but the buildings that enclose them are subject to a different set of Earthly laws. Some of the old legends tell us of Divine intervention, the stones of the structures flying about the countryside at the dead of night, and the fate of many of them was to have their ancient stones dragged away to be used in barns and houses. But there are not so many stories about wells that 'went visiting' to return eventually to their place of origin.

The well at *Rialton Priory* was a small stone building over a clear spring, containing a niche with a pedestal for an effigy, its Gothic arched doorway looking out onto the cobbled courtyard of the country residence of the Bodmin Priors. For centuries, this place was the hub of the great manor of Rialton, formerly 'Royaltown', with connections stretching back to the Black Prince and beyond. Monks came from St. Petroc's in Bodmin to the retreat in the valley, overlooked by ancient woodland and terraced gardens. Here, the old well had stood for hundreds of years used by all who passed this way. Until the steward of the Priory took a fancy to it in about 1840, that is.

When this staunch upholder of the faith left, moving him and his possessions to Somerset, so did the well. Stone by stone, it was carried off to a foreign county where it was re-erected in his private grounds. Evidently all hell broke loose when this was discovered by the great powers of Authority, and the well, stone by stone, was brought back to Cornwall and the erring steward was sacked. It stands to this day, looking none the worse for its adventure, in the middle of an immaculate lawn in the Priory garden, edged carefully with primroses and daffodils. This is now someone's front garden, a private place of tranquillity. It looks out to the walled garden with its ornamental trees and climbing plants, a quiet, enclosed haven strangely separate from the rest of the world. Standing silently in front of the magnificently kept Priory after chatting to the owner, I was sure I could smell the sweat of horses, and hear the sound of hooves on cobbles echoing from the stones. Pale ghosts were breathed into the frosty dawn air by invisible mounts, the silence masking a faint background

Well in the Court at Rialton Priory

noise of old voices and animals. A haunting place, a garden of the past with the intriguing centrepiece of the old holy well.

Not far from Rialton Priory stands another old shrine that, like the Priory, evokes images of hooded figures of the past. Built into the side of a wooded slope on a nearby farm, *St. Pedyr's Well* at Treloy is alive with the presence of other ages, but perhaps it is the Naiad, the elemental spirit of the well that is the hidden cause of the charged atmosphere that hangs in a cloud around it. Made from large lumps of granite masonry, it sits on a low wall of stones that stretches out into long stone seats, the water flowing into a central rectangular pool. Whether the waters were renowned for curing foot ailments or this arrangement was provided more for the weary pilgrims we cannot tell. It may be that the pool, now rippling through viridian water-weeds, was for the bathing of the entire body, a healing bath to soothe the diverse afflictions of Man's diseases.

Strewn around, half-hidden beneath leaves and dark green moss, are fragments of an earlier chapel that indicate that this place was once held important. Next to the well, which itself is built from much older masonry, lies a carved ecclesiastical arch at least twice the size of the one now over the doorway. Pieces of cut stone channel and worn carvings lie about, inviting the

THE WELL IN A FRONT GARDEN. . . . The old building of Rialton Priory Well, surrounded by neat lawns and spring flowers. In the last century, it was removed stone by stone to Somerset, but when this was discovered by the authorities, the Priory steward was dismissed and the well brought back to Cornwall.

touch of human hands once more. Gazing into the pool, the brimming waters hold the attention, the consciousness hypnotized by this fluid accumulator of the past. These waters are not of the Earth, they are ruled by the Moon. As the tides of the Oceans rise and fall, and the fertility of humanity and the other Earthly creatures depend on its rhythms, the Moon is the foundation of life as we know it. The whole planet is permeated by the monthly tides that course through its living body, ever-changing with pulses of activity and rest.

So it is with the human being. The Moon establishes an essential rhythm in the body and instinctive mind that dominates existence, and dictates that it is necessary to regularly withdraw from the realms of activity. We are revitalized by sleep at the end of the day, and if we have eyes to see it, the unconscious effect of the Lunar influences also bring us a monthly cycle that involves phases of personal projection and withdrawal. Sitting in the green shade at the side of the well, the waters also lead the mind to dwell on the other, more symbolic, Moon influences. All mirrors and other reflective surfaces have been traditionally associated with the sphere of our silver satellite, reflecting as it does the rays from the centre of our star system. This lunar looking-glass symbol is visualized as a hole in the sky through which the light from the Otherworld pours in, the Earth being but a receptacle to contain it, moulding it into its own shape as wine takes on the shape of a chalice or a grail.

Remembering that a pool of water was Man's first looking-glass, through the other side of the mirror lies the source of all power, the raw material of the Universe, the reservoir of archetypes. To peer into the reflective pool, where the image is destroyed by the slightest touch, is to look deep into the inscrutable fathoms of our own nature, and the physical crucible of primeval life as atoms and acids combine with the vital spark.

The water is a speculum, a crystal-gazer's ball. Through the reflection of your own self, a myriad of strange faces peer back from different worlds. The faces of people you have known, departed relatives and ancestors from ancient times, of images that well up from the depths of the psyche.

To 'Know Thyself' was the key to the stronghold of the soul for the old hermits. By looking within and tearing away the veils of the personality, a painful operation fraught with the possibility of insanity, a man can discover his True Will, his proper place in the Universe. By stripping away the layers of superficial accretions, a seeker isolated from the world penetrates beyond the mists of illusion to the reason for his existence. There is no better place for the western mystic than in the midst of Nature, at a place where the Moon fuses with the Earth to create a stream of secret power. With the help of those who have gone before and the hidden spirits of the supernatural realms, these sanctified sites are like batteries, storing the impressions of experience and supplying that extra bit of voltage to push you across the threshold into a world seen with different eyes. The attention is to be directed inwards, not squandered on the futile and transient outward appearances of civilization. As the Oracles of Zoroaster put it, for the benefit of the eastern mind;

'Direct not thy mind to the vast surfaces of the Earth; for the Plant of Truth grows

IN A POOL OF GREEN SHADE stands St. Pedyr's Well at Treloy. The mysterious moodiness of the place reflects the sanctity of the site in the past. Carved stones lie about, draped in moss and lichen, and the legends fill the mind with hooded hermits and weary pilgrims.

not upon the ground. Nor measure the motions of the Sun, collecting rules, for he is carried by the Eternal Will of the father, and not for your sake alone. Dismiss the impetuous course of the moon, for she moveth always by the power of necessity. The progression of the Stars was not generated for your sake. The wide aerial flight of birds gives no true knowledge, nor the dissection of the entrails of victims; they are all mere toys, the basis of mercenary fraud; flee from these if you would enter the sacred paradise of Piety, where Virtue, Wisdom and Equity are assembled.'

Such is the mysterious moodiness of St. Pedyr's Well that one is led off into the fathomless depths of strange inward reverie. It was once demolished by a large apple tree as it stood in the orchard of Treloy farm, but happily it was restored by the Newquay Old Cornwall Society in 1953, revealing the ancient pilgrim's benches. But the atmosphere of the place is so charged with an aura of introspection that it is as if the Naiad of the waters is still very much alive, coaxing deep and secret thoughts from the brain of which you were previously unaware.

The village of Crantock, once a medieval port, is an island in a sea of caravan sites, preserved and protected from the excesses of Newquay by the Gannel creek, a natural moat to keep the infidel planners at bay. It is something of a relief to find a Cornish village after the maze of modern roads with their staccato accompaniment of garish signposts, beckoning like Big Brother.

The air in Crantock breathes a slower pace; here you can sit on a wall watching old folk totter up the road to the Post Office with all the time in the world, children riding their ponies past cottages with polished brass and flowers in the window, and cats snoozing somnolently in shady porches.

St. Carantocus, who gives his name to the village, was the son of a Welsh King. At every twist and turn of the past, there seems to be some tangible connection between the Cornish and the Welsh. The early hermits nearly all had Welsh connections, mainly due to the formidable procreative power of King Brychan, who ruled from the Brecon Beacons, and the two Celtic countries have always shared that ancient heritage of earning their living by delving into the subterranean depths of the Earth. In the clay country, to the south, I have always been struck by the similarity of the mining communities to those of the Welsh valleys, rows of terraced houses with their strangely closed but friendly folk. True, the spoil-heaps that litter the landscape are shining white instead of black, and the sheep that graze the lowland are not as grey as across the water, but there is an indefinable quality that crystallizes in that independence of character that is inherent in Welshman and Cornishman alike.

About the year 432 AD, Carantocus joined St. Patrick in Ireland, helping to convert the Irish, and stayed in the Emerald Isle for many years. He returned to Cornwall in 460, bringing with him a large number of Irish hermits, and settled a little to the east of the community founded by St. Piran, further down the windswept north coast. Leland writes; 'Karantoc constructed an oratory for himself, in the place which was called Guerith Karantauc', the land being assigned to him by the owner with permission from the king. He gave his name to the parish, built his cell by the church, and after his death the College of Crantock was founded to honour the memory of the saint.

Well of St. Carantocus

This college was the Cornish equivalent of Oxford, attracting the attention of scholars and ecclesiastics from all over the country. In 1294 it was recorded that it had great revenues, an indication of the importance of this old seat of learning. But its fate was sealed by the shifting sands of the north coast, which blew up from the Gannel creek in vast quantities, engulfing the buildings as the winds of change had done further up the coast at St. Minver and St. Merryn. Nothing is now left of the college or the cell, but exhibiting an amazing resilience to the vagaries of the centuries, the holy well still exists in the centre of the village, not far from the church. It is a curious, bee-hive shaped structure with low walls around it, and seems to be unique in its position at the hub of the community. Its old stones must be impregnated with the past life of the village, a tranquil observer of relentless change.

Crantock used to boast no less than three holy wells within a short distance of each other, the ancient covered well dedicated to St. Ambrusca that once stood in the churchyard disappearing under the foundations of what is now 'St. Ambrose Villa'. But close by in a lane that leads down below the church, a carved wooden door encloses a small well that is of some antiquity, and dedicated to the same saint, despite the different spelling of St. Ambrews.

The door was carved by a local doctor as an exact replica of the original, which twenty years ago was decaying into a pile of wooden fragments. An old photograph shows the thick oak door in its death throes, marked by the use of centuries and worn by the hands of distant generations. A knot-hole is eroded by age into a gaping watery darkness, with wood the distinctive colour of old oak, grey-brown, shiny and polished by the ragged sleeves of long-dead children.

How they must have traced their grubby fingers around the incised image of St. Ambrew himself, wearing his square-topped hat reminiscent of a medieval bishop. A carved chain design encloses the staring face of the saint, looking very Celtic in its simple but powerful style. The modern door will never have the poignancy of that ancient piece of oak, but the doctor who carved it did a faithful job in preserving the image of the saint who has looked out from the side of this Cornish lane for countless years. And fortunately, we can still savour the delightful melancholy of the old, worn door, imprinted with the touch of a thousand hands, in the mesmeric painting of it by Penny Harris, who herself travels through the looking-glass of apparent reality in her unique glass-paintings, that peer transparently through time to the realms of a lost world.

Holywell Bay is famous today for its desert expanse of fine sand and the amethyst quality of its Mediterranean sea, the edge of what has been called 'the sweetest bay in England'. There is a serene symmetry, an exquisite harmony of surf-washed beach contained within lofty crags of headland and isolated by deep dunes. It is here that hordes of summer visitors come to prostrate themselves before the Sun God and frolic in the waves, restoring the elemental balance that is the essence of life. The whole scene encompasses a delicate equilibrium of Earth, Air, Fire and Water that condenses in the popular imagination as Sand, Sky, Sun and Sea, and leaves the human spirit revitalized and charged with a primitive potency.

The perfume of the place is sweet with ozone from the turbulent chasms on either side, and trudging through the soft sand of the dunes the mind assumes a lucid clarity that is pin-sharp. On the tufted sandhills, marram grass grows half-submerged in drifts, and then the sight of the expanse of ocean, disciplined by a rocky island that juts out into the horizon. The first time I came to Holywell, it was the middle of the summer and overflowing with humanity in all its diversity. Still, the spirit of the place struck deep to produce this delicious headiness that whispered that this was indeed a magical place. Walking up to the eastern end of the beach, not a soul invaded the silence that smothered the sound of distant babble, for the sunseekers were gathered in the centre of the bay, the swimmers contained by bathing markers because of the rocks and strong currents.

The tide was on the ebb, and I knew that the place I sought was further round, cut off by the foaming sea. I decided to sit it out, take the opportunity to soak up the elements, and muse about the penetrating natural sanctity of this spot. I comforted myself that this exhilarating experience was not simply the first symptom of some strange madness, for others had felt this way stretching right back into unrecorded history. The holy well that is a unique subterranean jewel in the rock of the cliffs proclaims its fame by giving its name to the bay visited every year by thousands of holidaymakers, most of them completely unaware of the existence of an actual 'holy well'. The chronicler Hals tells us that people frequented the well in 'incredible numbers' in his day, 'from countries far distant'. It seems, then, that this place has always exerted a

THE ANCIENT IMAGE of St. Ambrew stares out from the side of a Cornish lane at Crantock, eroded by time and countless hands from the past. This glass-painting by Penny Harris, based on an old photograph taken before the old oak door fell into fragments, preserves the atmosphere of a lost relic.

powerful attraction over people, sometimes those who must have gone through tortuous trials to reach it, travelling on foot through strange lands to visit the fabled holy place. And its most powerful pull was on the crippled and infirm, those whose sufferings were infinitely more acute than the usual pilgrim, yet who believed in its supernatural qualities so vehemently that they were prepared to risk their lives.

The receding tide beckoned provocatively. I walked into the welcoming waves, enchanted by some invisible sea siren whispering a mystic promise in the gentle breeze. I caught my breath as the cold sea surged around, sucking the sand from around the feet in an attempt to dislodge my delicate balance and insinuate its superiority. I continued, feeling for the hidden rocks and the undersea valleys carved by the currents, as grey boulders and the dark entrances to sea-caves reverberated with the muffled crash of the surf. I almost felt that I was out of my depth, as the level of the sea rose and fell around me, sharpening the exhilaration of intimate contact with the natural forces. Then, around the corner, was a small rocky cove, freshly washed by the sea. I arrived on dry land again slightly shaky, clothes dripping from my own elemental baptism.

At the foot of the cliff I could just make out rough steps carved in the rock, leading up into some dark recess. The entrance to the cave was dripping with emerald mosses that made the ascent very slippery, and I wondered how those crippled pilgrims of the past must have coped with such obstacles. The steps lead to a formation of unearthly beauty which can only be described in poetic imagery, for the essence of it lies in the realms of the supernatural. In the private gloom of this dark sea-cavern, a series of hollow steps sculpted by Nature cascade with water that drips from the stalactitic roof. The distilled drops hang like glass baubles for a moment from the calcareous deposits stained by minerals from the cliff above, white, blue, iron-red and malachite green.

A natural basin, enamelled in pink and white, brims with water that still has a briny tang, and is connected to another similar receptacle, leading up to a dark chamber in the womb of the Earth.

I could just squeeze into this tiny cave, sitting there in a puddle, lost in wonder at the primeval majesty of the natural architecture. A curiously formed pillar connects ceiling and floor, full of weird faces formed by the folds of dripping deposits, strange eyes peering out from the abstract designs like the images that loom up from the psychologist's ink-blot. It was through the space formed by this primeval pillar that mothers passed their deformed or sickly children, resulting, it is said, in the healing of the disease. Cripples also left their crutches in this hole at the head of the well, and in my imagination gnarled hands thrust crude supports into the blackness of the cavernous chamber where I sat.

It is not surprising, then, that this unique natural shrine excited the imagination of people down the centuries, who came here to cure all manner of disease and deformity with the aid of the miraculous waters, in a cave that

IN THE DEPTHS OF A DARK SEA-CAVERN, the rocks of the holy well at Holywell Bay are stained pink and malachite green from the mineral-rich waters cascading from a stalactitic roof. In medieval times, huge numbers of people came 'from countries far distant' to experience the miraculous healing qualities of the fabled waters.

must have struck simple folk as of unearthly wonder. The historical legend of this well tells that in 995 AD, Alchun, Bishop of Holy Island, took up the corpse of St. Cuthbert, who was once the Abbot of Lindisfarne. In escaping the ravages of the Danish invasion, he and his monks resolved to transport the saint's relics to Ireland, but were driven onto the north coast of Cornwall where they settled and built the church at Cubert. Told by an oracle to take the sacred bones to Durham, they left, but not before the relics accidentally touched the well, communicating healing powers to the waters. But people would have venerated this place long before Christianity, the primitive mind being a thousand times more receptive to the natural power flowing through it. This would appear to be a prime example of the new religion usurping the potency of a truly pagan shrine for its own ends.

Since that first day when I crawled, dripping, into that underworld cave, I have returned many times, captivated by its remarkable power to connect pre-history with the present. Once, in the middle of winter, I battled against a biting wind to find the cave completely changed. I thought for a moment that it had all been some fantastic dream that had got mixed up with reality. All the huge boulders that I had scrambled over had gone, smooth, silken sand stretched away up to the cavern. But there it was. A recent storm had deposited tons of sand in the cave, burying the vast rocks beneath a mountain but leaving the well untouched. As the tide recedes, the waters lose their salty flavour and become sharper, purifying themselves before being inundated once again as they have been every day for perhaps thousands of years.

And that is one of the fascinating aspects of this solitary and secret shrine. Other wells linger amidst the places of human habitation, affected by the atmosphere of those who visit them, storing impressions in the subtle ether of their fabric. This well, built by the very forces that shape the planet, is purified daily by the incessant sea, all taint of the confusion of human thought washed from its rocks by the pull of the Moon, to emerge cleansed and renewed, the very purpose and proof of a holy well.

But there is yet another well at Holywell Bay that was lost for centuries, and only rediscovered about 1916 by a local resident, who, wandering up the valley from the bay, happened to notice some stones and part of an arch lying beside the stream. Further searching revealed the floor of the well, and the building was rebuilt by the Newquay Old Cornwall Society in 1936 and christened *Cubert Well*. Walking through Trevornick, a Cornish farm that is in the last throes of turning into a caravan site, the wanderer passes a series of fishery pools stacked like locks on an old waterway. No colourful narrowboats and sweaty bargees here, though, the only traffic is a splash of ducks gossiping away to each other amongst the reeds. Following the stream down into the valley, the strange archway that leads to the well stands proud from the base of a tangled rocky outcrop like some castellated Victorian folly.

Through this archway lies an exceedingly damp enclosure, water flowing all about from the well at the far end. The building is very unusual, a curious creation covered with ivy and surrounded by brambles and feathery ferns unfurling their tight spirals. Inside, the strange structure looks like a cross between a medieval bread oven and a primitive footbath, with stone seats on either side and small, warming-oven niches in the wall that is built against the bank. The stone chute that channels the water into this dripping cavern is completely covered in thick, emerald green moss, and the interior is plastered as it would have been in the Middle Ages. A plaque above the entrance arch offers a blessing to the visitor; *'May God refresh thee with the water of life'*.

The Rev. Lane-Davies, in his guide to the Cornish wells, says that this was obviously the famous well which gave its name to Holywell Bay, discounting entirely the wonders of the far more impressive spectacle in the sea-cave half a mile distant. He accuses other writers as well as the Ordnance Survey of making the mistake of attributing the fame of the place to the weird natural formation in the cliffs. It all seems to be a question of vested interests. The Reverend, perhaps because of his chosen work, cannot, it appears, admit to anything that might smack of primitive paganism, cannot see that before Christ, places such as the well in the cave would have had an entirely natural fame amongst the animistic inhabitants of earlier ages. To compound this simplistic felony, he goes so far as to completely ignore the fabled spring that issues from a rock below the hermitage at Roche Rock, a well noted by historians and poets through the ages. You can't get more pagan than rocks and caves, of course. But then you really can't get more pagan than sacred springs either, whatever the bishop might think!

Travelling westwards from the interesting wells of the Newquay district, the tireless wanderer now comes to an area that is very rich in legend, but very poor in remains. Passing through Perranwell, he reflects that the famous arched fountain of *St. Piran* is now only remembered in its name, cottages having been built on the old site of the well that was considered especially valuable for curing rickets.

Tradition has it that the saint gave the tinners and miners in the area a valuable secret concerning the dressing and preparing of tin, and was held in such esteem by the local people that he eventually became exalted to the lofty position of Patron Saint of Cornwall, who celebrated his feast day on March 5th. This veneration obviously did not make any difference to the Victorian vandals who tore down the old well, which had an entrance porch large enough for three or four people to sit in and discuss the merits of the fabled waters. Fortunately, though, a certain Mr. Peters of Chiverton heard about the desecration and rescued the arch and a few remaining stones, erecting them on his nearby estate where they still stand.

Close by, *St. Agnes Well* suffered much the same fate at the beginning of the nineteenth century, although none of the stones were saved. The saint who gave her name to the spring was reputed to be a most beautiful and gifted Roman lady, descended from a noble family. Being one of the early Christians, when the faith was pure and unsullied by the political manoeuvrings of the Roman Church, she refused to marry the son of Sempronius, the governer of Rome, because he was still a pagan. Despite bribes and threats, she refused all advances, and in indignant fury, Sempronius condemned her to be burnt. As soon as the fire was kindled, however, the flames divided and encircled her on every side without doing her the slightest harm. In desperation, this young lady of such noble birth (she was said to be thirteen at the time) was dragged from the stake and beheaded by a common executioner.

Thomas Quiller Couch wrote of the well; 'My friend writes that this well existed in an entire state till about 1820. Over it was a little Gothic edifice, which gave the name of Porth Chapel to the spot, and Chapel Coombe to the valley and adjoining cove. It was on the western side of St. Agnes beacon, in a narrow dell descending to the sea. The situation, as is not infrequent with these buildings, is wild and weird in the extreme. Not a cottage nor a tree is to be found; a bleak heathy common, relieved by a few furze bushes, and rugged volcanic rocks, are the only objects that meet the eye.

'The destruction of the chapel and its well was effected by time, and lack of faith and reverence. It is said that the principle depradators, who carried away the stone to build a hedge, said, when remonstrated with, 'What's the good of a well without water?' The well had indeed been drained by the delvings of the miners in a working below. The name of 'Giant's Well' was given to it by the country folk, in memory of a Giant (called Bolster) who once lived near it, and was accustomed to drink of the fountain. There were the marks of his thumbs indented on a stone in the well, and near it, on another, the print of his foot, very large, and very like a footmark. Pins were dropped in with wishes as in many other parts of Cornwall.'

Standing in *Kenwyn Churchyard* amongst clusters of Celtic crosses and towering yew trees, your eyes are drawn down to the sprawling city of Truro below, framed by Brunel's gargantuan viaduct and dominated by the trinity of spires from the cathedral. The river writhes in serpentine splendour in the sunlight, the distance lending enchantment to the reality of the sounds and smells of modern traffic. But in this old churchyard, with lichen encrusted gravestones leaning out of drifts of virgin snowdrops, is a well that is said to be much older than the church itself. No legend tells of the mysterious qualities of the water, but it seems likely that the church was built on this site because of the existence of the old sacred spring, Christianity erasing the earlier traditions that would have been passed on from generation to generation. It wells up near the entrance to the church, a series of ancient slate steps worn by countless forgotten feet leading down below ground level. An old brickwork arch roofs over the subterranean pool, the water tasting unpleasantly of old musty leaves and lichen, and more likely to give you an upset stomach than cure your lumbago.

A similar well, reached by stone steps descending below the front garden of a house next to St. George's Hotel in the town, has more historical connections. It resides in a very old suburb of the town where a friary was established by

Dominican Friars in 1259, hence the name of *St. Dominick's Well*. Evidently, in its day it was an important missionary centre with its own farm, church and chapter house, and when it was destroyed during the Dissolution, boasted at least one Prior and ten friars. Who knows, but buried somewhere around here might be the gold vessels and treasures of the Friary, hidden from the desecrators and never rediscovered. There is a story telling of hidden treasure connected with *St. Clare's Well* at Idless, a couple of miles up the river from Truro. The seventeenth-century chronicler Hals writes; 'It was a walled well, chapelwise built by the nuns of the nunnery house of Poor Clares in Truro; but yet, alas! as tradition saith, they were not so poor as their rule obligeth them to be, for in the walls of this well they had deposited or hid away considerable sums of money, which, by tradition or some dream, was discovered during the time of James II, by some of the inhabitants of the parish, who one night pulled down the walls and totally defacing this chapel wall in quest thereof, and probably succeeding in their undertaking, for soon after some poor labourers in agriculture became rich farmers and landed men and others'. One can only hope that this antique precendent is not followed by modern well-hunters, spending furtive weekends at remote wells amidst the bleeping and buzzing of metal detectors.

These stories of hidden treasure seem to be common to this area, in a similar way that the curses of St. Nun's and St. Cuby's well in the Pelynt district were so prevalent in past times. Yet another tale tells of how *St. Cohan's Well* at Merther was demolished 'by greedy searchers for money', all that is left today is a spring bubbling up in the corner of a field.

But near the ruined church and the site of the now lost chapel, many interesting objects have been dug up from time to time, including a stone figure of St. Anthony boasting a carving of a pig with a bell round its neck at his feet, possibly from the fifteenth century, a holy water stoup with a human face on it, and fragments of a very ancient font with star mouldings, presumably from the site of the old well.

No-one really needs an excuse to visit the Roseland peninsula, an area of Cornwall that is saturated in mystic legend and soaked in an exquisite atmosphere of peace. Two thousands years ago, the Roseland was almost an island, with the rivers in full flood and ships travelling up the rivers and estuaries as far as Tregony, which was even navigable to smaller boats up to the Middle Ages. A thriving trade with the Phoenicians developed in this area during the Bronze Age, which may well stretch back to far earlier times, and recent aerial photographs have shown that there was a henge monument at Philleigh, as well as the formidable structure of Carn Brea, with a diameter of 137 feet. The legendary island of Iktis, recorded by the Latin historian Diodorus in the fourth century BC, may well have been situated here, for he tells of an island that was accessible only by a causeway at low tide and that it was a centre for trading in tin. Other possible sites in Cornwall include the magical island of St. Michael's Mount, but it is interesting to note that in 1812, a tin ingot was dredged up off St. Mawes' point that is now in the Truro museum, and is thought to be the oldest example known.

St. Just-in-Roseland Church is deservedly famous as one of the most beautifully situated churches in Britain, and it possesses an old holy well below the gardens near the shoreline of the intimate cove with its bobbing boats and air of intense tranquillity. H. V. Morton wrote of the place in the 1920's; 'I have blundered into a garden of Eden that cannot be described in pen or paint, there is a degree of beauty that flies so high that no net of words or no snare of colour can hope to capture it, and of this order is the beauty of St. Just-in-Roseland. . . . There are a few cottages lost in the trees, a Vicarage with two old cannon balls propping open the garden gate, and a church . . . in a churchyard which is one of the little-known glories of Cornwall. I would like to know if there is in the whole of England, a churchyard more beautiful than this. There is hardly a level yard to it. You stand at the lychgate and look down into a green cup filled with flowers and arched by great trees. In the dip is the little church, its tower level with you as you stand above it. The white gravestones rise up from ferns and flowers.'

The well is at the end of a little path that leads down below the churchyard, a primitive square building roofed over by a large slate, and with a heavy slate step. Although there is no legend attached to the well, the water was used as the main source for the Rectory for many years, and has been fetched for baptisms in the church since time immemorial. The area is surrounded by the tenacious legend that Christ came here with Joseph of Arimathea, who travelled this way as a tin merchant. The boy Jesus sailed into St. Just Pool and landed at the bay below the church, a place that was already held sacred in those pre-Christian days, and talked to the holy men who lived there.

Whether those feet did, in ancient times, tread this green and pleasant land, perhaps travelling to the famous Holy Island of Avalon at Glastonbury in search of the most enlightened men of his age, we may never know. But the persistence of such a legend, and the almost other-worldly peace that permeates the place has the effect of seeping surreptitiously into the deep levels of the mind, celebrated at the back of the guide-book to the church in a Christian invocation of the primeval four elements;

> *Deep peace of the Running Wave to you,*
> *Deep peace of the Flowing Air to you,*
> *Deep peace of the Quiet Earth to you,*
> *Deep peace of the Shining Stars to you,*
> *Deep peace of the Son of Peace to you.*

Travelling from Wales in search of the ascetic life, the solitary hermit who was later to become *St. Mawes* chose a remote spot at the side of Falmouth harbour. Reputed to be the son of an Irish king, he settled near a natural spring that was, like the hermit himself, to become famous for its healing powers. Whitaker records, in his 'Cathedral of Cornwall'; 'The existence of a well combined with the solitariness of the site and with the noonday sun to invite his settlement at this particular ground. There he lived as a hermit; forming himself a chair in the rock above the well for his enjoyment of the warm situation, in occasional surveys of the creek under him, of the harbour upon his right, and of the sea in front of the latter, then all assuredly solitary almost as the very site itself. Thence, however, the fame of his sanctity diffused itself all over the neighbourhood, he thus became troubled probably with the resort of people to him, removed himself across the Channel to find a more solitary situation, and settled in an uninhabited islet for the effectual preclusion of all visits. . . . After his removal, the chair and the well appear to have been visited and admired for his sake, the admiration of his character naturally attaching to every object connected with it. After he was dead and sainted, this admiration of course rose into reverence, the well was visited in greater crowds, the chair was viewed with deeper respect, and the hermitage was entered with devouter awe. This gave a commencement to the town, the votaries of the sainted hermit settling in houses around the hermitage, and the hermitage itself being reconstructed into a chapel for the devotees.'

If the saint took so much trouble to avoid the tourists of his day, his presence would certainly not linger long around the village of St. Mawes in the summer today. It still possesses a certain charm out of season that once gave rise to the description of a 'praty village or fischar town with a pere', but it is now a place primarily for the visitor, a long tradition initiated by the old saint himself all those years ago. In the last century, the well was 'cut deeply into the living rock, on the right of the road into the village; running endlong into the heart of the rock, arched over for its whole length, and faced with a slightly peaked arch of stone.'

In the reign of Elizabeth I the nearby chapel was closed and turned into a dwelling-house, and later, human bones were excavated when the chapel yard itself was built upon. Nowadays the well stands half-way up the hill from the Victory Inn, close to the original site, restored with a fifteenth-century arch and a modern carved oak door, tucked in beside a pink-washed cottage. It was renowned until recently for its curative properties pertaining to those who required to rid themselves of worms!

Wandering about the Roseland peninsular in the spring is an invigorating experience, for the whole area seems trapped in a time-warp where watches and clocks appear to slow down, producing an immediacy that is outside the circles of time. It is similar to the shock some people feel when they visit

Ireland, for time really does not matter in the same way you always thought it did. The events of the days and weeks of your life are not, in fact, governed by the passage of time as you had always supposed, for time is merely a by-product of the events themselves. This essentially Celtic feeling is particularly noticeable down in the promontary of the Roseland, especially if you have come across the river from the Falmouth side, where civilization rules, on the King Harry Ferry to embark on the shores of a part of the land that is timeless. Travelling through lanes like tunnels, cut in the rock of the hillside and arched with trees, past ruined mills and lovely old cottages that have yet to be modernised into the twentieth century and moulded into picture-postcard holiday homes, you can stumble across small villages like *Veryan* in a strangely sensitive frame of mind. The day I went to see the old well opposite the church, an interesting restored well rebuilt in 1912 and with as strange a cross as I have seen adorning the roof, a funeral was taking place in the church. The sound of mournful voices raised in sober song reverberated around the gravestones, the coffin trestles stood to attention outside the church door. A delicious realization of the total futility of hurtling around the face of the Earth like frenetic fruit flies, desperate to cram in as much as possible in case someone should swat us with a rolled-up newspaper, descended upon me as I thought about the slow refined elegance and natural harmony of the place, and of the cold body lying in its box in the aisle. Not a mood of morbidity, just an immediate understanding of the real need to find time to stand and stare.

11

THE WELLS
OF THE EAST

*Old ruinous places reveal themselves—Talking
heads—The curse of the Piskies and the Bog
Demon—memories of ancient warriors and Kings—The
magic elixir for a blissful marriage*

HE village of Lewannick is particularly well-endowed with springs, some of which are no more than open streams, although to this day dim memories of reverence remain in the minds of the locals. One such well, located in the woods of the Trelaske estate, is known as *Joan's Pitcher*, from which the water used to be collected for baptisms and was considered to be good for sore eyes. A similar story is told of *Penventon Well*, which a century ago was entirely unknown except to the Vicar, and we must suppose that the brambles and weeds that were engulfing it then have taken their toll and condemned it to be lost in the haze of the past.

Blaunders Well has been thought by some to be the origin of the foundation of the village, and is remarkable for its inexhaustible supply of clear water, much used by the locals of old. It rises in a boggy hollow at the side of a farmyard, overhung by beech trees, and flows, directed by small, displaced stones, to join another small stream that trickles down from above. One large stone serves as the foundation of the structure, three slabs of slate being arranged to form a square, open well, the water issuing from a round hole cut in one of these slates. Standing beneath the old tree that overlooks the spring, the farmer told how, as a child, he had played around the old well with other village children, and how it was famous among them as a place to collect frogspawn. Sure enough, the milky globules of spawn floated beneath the rippling water, protected from the surrounding mud by their sanctuary of slate. His cattle still drank from the spring, he said in an affable way as if relieved to stretch his legs after too much tractor-driving. He recalled how, as a youngster, he and his friends had greatly enjoyed the antics of the local vicar, who, robed in his vestments, would walk in a suitably dignified manner through the village from the church in order to bless the waters of Blaunders Well. From his vivid description, I left the old well with a clear mental picture of the cleric strutting off down the lane, the village children laughing and dancing after him as he strode off like the pied piper of Hamelin.

Old photographs of *All Hallows Well* at Halwell show a remarkable spectacle of the almost supernatural rapport between old trees and the masonry that covers these springs. Large chunks of the local freestone are trapped in the serpentine writhings of bulbous and distorted roots, growing directly from the crumbling structure in a weird celebration of the primitive pantheon of tree, rock and spring. Perhaps it is exactly this intimate union of the three realms of Nature that conveys an often lasting image of strange unearthliness, a primeval beauty that has little to do with our normal ideas of prettiness and cultivated pastoral romance. Whatever the images projected into the inner mind, they now only exist in these old photographs, for the peculiar phenomenon of All Hallows has now disappeared altogether, and has been replaced by a rectangular box made of tedious concrete blocks, the sort of structure that would be more at home on a sewage farm. Scattered about are the next generation of young trees, offspring of the venerable ancient parent who for so many years provided such singular support for the old stones.

George Bishop was not only fascinated by the existence of this well, he was intrigued by the whole history of the area around his cottage, and bulging files of documents were crammed into shapeless cardboard boxes piled on the table. He knew I was writing a book on the old wells, and in the course of tidying up the stone hedges at the bottom of his garden, had come across fascinating remnants of what must have been the original structure, or perhaps parts of the chapel that had once stood on this spot. We talked of the antiquity of the once-famous holy well, and of how Lord Treffry and his family were married, baptised and buried their dead at the chapel which stood within a hundred feet of the well, the waters of which were directed into the chapel yard by a stone channel. In 1332 Sir Reginald Bottreaux had a medieval masion here, a fact that interested me since that other haunt of the Bottreaux family, Boscastle, had been responsible for ensnaring me with its wild Cornish beauty. I had once come down for a holiday and never returned to the land across the Tamar, except for the occasional visit.

The old, moss-covered stones that George Bishop had rescued from the hedge were indeed intriguing. The worn, angled roof-stones he had discovered were piled up under a tree like miniature casing-stones from an Egyptian pyramid. Other, carved blocks lay about, and a crafted door-pillar of such exquisite workmanship that there could be no lingering doubt that here, on this spot, there once stood a building of great importance. And other than these buried stones, there seemed to be nothing left to remind us of those lost days except for the references of dusty historical records. We tasted a tiny thrill of archaeologists uncovering things buried for centuries.

Next to the piles of excavated stones lay a huge granite trough, of such size and weight that we must assume that it had not travelled very far in its time. It reminded me of a Saxon sarcophagus, such was its size, except that the shallowness indicated other origins. Too elaborate somehow for a mere animal trough, it seemed more like a bath, with a drain hole drilled through the stone at one corner, other slits cut in the sides and various grooves chiselled here and

OLD STONES REVEAL THEMSELVES. . . . An ancient granite trough and carved masonry are revealed at the site of All Hallow's Well, Halwell.

there, inviting speculation that it had once been a receptacle where the infirm could bathe in the healing waters. It was certainly a unique object, and as the drizzle collected and dripped from our damp, tousled hair, we headed back to the cottage past a huge slab of granite that had just been hauled from the ground, finely worked into a perfect crescent arc. The whole area seemed to be disgorging its hidden trove of relics. Only a few days before, another stone similar to the ornate door-pillar had been discovered reclining in a neighbour's garden. The past was beginning to come to the surface after centuries of obscurity, and it drew our minds to the treasures that lay buried the length and breadth of the county, perhaps hidden just a matter of feet below the unsuspecting surface.

Back in front of the kitchen stove, we began to steam gently as I theorized that Halwell could in fact be a contraction of All Hallows Well, and thought of the Celtic festival of All Hallows Eve, when, standing on a high point an observer would see great chains of bonfires stretching away across the countryside, the horizon aglow with the orange halos of the burning beacons, with legions of tiny, distant figures silhouetted against the flames. I was in a suitably romantic mood to set off to see the well of St. Melor, just a few miles to the south at Linkinhorne.

Sometimes I wish I had been a boy scout. If the mood is not quite right or there are some maleficent astrological influences doing their best to lead me astray, I have great difficulty in translating the lines and features of a map onto the real landscape, which to the human eye is a limited field of vision made up of buildings, trees and hills. But I could see that *St. Melor's Well* was somewhere down in the valley below the church, and, incidentally, past the village pub. After turning the map upside down a few times and exploring the churchyard for a possible path, I decided to head down into the fold of the valley where I hoped the granite building would loom up at me from around some unexpected corner. A photograph taken in 1891 shows three people sitting on the hill above the well, stiff-collared and starch-frocked in their Sunday best, and helped to give an idea of the lie of the land. Down a lane by the church, I wandered through a farmyard looking for the farmer who belonged there, but all was silence. Walking down through an idyll of a meadow, shafts of sunlight began to shine through the trees in an orchard as the weather changed to herald a bright mood of spring optimism. Young calves nosed amongst wild daffodils and a white horse edged forward inquisitively. I felt as if I were somehow intruding in some private dream, a little guilty that I had not been able to find the farmer.

Looking back over my shoulder at this scene of impressionist tranquillity, I crossed over a couple of hedges and passed another relic of the power of water, a rusting iron mill wheel set half-way in the ground, water still in its leat. What use was this put to, I wondered? No machinery remained and it is unusual to find such a monument to man's industry on its own in the middle of a field. On I went, following the cattle tracks past a hillside covered in yellow gorse, and there, in the corner of a field, its gurgling trickle drowning the birdsong, the old well stood in the middle of a marsh, huge irregular blocks of stone untouched by time except for the rounding of the once-sharp corners and a missing chink in the roof. A large blasted oak lay fallen just a few feet from the well, and the church steeple peered over the bright yellow gorse, the copious spring meandering its way down to the stream not many yards away. A gentle place, with the hypnotic sound of the water stilling the mind.

Sitting on the bearded trunk of the fallen tree, thoughts of the legend of St. Melor flitted through the mind. This saint of Cornish and Breton fame also gives his name to Mylor, near Falmouth, and was reputed to be the son of a king of Cornwall called Melian. In a tale of ruthless family ambition that could rival the Borgias, Melor's uncle Rivold invaded the county, murdered Melian and demonstrated his affection towards his nephew Melor by cutting off his head. But he must have got quite a shock when the severed head spoke and instructed him to set it on a staff in the ground. When this was done, the skull and staff was transformed magically into a beautiful tree from the root of which an unfailing fountain began to gush. Absorbed in the Celtic flavour of this tale

AN EARLY PHOTOGRAPH OF ST. MELOR'S WELL at Linkinhorne, which was obviously visited by people at the weekend in their stiff and starched Sunday best.

A sketch of Manaton Well in the last century, when it had a curious roof of turf. Today it looks very different, neglected and overgrown.

of the Cornish Aaron's Rod, I got quite a shock when the breeze blew a dangling piece of old man's beard into my face from the branches of the fallen oak, my mind awash with visions of severed heads.

An old sketch of *Manaton Well* shows a peculiar building roofed with turves, with large granite quoins forming the walls, a moulded doorway and a cut stone channel leading the water away. The garden of the private house on which an ancient manor house once stood is exotically atmospheric, with a picturesque pond containing an island with palm trees and a small stream flowing under tiny bridges. Water seems to rise everywhere. The owner told me that parts of the present house went back to the twelfth century, and there seems little doubt that the site stretches back into great antiquity, leading us to believe that the well, in a field below the garden was at one time a holy well, although no saint's name or legend is now remembered. It is now a pale and poignant shadow of its former self, preserved in that old sketch. An old holly tree sprouts from all around the building, the turfed roof has long since disappeared, and the whole structure is in a sad state of neglect and decay.

Tucked into a corner, below the level of the street in the town of Liskeard, is a well that has some intriguing peculiarities, its curative properties being famous in the past when crowds of people would swarm there to seek alleviation from their afflictions. In times gone by, it seems to have been known as both St. Martin's and St. Luke's Well, when the healing waters would obviously seem to be no match for a singular strain of saintly schizophrenia. Nowadays it is called the *Pipe Well*, and stands incongruously down some stone steps beneath the old market, complete with Victorian iron railings and the three protruding pipes from which the water issues. The best account of its virtues are given in Hitchens' and Drew's History of Cornwall;

> *'There is a house standing near the bottom of the town, which from its windows, gateway and sculptured ornaments, appears to have been formerly connected with some religious establishment. Near this building issues the spring which supplies the inhabitants with water, and the excellency of this salubrious fountain is deservedly held in high estimation. Conscious of its intrinsic value, the credulous inhabitants of former ages attributed to it some miraculous virtues, which fancy still continues to cherish with fondness, even to the present day. The source whence this water issues is acknowledged to be involved in a kind of indefinite mystery, so that even curiosity is content to let it remain unexplored. The stream on becoming visible is divided into three parts, all of which have some peculiar efficacy; but one branch far surpasses the others in its potent qualities. A stone that is deposited over the well is presumed by tradition to have a considerable influence over the matrimonial connections of any fortunate female, who, under given circumstances, and at an appointed time, shall have the happiness to touch it with her foot. These tales are still kept alive, and the ceremonials are practised by the young and thoughtless to the present hour.'*

The age obviously became less credulous as the years passed, for a later observer, Gilbert, in his survey of Cornwall, writes;

> *'Liskeard has one of the most commodious wells that we have seen in the county, and which was formerly crowded by superstitious visitors. The water falls into a stone reservoir from three shutes; and that which flows from the central one was in former times believed to possess the greatest healing efficacy. The well is still plentifully supplied with transparent water; but the credibility of its sanative virtues has evaporated like the morning dew which is exhaled by the rays of the sun.'*

Certainly, its credibility is now at an all-time low, the magic stone being covered over, its healing virtues unknown and unsought as the traffic and bustling shoppers hurry past this old spot. And the final indignity to anyone who might be presumptious enough to invoke the powers of the waters is emblazoned on a painted sign above the spouting pipes. An official warning states that 'This water is not for drinking'.

At the side of the country road that leads from Liskeard to the village of Duloe, where there stands an impressive stone circle made from solid quartz, the interesting well of *St. Cuby* lies in the midst of a tangle of rhododendron bushes and wild plants. The saint himself is of great interest, since he is virtually the only Cornish saint who we are definitely told was born in Cornwall. He was the son of Solomon, a Christian chieftain, who renounced his claim on his father's kingdom and devoted himself to learning and religion at an early age. He later settled at Tregony for a short time, then visited Ireland, and finally travelled to the Holy Druidic Isle of Anglesey, where he died.

The solid stone building of grey granite, topped by an equal-armed cross, is quite a wondrous place, especially as the only original part of the well is the rock wall at the back. A former Rector was responsible for restoring the well, and a fine job he made of it. A rough slate path leads to a dingy cavernous entrance, and stone seats are placed either side where you can sit and soak up the atmosphere. The rock wall down which the water drips into the pool below is glistening green with mosses, the water itself deliciously cool and pure. At one time, the water used to flow into a circular basin of granite, carved and ornamented around the edge with the figures of dolphins, shaped like a font and with a griffin on the lower half. In the past, the well and its basin were treated with the greatest respect by the countryfolk, who believed that some dire misfortune would inevitably befall anyone who attempted to move the font-shaped receptacle. The same story that hovers over nearby St. Nun's Well at Pelynt is also connected with this one, in that a farmer who tried to remove the basin was forced to give up the attempt when one of his oxen fell dead on the spot. Another story tells that when the basin was rolled down the hill by drunken workmen, it came to rest beside the cottage of an old lady who heard the Piskeys laughing over it all night. In the Old Cornwall journal of April 1928, a story is told which demonstrates that even at the latter part of the last century, the superstition was still strong. The squire of Trenant Park wished to take the basin to 'preserve' it in his grounds, but such was the belief in the malevolent power of the Piskeys that he had to pledge himself firmly to provide pensions for the families of anyone who fell dead before his men would touch the stone. Perhaps he bribed the Piskeys as well, for we have no record of any connected deaths, and the bowl was duly removed to Trenant. It stands today in the local church.

These tales of malefic intent directed at would-be desecrators of the old shrines might well strike us today as the ridiculous superstitions of simple country yokels, perpetuated down the centuries as some form of meagre protection for the wells. But the tales that we come across now are but a decaying memory of an earlier view of existence, a direct experience of the natural but unseen realms that were not only apparent to the unaffected people of old but were also more potent in their manifestation. As the original purpose of these places was forgotten, the memory of their power was bound up more than ever in the common consciousness with the pervasive tales of the creatures from the realms of Faery.

ST. CUBY'S WELL near Duloe is one of those wells that is connected by tradition with a curse. This, however, did not stop the local squire removing the carved stone basin to his estate towards the end of the last century. He did, though, have to pledge himself to provide pensions for the families of the men who moved the stone in case of mysterious death.

A succinct appraisal of this vision of the reality of the Otherworld is given by E. L. Gardner in the preface to Geoffrey Hodson's book 'Fairies at Work and Play';

> *'A vast variety of etheric and astral forms, large and small, working together in organized co-operation on what we must call the life side of Nature, stimulating growth, bringing colour to the flowers, brooding over beautiful spots, plunging in waves and waterfalls, dancing in the wind and sunlight, in fact, another order of evolution running parallel to and blended with our own.'*

In between eating, sleeping, procreating and dying, these diverse beings attend to their work according to their particular element, daily performing their special duties. Certain sub-species are connected with actual places and objects, and Naiads and Undines, the creatures of Water, sometimes appear to humans in flashes of second sight or clairvoyance as water nymphs 'lustrously speeding along rivers and streams or rising seductively from secret pools'. Behind this romantic imagery lies the actual creative reality of the potent energy forces of Nature, working together to create and maintain the incredibly complex structure of the natural world.

In the sixteenth century, such memories were collected from all over the world by a certain Theophrastus Bombastus Von Hohenheim, better known to us as Paracelsus. In his wanderings, the great mystic, physician and alchemist recorded the persistent legends from all corners of the globe, and concluded that the elemental spirits have a separate reality of existence which often interpenetrates with our own, and can become apparent to those of a sufficiently sensitive nature. This vision is remarkably well sustained throughout the ages, from the primitive shamans of the ancient world, through the Druids and the great Nature religions to the present day, where a similar outlook is common among the cottagers and crofters of the remoter parts of the Celtic regions. In the days when the wells and other Earth shrines were utilized for their primordial purpose of balancing the flow of terrestrial energies, humanity and the elementals worked in harmony for the same purpose, the health and fertility of the countryside and all its creatures. It is because of this rapport that some people are occasionally granted glimpses of the 'Faeries' or 'Piskeys' usually when they least expect it. The ancient sites of mounds, monoliths, stone circles and wells are quite notorious for the sighting of these secretive beings, the inherent power still attached to the old places opening up that part of the mind that is strangely receptive to their presence.

But these Earth spirits are not always as twee and loveable as Victorian nannies would like us to believe, for they control their particular aspect of the Life force, and can withold it or even turn it against those who destroy or interfere with their works, causing injury and even death! The offerings left in wells are often votive gifts to these spirits to ensure their help and co-operation. Think about it next time you toss a coin into a wishing-well!

An old granite basin, which fills mysteriously in its dim grotto, is practically obscured by a covering of rich moss, dripping with beads of quicksilver water which fall to the dank ground below. The ancient bowl of *St. Nun's Well* at Pelynt has been guarded for ages, so we are told, by a legendary tale that seems to have protected it from the destructive hand of man to this day, although the structure of the damp cavern grown about with the writhing roots of a gnarled oak is now in danger of collapsing completely. Looking out across a steep, wooded valley, the old well may still be haunted by a spirit which can show anger to those who would threaten it, as well as adopting the mood of a beneficent elf, so leading local people a century ago to call it 'Piskey's Well'.

An old farmer, so the story goes, decided that the stone basin would look much better in his pigsty, and no doubt encourage his unholy hogs to grow at a rate to be expected from those who would feed from such a sacred trough. Two oxen with chains were his chosen method of removal, and he arranged the chains and bade his oxen pull with all their might in the traditional manner, no doubt licking his lips and sniffing bacon in the air. After considerable effort, they finally dragged it up to the top of the steep valley, where the old stone antiquity showed its innate dislike for pigs and oxen by breaking free of the chains, rolling back down the hill, making a sharp right turn and settling neatly back into its place in the well. One of the beasts immediately fell dead, the farmer was struck lame and speechless, and the previously prosperous landowner found that his fortunes had turned like the twist in a pig's tail. It seems at first glance that no-one has ever been prepared to test the efficacy of the old legend, for peering into the gloom reveals that the revered receptacle still rests in the dripping twilight of its subterranean shrine, always full.

However, closer inspection reveals that this may well be a replacement, for it is damaged, and shows no sign of the carvings shown in old sketches. Did some foolhardy soul eventually scorn the old legend and drag the old bowl off despite the curse? Perhaps the ancient basin resides at this very moment in some corner of a Cornish farmyard, smouldering with resentment, while the owners, unaware of its power, wonder why their crops wither and their animals are always sickly?

When Thomas Quiller Couch came across this well in the last century, time and the storms of winter had almost ruined it, and the roots of a large oak tree had dislodged stones from the arch. The swaying of the tree in the wind had shaken down a large mass of masonry and the place was clothed with ivy and dense undergrowth of willow and bramble. The owners, the romantically-named Trelawneys of Trelawne, suggested that he superintended the restoration, which involved felling the old oak and rebuilding the well with Cornish slate. A hundred years later, the condition of this dank and dripping place again needs some sympathetic soul to rescue it from the ravages of wind and weather, and, I suspect, much damage caused by cattle. Another oak, or perhaps a remnant of the original, grows from the corner of the building, its twisted roots pulling apart the slates that sprout clumps of Pennywort. The single flat stone lintel is now leaning at a drunken angle away from the

St. Ninnie's, or St. Nun's Well at Pelynt, sketched in the last century by J.T. Blight. His friend Thomas Quiller Couch rebuilt the well at the suggestion of the romantically-named Trelawneys of Trelawne.

curiously-shaped tree root and the old slates are working themselves loose, giving the impression that at any moment, Nature might achieve what the human hand, perhaps thanks to the old legend, has not.

A small chapel once existed above the well, dedicated to St. Nun, the daughter of a Cornish chieftain, and an oratory, of which no trace now exists, was mentioned as being licensed in 1400. This ancient sacred site is found in an

DECLINE AND FALL. . . . The entrance to St. Nun's Well at Pelynt, rebuilt by Thomas Quiller Couch over a hundred years ago, and now desperately in need of more attention as the masonry slowly collapses. Inside, an old granite bowl, protected by a curse, fills mysteriously in the dripping twilight of the old shrine.

area famous for its eyecatching beauty, the part of Cornwall beween Liskeard and Looe swathed in the lush foliage of established woodland and verdant valleys. It lies on the western side of a river that flows on to the Looe estuary, and although it is completely hidden from view as you take the dead-end track over a cattle grid, it is clearly marked on the map. Despite the peace and natural sensuality of the spot, there is a strange air of brooding that surrounds it which is difficult to communicate. An indefinable suspicion of resentment is one of the moods I have caught on more than one occasion.

Once, sitting on the old thorn tree that has been torn from its roots and almost obscures the entrance, my eyes wandered skywards to a pair of buzzards circling overhead, and the lazy flapping of a heron winging its way upstream. As if some malignant spell had been cast, the sky darkened in a few fleeting seconds, and I watched a whirling grey squall of bad weather move rapidly up the valley, which made me dripping wet before I could react. The speed and unexpected force of these few moments, whilst being an entirely natural phenomenon on a late winter's day, somehow fermented the peculiar atmosphere of the place into a wary respect that caused me to look over my shoulder more than once as I made my way back towards the gate. Like the respectful people of old, who used to drop innumerable offerings into the antique granite font for cure and prophecy, and like the warning legend that hovers about the well, it left me with a feeling of having approached something distinctly other-worldly, a power almost primeval.

It would appear that the well has affected many others with its malefic mood, for the Rev. Lane-Davies relates how an old lady was horrified when her children brought home eightpence they had found in the well. She was greatly agitated and sent them back instantly saying she would not have the Piskeys in her house for untold gold. And a Pelynt girl told the story that anyone who visited the well without leaving an offering would be followed all the way home by clouds of Piskeys, a name given to small night-flying moths believed to embody the spirits of the dead! I suggest leaving a small offering would be the safest bet in this particular case.*

On the banks of the River Fowey stands the delightful church and holy well of *St. Sampson* at Golant, built on the site of a hermits cell that can be traced back to the sixth century. This solitary cell was once part of the church itself, extended and added to when the ancient site was taken possession of by a colony of monks from nearby Tywardreath during the religious revival that took place at the beginning of the thirteenth century. The well itself is built alongside the porch, the connecting aperture reopened during extensive renovations in 1938. But much of the legend of the saint who originally chose

---

* A recent visit reveals that the well is now in a far better state of preservation, and has been cleared from fallen trees. There is a far more peaceful quality around the old shrine.

this sylvan spot for his oratory is lost in the misty centuries, and it was not until many hundreds of years after his death that St. Sampson was sainted at the council of Lyons in 1244. The place is mentioned in Cornish romance by the Anglo-Norman Beroul;

> *'By the paved road they go up to the monastery of St. Sampson, the Queen and all the barons, a great number are met together. . . . The great baron, Dinas the Brave, carried thither a garment of rich silk embroidered with gold; it was worth fully one hundred marks of silver and the like was never possessed by count or king. And the Queen Iseult took it and laid it on the alter as an offering. It was made into a chasuble, which was kept in the Treasury and used only once a year on the great anniversary feast'.*

Tradition tells us that King Mark of Cornwall lived at Lancien, close to the monastery of St. Sampson, and the name Lantyne still lives on in the name of a nearby farm, a remnant of what must once have been the administrative centre of a great feudal empire across Cornwall. The romance and legend have become inextricably tangled over the centuries, tantalizing us with snatches of half-forgotten historical reverie. The life of the saint was set down about fifty years after his death, and tells how he founded the sacred site on the banks of the river, near a cave in which the saint had subdued a dragon. And, to tantalize us further with the fascination of the old romances, obscure facts may sometimes lead us to believe that there is more to them than we might otherwise suppose. For between Fowey and the ancient fortress of Castle Dore, a seven-foot high monolith that appears to date from the sixth century once stood in the middle of the road opposite the gates that lead to Menabilly and is now located near a roundabout leading to the town. The inscription reads; 'Tristram lies here, son of Cynvawr'.

St. Keyne is reputed to have lived towards the end of the fifth century, one of the progeny of the prolific King Brychan, without whom Cornwall would possess hardly a saint to call its own. Of the fifteen sainted children of the illustrious King of the Brecon Beacons, she stands out as the most saintly and the most beautiful in mind and body. Despite her bewitching loveliness, she is remembered as wandering about the country, safe from insult or wrong-doing by 'the strength of her purity', performing the most astonishing miracles in all the places she visited. One such miracle, performed in Somerset, is remembered in the name of Keynsham, where she changed all the serpents which infested the place into stone.* After a long life spent doing good works, the goodly saint retired to Cornwall, an idea much prevalent today as well as in

---

* Some claim that this is an allegory of the erection of monoliths or crosses to neutralize unbalanced energies, others point to the large number of fossil ammonites that are to be found in the area.

THE PICTURESQUE SITE OF ST. KEYNE'S WELL about a hundred years ago. The cottage has long since disappeared, but the spring of St. Keyne, one of the most famous in Cornwall, still flows on at the side of the road.

the past, to make her home in the beautiful valley near the well that bears her name, the famous holy well of *St. Keyne*. Over the spring she planted an oak, an ash, an elm and a withy, blessing them and endowing the waters with their peculiar virtue, and on her deathbed, soothed by the murmur and ripple of the stream, this saintly precursor of the feminist movement blessed the waters 'desiring above all things peace on Earth; and she hoped to benefit the world by giving to woman a chance of being equal to her lord and master'. The legend is enshrined in Southey's quaint poem, which is of interest in relating the properties of the fabled spring;

> *'A well there is in the west-country,*
> *and a clearer one never was seen,*
> *there is not a wife in the west-country,*
> *But has heard of the well of St. Keyne.*
>
> *An oak and an elm tree stand beside,*
> *and behind does an ash tree grow;*
> *And a willow from the bank above*
> *Droops to the water below.*

A traveller came to the well of St. Keyne,
Joyfully he drew nigh,
For from cock-crow he had been travelling,
and there was not a cloud in the sky.

He drank of the water so cool and clear,
for thirsty and hot was he,
and he sat down upon the bank
Under the willow tree.

There came a man from the house hard by
at the well to fill his pail;
On the well-side he rested it,
and he bade the stranger hail.

Now art thou a bachelor, stranger? quoth he,
For an if thou hast a wife,
The happiest draught thou hast drunk this day
That ever thou didst in thy life.

Or has thy good woman, if one thou hast,
Ever here in Cornwall been?
For an if she have, I'll venture my life
She has drunk at the well of St. Keyne.

'I have left a good woman who was never here,'
The stranger he made reply;
'But that my draught should be the better for that,
I pray you answer me why.'

'St. Keyne', quoth the Cornishman, 'many a time
Drank of this crystal well;
And before the Angel summoned her,
She laid on the water a spell.

'If the husband of this gifted well
shall drink before his wife,
A happy man thenceforth is he,
for he shall be master for life.

'But if the wife should drink of it first,
God help the husband then!'
The stranger stoopt to the well of St. Keyne
and drank of the water again.

'You drank of the well I warrant betimes?'
He to the Cornishman said,
But the Cornishman smiled as the stranger spake,
and sheepishly shook his head.

'I hastened as soon as the wedding was done,
And left my wife by the porch;
But, i' faith, she had been wiser than me
for she took a bottle to church.'

It is quite remarkable how this legend still persists in the county, for I have met many women who have tasted the waters 'just in case there's anything in it'. Thomas Quiller Couch relates a story from his day when the rector of the parish sent two dozen bottles of the fabled water to a bazaar in the grounds of Mount Edgcumbe, where they sold quickly at the amazing price of two shillings a bottle, and a loud demand for more!

Old photographs show the picturesque well opposite a quaint thatched cottage, and overshadowed by the celebrated trees, but towards the end of the last century the arch was tumbling to pieces and the trees in decay. Later, the lane was widened, the cottage disappeared, the remaining trees came down, and the Liskeard Old Cornwall Society undertook a complete rebuilding of the well in granite to give us the structure as we see it today, well signposted for miles around and much visited by our modern equivalent of pilgrims throughout the summer months.

Another famous well is *Dupath Well*, about a mile outside Callington, and which by a curious quirk of fate is a stone's throw from the printers of this book. Signs point the way, and you walk through a farmyard to see a curiously imposing structure, unique and idiosyncratic in its architecture. This building, made entirely from granite blocks, is the largest well building in Cornwall, and is said to have been erected over the spring by the monks of St. German's about 1510. The roof is formed by long stones laid horizontally, overlapping each other, the weight being supported by an internal arch springing from crude capitals, and supported by square piers. A square-headed window of two lights is in the east wall, with sunlight filtering in to dapple the copious cascade of water as it flows through its channel, bright coins glistening coppery gold in the shafts of morning light.

When it was re-discovered by the rector of South Hill, the Rev. H. M. Price, an enthusiastic antiquarian, it was in a very dilapidated condition with ivy and foliage concealing the ruins. He carefully picked out the stones that lay about, and succeeded in restoring the complex three-dimensional jigsaw puzzle to its present state. Later, a member of the local Old Cornwall Society bought the well from the local farmer for £100, a reasonable enough price for such a monument! The tradition connected with the well is as follows;

'A duel was fought here between two Saxons, named Gotlieb and Sir Colan, as rival candidates for a young lady. Gotlieb was a private gentleman of considerable wealth, while Sir Colan, though a knight, was poor. The father of the lady wished her to marry Gotlieb, on account of his wealth, but she

Dupath Well, or Baptistry

preferred Sir Colan, whom she had known from childhood. Sir Colan received the first wound, but ultimately overcame Gotlieb and killed him. The contest was long and desperate, Sir Colan's wound would have healed but for his impatience, to which he fell a victim'. Various versions of this romantic tale differ in the names and outcome of the story, but it is usually the victorious one that is remembered as surviving the effects of the duel, and building the well as an act of atonement for his sin. The romance of the fabled well was too much for even stout hearts to bear, though, for the poetic Vicar of Morwenstow, Robert Stephen Hawker, could not resist penning his own individual fancy in the ballad of Siward and Githa, an ancient fable of distinctly modern origins, no trace of his story being connected with the well outside his inspired imagination.

A grey, seeping mist hung in the still air the day I pulled up outside the church at *Landulph*, on the banks of the river Tamar. I knew that the remains of an old well were to be found in the garden of a house still called St. Anne's after a nearby chapel, but they were sparse remnants almost obliterated by wild growth. I was more intrigued by the possible remains of another well, marked on the Ordnance Survey map and to be found in a plot of land noted as Holy Well Meadow on a much earlier example of the mapmaker's art in 1788. One of the local residents pointed me down into the marsh on the edge of Kingsmill Lake, commenting wryly that it was just as well I'd brought my wellingtons. I saw instantly what he meant. I splashed though the misty marsh feeling my way with great care as I sank up to a foot every time boots connected with the spongy mass of weed and grass that was the bed of the marshland. A strange experience, as if the Earth itself had melted into something insubstantial, like wandering about in some primeval swamp from an age before man. But in the murky distance, I could see the blurred shapes of tiny vehicles crossing the Saltash bridge between Devon and Cornwall, and beyond, the sweeping Victorian curves of Brunel's Royal Albert bridge. In the foreground, like some carefully chosen location for a horror film, great leaning timber piles glowered in the swirling mist, the decaying remains of piers and jetties when men plied these quiet waters in rowing skiffs.

I must have trudged about for an hour, diligently peering through the Cornish mizzle in search of any clue to the site of the old well. It did seem quite remarkable to have had a holy well in the middle of a watery marsh, and I began to feel a little like the victim of some hoax that had been set in motion centuries ago. No sign of any remains could I find, until at last I came across a small clump of dank trees that looked as if they may have once indicated something other than a watery mire. And then the joke was really on me. As I tentatively set foot near the site, a great hole opened up beneath my feet, swallowing me in a sudden surge as I floundered helplessly, sinking fast. My wellingtons immediately filled up with a sort of fine sludge, and as I went down, my thoughts were to hold my camera gear aloft as the greatest necessity, and then a distant recollection that the worst thing you could do in a situation like this was to struggle! My eyes darted around the deserted marshland as I trod water hysterically in an effort to preserve some sort of equilibrium. If anyone had been around I would have made a comic sight, up to my waist in the bog, two arms stretched heavenwards in an attempt to keep my cameras dry. And then a strange power seemed to take over, something that has happened to me in other tight spots on cliffs and in the sea. The memory does not register exactly what happened in those few crucial moments, but the next thing I knew I was treading not water and sludge, but the spongy mass that was the bed of the surrounding marsh. I plodded and plashed my way back to higher ground, sat on the decaying hulk of an upturned boat, and collected what wits I still possessed. I was considering myself very lucky indeed, and found myself wondering whether I had actually fallen into the well itself. Then I discovered that my bunch of keys were no longer in my dripping pocket. They had been claimed by the grasping watery hands of the Bog Demon!

Fortunately I didn't bump into anyone as I headed back to the car, otherwise I would have felt even more sorry for myself as I left a trail of slime behind me like an antedeluvian reptile crawling from tl e primeval swamp. Sitting in a muddy puddle, staring at the smirking keyhole of the ignition switch, I cursed the Bog Demon wholeheartedly and determined not to be beaten. By some miracle, I managed to start the car with my Swiss Army penknife, and was never so glad to leave anywhere as I was when I drove, a limp and soggy mass of steaming self-pity, out of the cursed Landulph swampland. I comforted myself by invoking the 'Oh well, you can't win them all' philosophy, and deciding that some more intrepid well-hunter than myself could experience the joys of discovering the wells of Landulph, I headed off home to a dry armchair and a warm fire.

Almost at the eastern tip of Cornwall is *St. Julian's Well*, raised above the level of the road on the fringe of Mount Edgcumbe Country Park. This must have been the first well that travellers and pilgrims came to as they crossed on one of the ferries from 'England', from Western King Point, always in sight of Drake's Island, to Devil's Point on the Cornish side. What strange visions of this ancient and isolated part of the world must those travellers of old have conjured up in their minds as they embarked on the shore of this mysterious land of fable and legend? The old well sits high above the road which leads away into the country, aloof from the stone trough beneath an archway where the weary animals that would have struggled up the hill from the ferry slaked their thirst. The well is tucked in beneath a small hillside copse, standing solidly in a mood of Gothic transcendence. Grey-green stones, first shaped by the hand of man and then by the elements, form an arched doorway of perfect Gothic symmetry. Burnt sienna leaves scurry like mice around the entrance leading to the twilight pool of water beneath a corbelled roof, with niches placed for an effigy of the saint and another for votive offerings. A stone plinth in the corner is being eroded away by the earth-red seepage from behind, and through the doorway, setting the eyes beyond the gaps in the trees, grey warships rest easy in mid-river, against a backdrop of the modern bustling buildings of Plymouth.

About a hundred years ago, St. Julian's Well had become very ruinous, and was restored by the Earl of Mount Edgcumbe under the direction of the architect James Hine. He leaves us a lucid description of the building in his time;

> 'Probably the most ancient example of that curious and to some extent unexplained class of buildings, the Cornish well-chapel, is that of St. Julian's at Mount Edgcumbe. It is very small, its internal dimensions being only six

The neat Gothic building of St. Julian's Well at Mount Edgcumbe, from an old sketch.

feet three inches by four feet nine inches, and it was vaulted over by an equilateral stone arch formed by level bedded courses of masonry with a central chamfered rib resting on a moulded corbel. The doorway, or rather gateway (because there was no door), at the entrance end had also a pointed arch springing from the same line as that of the vault. The proportions are as simple as they are beautiful, and the details and character of the masonry fix the period approximately as that of the early part of the fourteenth century.

'It appears not to have been thought essential that these well-chapels should stand east and west, like our parish churches; and whilst the one at St. Cleather follows that position, this little building is placed north and south. At the southern end or fountain end is a niche which probably contained the figure of the patron saint. In the western side-wall, near the fountain, is another and lower recess, with an ogee chamfered arch corresponding with the other. The jambs, existing, of the doorway, the rib and corbels of the roof, as well as the niches, are of green freestone from the parish of Landrake; the rest of the masonry is of more local stone. The pavement was of red and green glazed tiles, fragments of which we have found.'

It may be that this well, unusual in its neat Gothic beauty, was dedicated to St. Julian of medieval mythology, condemned by fate to kill his parents. Perhaps more likely is that the patron saint is the St. Juliana of nearby Maker church, yet another of the innumerable saintly progeny of the Welsh King Brychan. There are many others throughout history of the same name, but there is no way of tracing such an attribution. For the Church always seemed to have had a disconcerting way of dedicating remote churches and chapels to obscure saints whose feet had never come within a thousand miles of this western land, as if in a deliberate attempt to throw a veil over true history, confound the natives, and bewilder hagiographers all at the same time. You leave your offering and you take your choice.

12

THE WELLS
OF BODMIN AND THE MOOR

*Disappearing chapels—the quick and easy method of
curing lunatics—a famous and saintly dwarf and the
Rime of the Ancient Ecologist—a little innocent
hydromancy—Prehistory is alive and well and living on
Bodmin Moor*

ODMIN Moor is the ancient heartland of Cornwall. Its rivers rise in the barren uplands, threading their way through ever-steeper valleys that grow greener and increasingly forested the closer they get to the sea. Nowadays the remote wilderness seen by the passing visitor is largely being spared from the destructive ravages of some modern farming methods by the continued existence of the small landowners who tease a precarious living from this wild land in much the same way that their predecessors have done since those early times. What appears to us as a vast windswept tract of open land was in those days densely forested, wild animals roamed free, and there was a settlement of Neolithic folk on the slopes of every tor. To inhabit the jungle-like valleys of those days was far too dangerous for our ancestors, they found bleak refuge on the hills above, building their stone huts, walled enclosures and Nature temples. They are there to this day.

It is difficult to imagine just how densely populated the moor was in those days of stone, but a fair idea can be gleaned by the remains of their villages and religious monuments, still braving the Cornish weather after many thousands of years. Hut circles and standing stones are scattered around the moor in great profusion. The Stripple Stones, The Hurlers, Nine Stones, Trethevy Quoit, countless relics in granite of the time before Man had mastered the use of metals. The wells which were venerated in their primitive animism have not stood the test of time in the same way as the implacable monoliths. Who knows if that boggy patch on the slopes of the tor was once kept clean and clear by the hands of the beaker folk, enclosed by slabs of crude stone for the worship of the spirits of water? It was all so long ago.

The only mention by Cornish historians of a well on the summit of a tor, which might take us back to these early days, is of a chapel and well on *St. Bellarmin's Tor* near Cardinham. In ruins for hundreds of years, no more than a few stones existed in the last century. Now a soggy spring is all there is to mark the once-venerated site. As the ages gathered momentum, the men of stone moved down from the hills, clearing the virgin forests for cultivation and grazing, and establishing settlements which have been almost continuous places of habitation through the aeons, and these are the places that have come down to us today, covered in a thin veneer of modernity. On the sides of moorland valleys, where the bleakness changes into scenes of pastoral picturesqueness, many of the old wells still exist, modified and changed by the vagaries of human evolution, as do other, younger wells founded by mystics whose names are sometimes remembered in legend. But many of the old shrines are simply remembered in the names of particular places or farmsteads which have been dwelling-places for millennia, as in the case of the ancient spring that still rises at *Maidenwell* near Cardinham, now the home of the explorer Robin Hanbury-Tenison.

Right in the middle of the moor, its name subtly charming you with visions of heaven-on-Earth, is the village of Blisland. Charming it certainly is, with the Royal Oak Pub, a most pagan-sounding hostelry, the Post Office and shop, and the church all flanking the village green, the only one of its kind in Cornwall. Those drawn to the dualist philosophy, however, will be pleased to note that only a couple of miles away is the complementary village of Helland, thoughtfully provided by the Great Architect to achieve the necessary balance between good and evil.

One old well is remembered only in the name of the track that leads down near the village shop, called Fairies' Well Lane, immortalizing the forgotten superstitions of the old village folk. Another spring from the past trickles away by the side of the road, down the hill from the church. This is the holy well of *St. Protus*, or St. Pratt, an early Christian martyr who sealed his faith with his blood when the Emperors of Rome were determined to crush the new faith into oblivion. A supreme irony as the political powers themselves were to avidly encourage the faith a few hundred years later to bolster up their crumbling Empire, a magnificent example of politicians changing with the wind.

At the turn of the century, the well was covered over, and the water directed down a chute, the sexton fetching water from the stream for baptisms. It was also said that the water used for building the church was brought from the stream that now flows through a cut stone channel, eventually to join a tributary of the river Camel below.

A far more prestigious affair was the well at a lonely spot near the hamlet of Tregenna, just outside Blisland village. Pulling into a lane in the midst of the small huddle of houses, one of the residents was stoking a bonfire with a tangle of bramble clearings, and the sweet smell of woodsmoke hung in the air. Delighted to be interrupted from his garden chores, he pointed out the farmhouse just a few steps away, belonging to the farmer on whose land *Blisland Holy Well* and chapel stood, and offered to show me the way, which I was very grateful for as it was entirely hidden from sight. We set off across the fields, passing a holding tank fed by a pump from the stream below the well, supplying water to my guide's cottage. Down the side of the valley, through a weird wood strewn about with huge mossy boulders, we followed the sound of running water to the ruins of the ancient chapel. A surprising, isolated place to find such a building, made from large, rough chunks of granite like the moorland cottages, and completely ruinous, two of the walls having collapsed almost completely.

A tree growing out of the masonry had fallen over, pulling the stones away amongst its roots and filling the interior of the chapel with its impenetrable branches. Beneath it, mossy mounds filled the cavity, and no timber or slates were to be seen, the whole structure impressing the mind with a feeling of great solidity and age.

The well rose from inside the chapel, somewhere beneath the mossy mounds, to flow through a small square doorway into a weedy quagmire and away to join the De Lank river which rises beneath Roughtor. As with all these sites, it possessed an individuality all of its own. It is a great pity that we know nothing whatsoever about its origins, history or legend, for it was surely an important place of the same order as St. Clether.

All we have, beside the ruins hidden in a wooded valley, is the recollection that the water was thought good for weak eyes, and the superstition that the field above the chapel and well should never be ploughed, some terrible disaster being likely to befall any transgressor. However, in the year 1878, a crop of corn was grown in this field, and during the harvest the ten-year old son of the farmer fell while taking down a scythe. The scythe fell with him, and cut his knee so severely that it was found necessary to amputate the leg, so strengthening the dire warning in the minds of the locals.

The old well next to a footpath at *Chapel Farm, St. Breward* shows the sort of resilience in the face of decay that might almost seem supernatural. In 1856, Thomas Quiller Couch visited it and found a 'dilapidated building standing in a sequestered valley, the old structure tottering to its fall'. He goes on; 'My original drawing is not without small value as preserving a memory of an interesting relic'. In 1891, visitors to the well were surprised to see it in very much the same state, except that a large opening had been made by miners at the back of the building. And growing out of the top, demonstrating some strange pagan affinity, was a thorn tree. I have lost count how many of these old structures have these trees, ancient symbols of spring and rebirth, growing out of their masonry or right next to the well. A huge thorn grows as a canopy over St. Nonna's Well at Altarnun, and there is a thorn tree growing above Jetwells holy well that was mentioned a hundred years ago. A thorn sprouts from the stones at Davidstow, and the trees spread all over the bank above the well at St. Clether. It is obviously true that they thrive on old masonry, but whatever the reason for this strange sympathy, it is quite extraordinary how often this particular type of tree thrives in such close symbiosis with the old wells, both being primeval symbols of that aspect of the Life-force representing rebirth.

IN SEARCH OF THE WELLS. . . . The author at Chapel Well, St. Breward. A dry and crumbling ruin for the last hundred years, there is little left to show that monks once inhabited this place up until 1442. Just the remains of the old well, the history hidden in the name of Chapel Farm, and a distinctive aura of sanctity.

Holy Well, St Breward

However, the old tree at St. Breward seems to have deserted its post, not content with a well that has no water. It used to be a perennial spring, visited by those afflicted with sore eyes and other infirmities. The spirit, or later the saint, was invoked by an offering, a farthing or a pin being usual in the days before its neglect. Offerings of more substance were probably made in the days when the chapel existed that gave Chapel Farm its name, providing a small but steady revenue for the monks who inhabited this place, their historical presence being last recorded in 1442.

Many stones from arched doors and windows were incorporated into the farmhouse during its construction, and other remnants of a religious edifice have been dug up near the well, indicating a place of some prominence.

Since the well itself was 'tottering to its fall' over a century and a quarter ago, it is a little astounding to find that it is in almost exactly the same condition as preserved in Thomas Quiller Couch's sketch, despite being a little more overgrown with ivy and moss. Damp leaves inhabit the interior, a modern pipe draining the water from below, and presumably, off to the farm. In earlier times, the water was channeled off into chutes to the back of the farm, and the remnants of this arrangement still exist near the back door. The old track that leads to the well, and the stone walls sprouting trees that surround it, have that distinctive atmosphere that envelops these sites of ancient sanctity, and which someone who searches out these places instinctively recognizes. To explain it is difficult through the medium of words, being a subjective experience, absorbed whilst pondering silently about past ages. But ultimately it is a question of imagination, of trying to keep the pigeon-holes of our preconceptions under control. You start to wonder about hooded monks, and a thousand images from books and films crowd the vision. But we can know little about the way that earlier minds functioned. An anthropologist (or should we say an anthropoid apologist?) would tell us that a primitive tribe discovered in the remote jungles of Papua New Guinea shows us how the tribal rituals of Stone or Bronze-Age man operated thousands of years ago. But that tribe has become trapped in time, stuck in the evolutionary mud. The people of old who held these places sacred were caught in a continuing vortex of gathering momentum, their attitudes drawn from different stimuli than our own. To them, Nature was an all-encompassing flowing power, not something you left outside as you shut the door when you got home from the office. The sense of wonder is the attitude to be cultivated in approaching these places, that is, an attitude that is diametrically opposed to the 'ignorant, primitive people of the past' stance that elevates us, and denigrates them.

In a field below the vicarage at Altarnun, the waters of the ancient *Well of St. Nonna* flow into a pool that has achieved great fame as a 'bowsening pool', where unfortunate lunatics were pitched backwards into the water in the hope of curing them by the early adherents of the short, sharp, shock principle. No better description of the prescribed treatment can be given than that recorded by the Cornish historian Carew in the sixteenth century;

> *'In our forefathers' days, when devotion as much exceeded knowledge as knowledge now cometh short of devotion, there were many bowssening places for curing madmen; and amongst the rest, one at Alternunne in this hundred, called St. Nunne's Pooll, which saint's altar it may be, pars pro toto, gave name to the church.*
>
> *'And because the manner of this bowssening is not so unpleasing to heare as it was uneasy to feele, I wil (if you please) deliver you the practise as I receyved it from the beholder.*
>
> *'The water running from St. Nunne's Well fell into a square and close-walled plot, which might bee filled at what depth they listed. Upon this wall was the franticke person set to stand,. his back towards the poole; and from thence, with a sudden blow in the brest, tumbled headlong into the pond, where a strong fellowe, provided for the nonce, tooke him and tossed him and tossed him, up and downe, alongst and athwart the water, until the patient, by*

forgoing his strength, had somewhat forgot his fury. Then was hee conveyed to the church, and certaine masses sung over him; upon which handling, if his right wits returned, St. Nunne had the thanks; but, if there appeared small amendment, he was bowssened againe and againe while there remayned in him any hope of life for recovery.

'It may be, this device tooke original from that master of Bedlam, who (the fable saith) used to cure his patients of that impatience, by keeping them bound in pooles up to the middle, and so more or less after fit of their fury'.

This extreme method of restoring a person's wits certainly appeared to work in some cases, curing epilepsy and some nervous disorders by this primitive shock treatment. But one cannot help feeling sorry for those bewildered wretches, frightened out of what wits they had left, standing, dripping in the church with the prospect of repeat performances until all hope was lost, an early aspect of the 'kill or cure' philosophy. And it really does seem a far cry from the benign healing qualities of other, more soothing, curative waters, sipped reverently or used for gently bathing the body. The practice of bowsening was eventually discontinued as orthodox Christianity attempted to defend itself against charges of cruelty (despite its appalling record!) and stamp out well-worship.

There are various legends concerning the life of St. Nonna, but it is generally agreed that she was the mother of St. David, patron saint of Wales, and it is interesting that St. Non's Well is near St. David's Cathedral in Wales, and that Davidstow adjoins the parish of Altarnun in Cornwall. Living in the sixth century, a time when there were few records kept, the details of her life were passed on by word of mouth in the same way that the legends of other saints come down to us. That is, some facts were forgotten by the passage of time, and others were embroidered to turn a good story into an even better one. The legends agree, however, that she was famous for her beauty, and that she was of noble birth. One story then goes on to tell us that King Caractacus of Cornwall fell in love with her and married her to produce St. David. Another relates how she fell into the clutches of a local chieftain by the name of Sant, who had no respect for her vocation and still less for her virtue. He forced his attentions on her, and as a consequence, she gave birth to a boy, the young St. David. Tradition has it that Sant repented his evil deed, and founded a monastery at a place some eight miles from Altarnun, now called Lezant. That there is an element of truth in there somewhere seems to be verified by William of Worcester, who states that St. David was born at Altarnun, and was thus by birth a Cornishman. And it is good to know that Cornwall gave at least one saint back in return for all those holy progeny of King Brychan.

Other stories tell of how the vicarage was built from the stones of a nunnery, and that the altar of this place was held in peculiar veneration by the country people. A lichen-smothered granite cross still stands in the churchyard from the sixth century, the time of St. Nonna. The well, however, fared badly after its use as a bowsening pool came to be regarded as primitive cruelty. In the last century there was little remaining, a triangular plot of hedges and fencing enclosing the pool, the walls, like some Roman bath, trodden down by cattle, and overgrown with rank grass and weeds. The pool itself was dry, the spring being drained off. An old thorn tree grew close by, which is still there today, and a covering stone was placed over the old well, carved stones lying about from some ancient sanctuary. And so it lay, dry and forgotten, for years.

Then Morley Brown bought the land on which it stood, and became fascinated by the legend of the well and appalled by its condition. An overgrown corner of a field, some old stones and a weedy depression beneath the old thorn tree was all that existed, the waters of St. Nonna nothing more than a hazy legend in the history books. And so he became the creator of a new legend, one which may well be told by future generations, and added to by those storytellers whose tales grow a little taller in the telling. They may well hold their audience spellbound as they relate how John Tryner, a local water-diviner, was called in to trace the underground course of the holy waters. Of how Morley Brown and his helpers dug down time and time again to find the spring, only to see each time, the water break away from the course intended for it; of how, with a hole twenty feet deep and still no result, they were on the point of giving up when rain came, days of it, filling the rivers and springs; and of how finally, one morning it was discovered that the water had itself taken to its ancient course, and that once again the old well was filled.

And so, thanks to Morley Brown, the well of St. Nonna lives on. Carefully tended, and planted about with herbs and foxgloves, the old bowsening-stone that was found buried deep in the earth, unused in this more enlightened age, at the side of the pool. Over the well, the old thorn tree still breaks out in a flurry of snow-white blossom in the spring, and what better thoughts to leave this place with than the words of Morley Brown himself, at the end of his short address to visitors to the well;

> *'All of us need to escape from this worldly madness, and to find peace, and rest. We trust that here you will find such peace, as St. Nonna did, and that you will take it with you wherever you may go'.*

St. Neot's Well is a monument to Victorian restoration. The top is secured in place by two bent bits of rusty iron and a stone cross stands guard aloft, looking like a lost tombstone with no graveyard to call its home. Two of the huge granite lintels in the roof have cracked, a grey slate rests inside on a decrepit bracket once wrought of iron, and the crowning glory is the memorable motto 'RESTORED IN 1852' in two-inch high letters above the door, deeply incised and painted black so that the eye can perceive nothing else.

The old oak door and its clanking irons are the most evocative feature of this paragon of partnership between blacksmith and mason, until, that is, you

A MONUMENT TO VICTORIAN RESTORATION. . . . St. Neot's
Well, on the edge of Bodmin Moor, photographed in the last century.

notice that almost illegible letters, battered by age, spell out the immortal word
'PRIVATE'. Three steps inside lead down to a pool of water, which laps
around a collection of stones and broken slate and does nothing to encourage
you to stoop and drink from the fabled fountain. In the time of the Rev. Henry
Grylls, who built this edifice, some of his more elderly parishioners could
describe a stone arch over the well, with a large oak springing from it, and
doors at the entrance. The water was of the purest quality, and furnished the
surrounding village with a constant source of unfailing supply. The great
spreading oak which grew horizontally from the bank, and overshadowed the
well with its fan-like form was cut down for timber after centuries of protection
by those more sensitive to the sanctity of the place, and soon after, the well was
'restored', thus marking the end of an era.

Despite all this, the setting of this ancient sanctuary is an idyll. You approach it by a narrow lane a little to the west of the church, which opens out into a broad meadow, a natural amphitheatre on the banks of a brook wending its way to the river Fowey. This sequestered dell breathes an atmosphere of tranquillity which may well have attracted St. Neot himself in the ninth century, and the peace of the place may be infused with the meditations of countless pilgrims with minds focussed on affairs of the spirit. The well lies at the foot of a rocky outcrop covered in trees, and on my last visit rippling sunlight filtered through the branches to fall on two grazing donkeys, content with their world and somehow putting the finishing touches to a scene of rare natural harmony.

Legend relates how St. Neot, a dwarfish man of noble birth, was visited in his wooded cell by the pious from near and far. Traditionally, even King Alfred the Great, a close relative of Neot, came to the holy man for advice on matters spiritual and temporal, and the whole area is still surrounded by a halo of myth and mystery which leads one to believe that these stories must have some basis in reality. In the church dedicated to the saint a few minutes walk away, the faded kaleidoscope of colours in the stained-glass windows tell his story. He resigns his crown to his younger brother and takes the vows of a monk. He sits with his feet in the holy well, chanting psalms, when a hunted fawn falls before him and pleads for protection from his pursuers. The dogs are abashed and run off, the huntsman throws away his quiver and immediately becomes a monk himself, prostrating himself before Cornwall's own 'St. Francis of Assisi', with his great mystical love of animals.

Another window tells the story of the well. An angel or supernatural being shows Neot the spring in which there are three fishes, with the instruction that as long as he takes one, and only one, for his daily food, the supply will never be diminished. The saint, sick in bed, orders his servant to bring one of the fish for his dinner, but he rashly takes two and arrives at Neot's sickbed with the delicious aroma of both roast and boiled fish enveloping him. The saint, much alarmed at this, orders him to immediately return both fish to the well, where they are miraculously restored to life. These ancient myths and parables have a quality of timelessness about them that often embody eternal truths which are untarnished by the centuries. It is not necessary to think too hard and long about St. Neot and his fishes to see that on one level, this is the Rime of the Ancient Ecologist. The principle of taking only as much as you need from the environment is more crucial for us today than ever it was for the conscientious saint, and the old warning comes echoing down the centuries to our modern world. To rape the natural resources of our abundant planet for profit over and above necessity is to create a situation of inexorable imbalance.

Bodmin lies more or less in the centre of Cornwall, and with its priory, its position on the southern edge of the moor and its famous jail, it has always regarded itself as the county's premier town. Some historians say that this was an ancient sacred place which once had a temple dedicated to the God Apollo a millennium before the birth of Christ, but whether or not this is true, the more modern temple to Christianity has been referred to as the largest and fairest church in Cornwall. An ivory casket lies inside that once held the bones of St. Petroc, who founded Bodmin Priory during the Age of the Saints.

A few years before Petroc's arrival, another wandering holy man came to Bodmin, then a deep-wooded glen surrounded by trackless moors inhabited by wild Celts. Bearded and with the front of his head shaven leaving long flowing hair behind, he set about collecting wood and stones to build a hut and surround his holy well. He set up a roughly carved standing stone and fasted and prayed for forty days to dedicate this site to the new well. As the local people took to this saintly figure, called Gwrin or Guron who had travelled from Wales, some built their own small huts within his enclosure, the foundation of a monastic settlement that would become one of the most influential in Cornwall.

Guron, however, having sown the seed of the new faith, moved on to continue his work and eventually settled on the south coast at the place which was to take his name, now known as Gorran. Petroc, a dynamic and persuasive personality, took over the task of converting the local chieftains with such success that his fame spread far and wide to immortalize him in the annals of Cornish history.

When he died on a Cornish cliff on June 4th, 564, an immense crowd mourned his passing.

St. Guron's Well still exists near the western doorway of St. Petroc's Church, looking out above the traffic and bustle of a modern town. A plain, unassuming building, it has a high-pitched roof and a Tudor doorway, most of the original granite slabs being replaced by masonry of local stone. Above the door, an unusual carving of St. Guron worshipping at his well exists, but one wonders if the figure of the saint was based on an earlier, Celtic model, for the cult of decapitation that was so strong in Celtic myth and legend seems to be reflected in the effigy of the saint himself. The unfortunate Guron has lost his head at sometime in the past! Not an edifice to excite the imagination, it was probably originally built in the sixteenth century, but the water is led away by underground chutes to spout from the mouths of two time-worn gargoyles, one horned, the other with pendent ears. Above the hideous heads, dim echoes of pagan well-spirits, is carved the date AD 1545, and a side-trough stands to refresh any horses or cattle that might brave the dangers of the twentieth-century traffic that roars past this old spot, once the centre of the town.

Night and day, even in the driest and hottest seasons, this stream of crystal water has flowed uninterrupted for millennia. It has served the passing generations of Bodmin folk with a never-failing supply of cool, and not a little holy, water to slake their parched throats and lay the dust of the town streets. It flows on, as ever, under the roads and pavements and away down into the valley to join the River Camel at Dunmere. But there was a time when the water fell out of favour with the townsfolk because of its course through the old graveyard. Carew writes that it 'runneth thorow the churchyard, the ordinary place of buriall for towne and parish. It breedeth therefore little cause of marvaile that every generall infection is here first admitted and last excluded'.

In the immediate vicinity, Bodmin used to possess three other holy wells of note. One was located in what used to be called, appropriately enough, Fairwash Coombe, and was no more than a limpid stream running into a trough. Its waters were held in high esteem by the long-dead folk of Bodmin who would frequent it to indulge in a little innocent hydromancy. The future was divined by rushes from the marsh below, tied crosswise. With the recital of a forgotten invocation, these were set to float on the water, their movements indicating the likely course of future events. *St. Petroc's Well*, a small stone building near the football field, still exists although much neglected and devoid of any story or legend.

The most renowned of the Bodmin wells was *Scarlet's Well*, located in the valley through which the waters of St. Guron's Well wend their way to the Camel, down below the old jail. It once reverberated to the hissing and rushing of the steam trains that ran on the Bodmin-Wadebridge line, and which passed within a few feet of it. Elderly residents of the town used to take their morning constitutional through the woods to this well, for a drink or an eye-bath in the healing waters, reputed to be a never-failing cure. Again, we have Carew to thank for preserving the beliefs surrounding this well;

> 'Within short space after the great fame dispersed touching the rare effects of Warwickshire wells, some idle envious head raised a bruit that there rested no less virtue, forsooth, for healing all diseases; in a plentiful spring near unto Bodmin, called Scarlet's Well; which report grew so far and so fast that folk ran flocking thither in huge numbers from all quarters. But the neighbour justices, finding the abuse, and looking into the consequence, forbad the resort, sequestered the spring, and suppressed the miracle. Howbeit, the water should seem to be healthful if not helpful; for it retaineth this extraordinary quality, that the same is weightier than the ordinary of his kind, and will continue the best part of a year without alteration of scent or taste; only you shall see it represent many colours like the rainbow, which (in my conceit) argueth a running through some mineral vein, and therewithal a possessing of some virtue'.

Thomas Quiller Couch, testing out this report of Carew's for himself, found that the water was invariably the same specific gravity as that of distilled water. Whether the spring had changed its composition or Carew was misinformed we cannot tell, but he did find by keeping records through the seasons that the temperature of the water was always 53 degrees Fahrenheit in hot sunshine and hard frost alike, indicating that it springs from a considerable depth. The spring, still known by its ancient name to this day, seems to have been called after a family of ancient inhabitants of the town by the name of Scarlet, one of whom was M.P. for Bodmin as early as 1312.

There are two ways to approach the remote region around Cardinham, on the edge of the wild moor. From Bodmin, you can take the main A30 road which follows the original route that has bisected Cornwall since men first trod this land, or you can take the Liskeard road along the steeply wooded Glynn valley, one of the most beautiful in the county. Whichever way you go, I hope that your powers of navigation are considerably better than following your nose, and that luck and St. Christopher will accompany you. In the years that I have negotiated these narrow, winding lanes that go up hill, down dale and disappear without trace into the moorland mist, I have invariably ended up not quite irretrievably lost, but considerably confused at the very least. As soon as I turn off the main road, some powerful magnetic field seems to send my internal compass, which is usually fairly efficient, completely haywire. I end up going round and round in ever-decreasing circles that appear to be modelled on the Universal archetype of the double helix, rather than the more straightforward spiral. I keep coming to roads that I have been down a thousand times before.

Maps are useless. The scale varies from field to field in a deliberate attempt to baffle you. Directions are useless. Knowledgeable old retainers always refer to invisible junctions or buildings that have apparently been demolished years ago.

I have never yet found myself wandering aimlessly at the dead of night, but if I ever do, I am sure that the Pole Star will have slithered off to hide behind the Plaiedes, or that the Plough will be occupied tilling some distant meadow.

After protracted adventures involving stories that would only be believed by Dr. Livingstone or an Amazonian tribal scout, I finally found Cardinham Church, and decided to stop and take stock of my position while the going was good. This area was heavily populated in the early days, and you can see the shape of the old Celtic camp on the moorland skyline, looking across from the north side of the churchyard, which has been there for over 2,000 years. The site of Cardinham Castle is on a steep hill to the south-east of the church, built about 1080, and never attacked by anything more formidable than erosion. After the fourteenth century, it wore away until now only the earthworks remain. The Celtic cross outside the church porch is possibly the finest in England, and has intriguing Scandinavian markings on it.

The Gods that rule over disorientation were a little kinder to me after I had paid my respects to this old cross in the churchyard, and led me to the site of *Cardinham Well* by drawing my attention to another stone cross by the side of a winding hill that led past a farm entrance. About a quarter of a mile north of the church village, this place has a detectable presence about it in accordance with its history of having once been one of the largest and most important holy wells. Sacred before the saints, this site once boasted one of Cardinham's parish churches, the other being built at the old castle. Later, a chapel existed which a century and a half ago still had a corner standing. A few years later the spot bore the appearance of a burial ground, owing to the fallen stones being grown over by grass and moss. The stones were removed and used in nearby

Holy Well, Cardinham

farm outbuildings, but feelings of guilt or shame must have overcome the farmer, for he arranged the old stones with their carved faces concealed, in an attempt to obscure their origins. Ancient pieces of arched granite still lie about in the farmyard below the raised site of the chapel, with its unusual stone cross standing in defiance of the desecrators of the past, practically all there is to remind you of the extreme antiquity of the place.

All that remains of the well itself is a spring of delicious, cool water that rises in a stone-lined chamber the size of a Hobbit's parlour near a farm entrance quite a way up the road, tumbles through a drain below the level of the lane, and cascades through an arch of twisted roots belonging to a stately oak, falling into an antique stone stoup in the corner of the farmyard. The old rock-hewn

IN THE MIDST of an area that is studded with the ancient remains of our prehistoric ancestors, St. Cleer Well stands by the side of the road leading out of the moorland village. Restored in grand Gothic style, old tales tell of miraculous cures, and of how the well was used as a bowsening-pool to cure the insane.

bowl is completely covered with a great beard of green, dripping moss, with no remnants of a building around it. In the last century, a doorway having an arch of shaped granite was erected, originally part of the old chapel. The water was still used for baptisms, although later a wooden door appeared, furnished with a lock and key, not to protect the holy waters, but to prevent the unwanted attentions of those who may have taken an unhealthy interest in the butter and cream, kept nice and cool inside. Except for the old stoup, the stone cross above and the remnants of masonry that lie about, there is little to indicate that this was once the site of one of the most venerated wells in Cornwall.

The moorland village of St. Cleer is in the midst of a whole array of the remains of our ancestors. A mere stone's throw from Trethevy Quoit, the Hurlers, the Cheesewring, King Doniert's Stone and a landscape studded with hill-forts, barrows and tumuli, it also possesses an interesting holy well, rebuilt in 1864 in grand Gothic style. Being close to Minions, the highest village in Cornwall, and being a tall, substantial building, the well itself may claim the title of one of the highest holy wells in the county, and one of the nearest to heaven! Unfortunately it stands at the side of the road surrounded by a mass of unsightly bungaloid growths, which considerably detract from its imposing demeanor, and the visitor is warned by a notice not to drink of the sacred waters for fear of some unhealthy contamination.

In 1850, all that existed were the remains of what must have been an important building. The entrance was by an ivy-clad double arch, the central mullion being broken. Ruins lay about, and the locals muttered abstruse and tantalizing tales about its miraculous virtues, of how it had once been used as a bowsening pool to cure madmen. They also told of how some of the stones had been carted away at various times to serve meaner purposes, but had always been brought back by some mysterious agency during the night. A year later, Wilkie Collins' delightful book 'Rambles Beyond Railways' was published, preserving a glimpse of the old Cornwall before its isolation was stolen by the age of steam. He waxes evocatively about his visit to the well;

> 'Half-an-hour's walking brought us to the village, a straggling, picturesque place, hidden in so deep a hollow as to be quite invisible from any distance. All the little cottage-girls whom we met, carrying their jugs and pitchers of water, curtseyed and wished us good morning with the prettiest air of bashfulness and good humour imagineable. One of them, a rosy, beautiful child, who proudly informed us that she was six years old, put down her jug at a cottage gate and ran before us to show us the way, delighted to be singled out from her companions for so important an office. We passed the grey walls of the old well, the position of which was marked by a ruined Oratory, situated on some open ground close to the side of the public pathway. . . . Poor St. Clare! If she could look back, with the thoughts and interests of the days of her mortality, to the world that she has quitted for ever, how sadly would she now contemplate the

Blight's sketch of St. Cleer Well at about the same time that Wilkie Collins
visited it and wrote so evocatively of its air of melancholy decay.

*Holy Well which was once hallowed in her name and for her sake. But one
arched wall, thickly overgrown with ivy, still remains erect in its place that the
old Oratory occupied. Fragments of its roof, its cornices, and the moulding of
its windows lie scattered on the ground, half hidden by the grasses and ferns
twining prettily around them. A double cross of stone stands, sloping towards
the earth, at a little distance off—soon perhaps to share the fate of the prostrate
ruins about it. How changed the scene here, since the time when the rural
christening procession left the church, to proceed down the quiet pathway to
the Holy Well when children were baptized in the pure spring; and vows were
offered up under the roof of the Oratory, and prayers were repeated before the
sacred cross! These were the pious usages of a past age; these were the
ceremonies of an ancient church, whose innocence and reverent custom it was
to connect closer together the beauty of Nature and the beauty of Religion, by
such means as the consecration of a spring, or the erection of a roadside cross.
There has been something of sacrifice as well as glory, in the effort by which
we, in our time, have freed ourselves from what was superstitious and
tyrranical in the faith of the times of old—it has cost us the loss of much of the
better part of that faith which was not superstition, and of more which was not*

tyrrany. The spring of St. Clare is nothing to the cottager of our day but a place to draw water from; the village lads now lounge whistling on the fallen arches under which their humble ancestors paused on their pilgrimage, or knelt in prayer. Wherever the eye turns, all around it speaks the melancholy language of desolation and decay—all but the water of the Holy Well. Still the little pool remains the fitting type for its patron saint—pure and tranquil as in the bygone days, when the name of St. Clare was something more than the title to a village legend, and the spring of St. Clare something better than a sight for the passing tourist among the Cornish moors'.

Left alone among the ruins, Wilkie Collins and his friend were approached by the 'keeper of the well'; 'a poor old woman, bent and tottering with age, who lived in a little cottage hard by. *'She brought us a glass, thinking we might wish to taste the water of the spring; and presented me with a rose out of her garden. Such small scraps of information as she had gathered together about the well, she repeated to us in low, reverential tones, as if its former religious uses still made it an object of veneration in her eyes'.*

Today, the building stands aloof from its suburban sprawl, even if the waters are polluted by seepage from drains. In something approaching genuine Gothic splendour, it is a memorial to the Rev. John Jope, vicar of the parish for sixty-seven years, and a finer and more imposing tribute could hardly be imagined.

13

THE WELLS
OF THE CLAY COUNTRY

The Great Pyramids—a favourite place of Victorian
matrons—The hermit of the Rock—a site for sore eyes

EFORE William Cookworthy stood looking out across the windswept Hensbarrow Downs with a handful of white clay and the germ of an idea in his mind, the area around St. Austell was a landscape of rolling meadows, wooded valleys and bleak moors. In the centuries that followed, the features of the land were radically altered by men who continued to exploit his idea in search of the natural wealth that lay beneath their feet, and the gentle undulations of Nature were transformed into a moonscape of weird white mountains. Those that are more familiar with this strange landscape of pyramid and pit may rarely cast their eyes skywards, being more involved in earthly matters. But the unsuspecting visitor may well catch his breath at the sight of the horizon of lofty peaks and gaping chasms which lurk round every bend. Steeply shelving slopes stretch away to the sky and great craggy caverns appear precipitiously as if scooped out by some vast elemental giant, of which Cornish legend is full. Huge metal monsters clank and clatter their way between lunar craters, looking like fearsome and predatory metallic insects burrowing and hauling around enormous ant-hills, a scene straight out of some gigantic science-fiction nightmare.

It comes as no great surprise, then, that the wells that must once have existed here as they still do in other parts, have been all but destroyed by the diggings and delvings of industry. Of the ancient landscape, little is left. Standing stones and sacred springs have been lost in the quest for a white powder called China clay, which, surprisingly, has a thousand and one uses in our modern world, but very little to do with the manufacture of china. All that survives in the ravaged area is a fascinating and unique spring below the stark outline of Roche Rock and a dry well in the village of Luxulyan. Another is located on the other side of the main A30 road, but still in the parish of Roche, and the remainder are on the south coast, away from the clay workings except for the beautiful Menacuddle Well at St. Austell. Despite the unnatural landscape, I have to admit that I find the unearthly romance of the white mountains

160

stimulating, revelling in the sheer, fantastic vistas of industrial creation, peering into the depths of the arctic green pools as if looking through into another universe. And this poetic imagery somehow heightens the effect of these few remaining wells, rare fountains sparkling in a dry and dusty landscape. There are probably many lesser remains unknown or half-forgotten, like the one mentioned in a letter to me from a Mrs. Nunn, from St. Stephen. She says that the well on her land, which never dries up and has steps leading down to the pool, is remembered to have been used to baptise children and to have been used as holy water by one of their past vicars, Canon Gilbert. Evidently a neighbouring farmer was much worried at the thought that it might be filled in and was greatly relieved when his mind was put at rest by Mrs. Nunn. Just a small demonstration of how these old springs live on in the minds and traditions of the local people, even amidst an industrial landscape.

Menacuddle Well is an enchanting place. All the more because of its proximity to the busy clay capital of St. Austell, just a few minutes walk from the shops and offices and the great railway viaduct that strides across the valley. A sign on the main road points down the hill to the well, situated in what are now public gardens with a character rare in the field of recreation grounds. A magical air stirs in the nostrils as you drop below the level of the road carrying the cars and clay lorries, and you find yourself in a rarified, enclosed woodland of ancient trees and towering rhododendrons. A stone seat, carved from a boulder, is placed in just the right position to view the beautiful Gothic building sunk in dappled shade beyond the barrier of a stream flowing milky-white with china clay. A mood of strange harmony pervades the place as the traffic rumbles along twenty feet above your head.

Crossing the tiny bridge to the well, I approached in a dream as the shafts of sunlight filtered through the trees, falling on the old stones in a carefully composed canvas of grey, green and gold. Inside the Gothic archway the peace was even more profound, a delicate silence a world away from the twentieth century. And then, like a whirlwind, a group of young boys appeared as if from nowhere, dropping their bicycles in a clatter outside the open doorway, and converging in a cacophany upon the lonely figure standing inside, lost in reverie. Just a few seconds of raucous ebullience, and they were gone again, except for one, left squatting and peering into the clear water. I asked him if he often found coins in the well, imagining the generations of young children who must have made regular pilgrimages to collect the bounty of the superstitious. Oh yes, he said. Lots of people still tossed their offerings into the well. And then, he stood up, and thrusting his grubby hand deep into his pocket, he pulled out a bright penny, flipped it with casual nonchalance into the rippling water, and was gone!

In the Middle Ages, Menacuddle possessed the most important chapel in the area, adjoining the holy well. It must surely be this connection that gives the spot its exquisite aura of sanctity, although the present building, one of the most beautiful in the county, was made from its squared granite blocks in the

MYSTERIOUS MENACUDDLE. . . . There is a strange magic in the air at the Gothic Menacuddle Well, St. Austell. The writhing roots of an ancient tree are washed by the overflowing waters of the milky-white stream that comes down from the clay mountains above, giving a weird supernatural quality to this haunting place.

late fifteenth century. As a plaque on the wall records, it was in 1922 that Sir Charles Graves Sawle restored the building and granted the gardens to the people of St. Austell as a memorial to his only son who fell in the Great War. The waters are crystal clear and very pure, and in the past were held by local people to possess extraordinary virtues for cure and prophecy. Samuel Drew, once a cobbler in the town, records in the 'History of Cornwall';

> 'Weakly children were carried thither to be bathed, ulcers have also been washed in its sacred water, and people, in seasons of sickness, have been recommended by the neighbouring matrons to drink of its salubrious fluid. In most of these cases instances may be procured of benefits received from the application, but the prevailing opinion is that the advantages enjoyed result rather from some mystical virtue attributed to the water from ages past, than from its natural qualities.
>
> 'Within the memory of persons now living, this well was a place of general resort for the young and thoughtless. On approaching the margin, each visitor, if he hoped for good luck through life, was expected to throw a crooked pin into the water; and it was presumed that the other pins, which had been deposited there by former devotees, might be seen rising from their beds to meet it before it reached the bottom. But though many have gazed with eager expectation no one has yet been permitted to witness the traditionary phenomenon.'

Following Thomas Quiller Couch's footsteps in search of *Chapel Well, Towan*, I headed through the oddly named 'London Apprentice', a name, he noted, 'suggestive of some tale of wild roystering and lawless riot, or of venture and success', but could find no path across the river to climb the steep wooded valley. An ancient inhabitant, however, in cloth cap and coat, was painting the windows of the Methodist Chapel in the rain, and said he had seen it as a child, but that the approach was from the other side of St. Austell. From this approach, I found myself at Chapel Farm, and was pointed in the right direction by the farmer, who much lamented the pressures and strains of modern farming, and the demise of those halcyon days of a slower time. I agreed wholeheartedly, and set off through the quagmire of thin farmyard mud, past decaying outbuildings that hung in a cloud of that penetrating country aroma that finds its way to the very bottom of the bronchial tubes and is strangely delicious and invigorating. I remembered that Gurdjeiff once commented that such smells were very beneficial, and swallowing a controlled gulp, set off past old trucks once belonging to the Great Western Railway and an impressive collection of rusting rural Victoriana.

Crossing the field, I came to the well building in a small hollow, so sturdy that another thousand years might not have changed it overtly. Built against the raised bank, the carved doorway and arch had strange holes in the

Pentewan stone from which hung pupae and small snails that seemed to prefer the protection of a stone home to the more usual cover of a Cornish hedgerow. Inside, two feet of crystal water filled the reservoir, and raised up on the back wall, a superb carved corbel, green and mellow, which must have once supported the figure of a saint, and now empty for the imagination to fill with its own fantastic effigy.

A few yards away, a modern concrete bore hole, round and raucous in the solitude of the old sacred spot, and across the stream, a respectful farmer had built a small pump-house from blocks and corrugated asbestos, almost a replica of its ancient brother, the dimensions appearing almost exactly the same. A great oak lay shattered not a few feet from the well, its roots torn from the ground by the recent storms. The farmer had told me how the old fellow in the house opposite him now long since dead, had related how a distant clergyman had changed into holy vestments in his front room in some almost forgotten time, and then led a group of people to the well to bless the waters. He also mentioned that there was a replica of Chapel Well in the narrow streets of Mevagissey, a story that intrigued me as to its origins and purpose. And, sure enough, after wandering through the streets of the fishing village with the plaintive cries of the seagulls filling the skies, I came across this enigma, a dry model, an echo of the well to be found miles away in rustic isolation. I could find no-one who knew anything at all about this curious structure, and musing over a pint in a Mevagissey pub, gave it up as an unsolved puzzle as I leafed through my old copy of the Quiller Couch book, now showing noticeable signs of wear after accompanying me up, down, and across Cornwall. He noted the memory of two other wells in Mevagissey, found at Trelevan. One, *Lady's Well*, gushed from a rock at the foot of a steep hill, famous for giving increased vigour and strength to the constitution. Another, known as *Brass Well*, bubbled forth nearby and was once spoken of as the 'Tunbridge Wells of the West', a somewhat dubious accolade, its waters being strong chalybeate and having a peculiar appearance from the sulphurous scum that floated on the surface. According to the old accounts, fading fast in the middle of the last century, it was notable for many famous cures and healing properties, perhaps working on the principle that the worse it tastes the better it is. I drank up and left.

In the heart of the clay country, the parish of Roche wanders across the downland to jump the division imposed by the main A30 route to the west, having two interesting wells within its boundaries. But whenever you travel in this area, the imposing spectacle of *Roche Rock* rises from an oasis of flatland in the midst of a sculpted landscape to peer out from its rocky pinnacle, dwarfing the trivial movements of man as it stands impassively observing so many ants going about their business. Below this hermitage built on top of the great crag of Roche Rock is one of the most peculiar wells in Cornwall, said to flow in mysterious sympathy with the ebb and flow of the sea. Surrounded by

THE LEGEND OF ROCHE ROCK tells how the chapel built on the rocky pinnacle was once inhabited by a solitary leper, wishing to avoid infecting others with his contagion. Looking after him was his daughter, Gundred, who fetched water from a hollow boulder that is said to ebb and flow with the tide.

superstition and haunted by legend, this ancient chapel exerts a powerful fascination that has led to many visits in search of this mystery, until I began to despair that I would ever locate it.

Throughout the changing seasons, I have searched amongst the boulders and rocks that lie strewn about, many of them exhibiting those shallow basins that are linked in the minds of some antiquaries with the religion of the Druids. Many times I have found myself scaling the heights of the rocky outcrop to stand in the exposed doorway that stands aloft, listening to the screeching rooks wheel and wail high above the landscape, the eerie sound of the wind howling, as the legend says, like the great ghost of Tregeagle begging shelter from the demon hounds of Hell. The weird whistling and shrieking of the wind around these rocks is one of the most disturbing sounds to be heard on the Cornish moors.

After many hours spent looking for this spring, I arrived one day in a clear and lucid state of mind, determined to attempt yet another search. And, as if I had paid the price of knowledge with my previous visits, the spell was lifted and I instantly saw what I had been looking for as I crossed the old slate stile from the road. A large boulder lay amongst a tangle of bracken just a short way from the stile, invisible or overlooked before. A hole, bored by some nameless power, full of water, stands gaping from the smooth outline of the rock, and an arm thrust into this winding passage disappears down into the granite for about a foot. Whether it is actually connected to a spring or in some way collects rainwater is difficult to tell, or if it does rise and fall with the tide outside the imagination of the old inhabitants of Roche is perhaps a little dubious. But on subseqent visits, there has always been water present in this hole at varying levels. Hals, writing in the early part of the seventeenth century, tells us the legend concerning the well. He writes that after the chapel was abandoned by the rock saint who made it his abode, the hermitage was occupied by a solitary leper, who, wishing to avoid infecting others with the dreaded disease, spent the rest of his days on the crag of Roche Rock. His daily needs were brought to him by his devoted daughter Gunett, or Gundred, who fetched the water from this curious well. And Carew immortalizes the fable of the well as follows;

'You neighbour-scorners, holy proud,
Goe people Roche's cell,
Farre from the World, neere to the heavens,
There, hermits, may you dwell.
Is't true that spring in rock nearby,
Doth tide-wise ebbe and flow?
Or have we fooles with lyers met?
Fame says it; beit so'.

From the mysteries of this strange rock basin, below the stark solitude of the cell where St. Conan, one of the first bishops of Cornwall, sought enlightenment, the well-seeker travels across Goss Moor to a very different sort of spring, one which has often been confused with the well at Roche Rock. To the crossroads at Victoria, turning westwards leads to a small lane leading off to the right of the main road. Stopping to open the gates of a level crossing, the country lane that stretches away to the farm at Roche called *'Holywell'* is moodily rustic, its hedges untouched by the ravages of machines. Over the ages, a vast procession of humanity has walked down this old trackway, leaving their presence in the spirit of the place, teasing the mind back to older days and older ways when the rhythms of life were slower. Continuous hurrying is a modern disease, born of insecurity and our alienation from the natural world. It may seem amazing to us, but up until the last two hundred years or so, nobody lived to a schedule, except monks and nuns who imposed a regime upon themselves deliberately to achieve mental discipline. Celtic seafarers never knew exactly when they were going to arrive at their destination, they allowed a few weeks either way to take account of unforseen adventures. And pilgrims likewise travelled in empathy with the unpredictable situations and changing circumstances of a personal odyssey, moving with the tide of events like a tree bending in the wind.

Past a crumbling cottage, dropping down to the right by the old farmhouse where one of its younger inhabitants has scrawled 'I live at Holywell' on a window pane, the path cuts through a steep bank to open out into an unkempt copse where the ancient arch stands, looking much the same as it did a century ago. Once, it was a fine structure of massive granite blocks with a stone figure of a saint on its roof, but stories from old books tell us that this was thrown down and carried off, and that the font from the chapel that stood here previously had been removed by a mason for making mortar and limewash. Considering that there is nothing to see of this chapel now, it is remarkable that the well still exists, although much ruined, despite the hand of desecrating man. Its waters are renowned for the cure of eye diseases if resorted to on Holy Thursday and the two following Thursdays, before sunrise. An offering of a bent pin was dropped into the well whilst calling upon the healing virtues of the saint, and this practice was much in evidence at the end of the last century, when quite a collection of pins could be seen in the bottom of the healing well.

The decline from an influential place of pilgrimage to a moody ruin seems to have happened in the last couple of hundred years, the unmarried girls of Roche tossing their pins and needles into the spring being a superstitious shadow of the old power of the well. But in the prosperous mining days, the underground stream that feeds the well was intercepted and used for the mine workings, and the remaining stones of the chapel carried off to be used in farm buildings. One of these stones, which may have once been part of a cross that stood near the well, was used in the farmhouse fireplace. But the disappearance of the old buildings, and the stubborn resilience of the well-building itself is strangely significant, for it was the existence of the natural spring that first gave rise to the sanctity of the site, perhaps many thousands of years before Christianity came to these parts, and now, when everything else has long gone, the well still stands defying the centuries. It shows how these

SITE FOR SORE EYES. . . . The waters of the holy well at Roche are renowned for the cure of eye diseases if resorted to on Holy Thursday and the two following thursdays, before sunrise. The young fellow in the photograph would never suffer such maladies, though. The water from the well is pumped up to the farmhouse where he lives.

Roche Holy Well in the 19th century. Stories tell of the figure of a saint once standing on the roof, which was thrown down and carted off to oblivion. At the time of the sketch, many bent pins were to be seen in the spring, offerings from those who would ask favours of the well spirit.

old sacred springs are truly the immoveable focus of a primitive aspect of human development, continuing to function throughout the vagaries of the ages despite successive epochs, religions and the transient fashions of civilization.

In those halcyon, rustic days when Thomas Quiller Couch would spend his weekends wandering the lanes of Cornwall in search of the old, ruined wells, the countryside would have appeared very different than it does today. Those landscapes full of trees that would have delighted the eye of Constable or Samuel Palmer now fulfil the role of an urban conception of the countryside, with neat hedgerows that would now only delight the myopic eye of a trendy town-planner. The chain-saw has, in a few short years, changed the aspect of our ancient land, as places that were tended in a rough, wild manner for centuries have been tidied up and made more acceptable to the mass mind of mediocre modernity. And when the trees come down, no saplings are allowed to grow to disturb the neat precision of the hedge, for the flail-cutter sees that everything is reduced to a tedious uniformity in a clatter of destruction, leaving in its wake the bruised and battered stumps of living wood staring like broken bones in a battlefield. Soon, there may only be trees that have been allowed to grow under the protection of a telegraph pole, where the flail-cutter cannot reach, a grim testimony to the ignorance of man towards the King of plants, worshipped by the Druids for its magical and medicinal properties and the crucial role that it plays in the harmonizing ecology of the planet. It is significant that they worshipped in sacred groves, encompassed by the cloistered pillars of the great tree-spirits.

Trees are the greatest friends that mankind possesses. They give cradles to the newborn, chairs to sit upon and tables to eat at as they grow, beds for slumber and love, and coffins for the last final journey. Our entire lives are connected intimately with the tree-spirits, providing humanity with the life-protecting warmth of fire and replenishing the essential balance of the atmosphere. They are crucial to the weather-patterns of the planet, and it is now all too obvious that places like the Sudan and other African countries, have condemned themselves to many years of drought and famine as a result of the systematic removal of the great forests that once inhabited the land. Such destruction is still currently taking place in Central America, despite the warnings. With the trees gone, the rains wash away the remaining topsoil ensuring that nothing will grow again, and the topsoil silts up rivers and brings a whole new set of problems in its wake. On a less dramatic level, exactly the same thing occurs when fields bordering Cornish rivers and streams are brought into cultivation. And yet, such is the arrogance of man that we continue to slay our friends, those who have nurtured, protected and fed us since the beginning of time.

This is no new problem, it is just that with the aid of machines, a century of destruction can now take place in a week. Even in the last century, the trees were under great pressure. A great spreading oak that grew in sympathy with St. Neot's Well on Bodmin moor was cut down for timber, and many examples of that curious rapport between tree and spring were destroyed as the wells fell into disuse. Thomas Quiller Couch lamented this state of affairs when he visited *St. Cyr's Well* at Luxulyan, a well which he had sketched in 1855 surrounded by an abundance of wild greenery, as the old stones began to show their age;

> 'This once fine well is a little below the parish church at Luxulyan, struggling against undeserved neglect, and, I fear, unavoidable destruction; its stones decayed and disrupted, and its basin utterly and forever drained by the excavations necessary to form the mineral railway which passes near.
>
> 'When I first knew it, many years since, its condition was fairly perfect, although a newly built house above, and a rough garden wall below, which encroached on it, had done much to spoil its picturesque surroundings. It was then a stately little well, with a constant supply of good water, built of large cut granite blocks throughout. Outwardly it was a slightly oblong building, with a highly pitched roof of slabs overlapping inwardly to the ridge, which was

rounded by slight cavettos; in front, a narrow pointed archway with two rounds from basement to point. Within was a vaulted and pointed ceiling. In the further end was a projecting corbel or bracket, which I guess may once have supported some effigy of the saint; and on the left, an oblong recess, on which were probably placed the ovations of those seeking the help of the water, or perhaps for resting the drinking vessels. All recollections of the particular gifts of the well have vanished, all respect for its sanctity has gone, and the utter fall of its structure will soon follow'.

The trees may have gone forever, but some years later, the old well was carefully restored and supplied with water from a tank. Today every last vestige of greenery has been eradicated, and the whole structure has been built around with cemented stones so that even the odd redeeming weed cannot secure a hold. The impression is one of a sterile pedestrian precinct, a grey courtyard in the middle of a Cornish village. Evidently a local resident paid thousands of pounds for the work to be done, executed in a thoroughly professional manner with hardly any redeeming feature that would have made up for the lack of sympathetic greenery. The place is cold and dead. The well is dry. A sundry collection of damp litter moulders where the spring used to bubble up.

The newly-restored well of *St. Columba* at Ruthvoes marks the site of an ancient spring that was venerated for many centuries, the bare remains of a chapel still existing along with tales of carved stones and crosses being found by the local schoolmaster. The legend, related by Nicholas Roscarrock in his life of St. Columba, tells how 'the saint pursued by her pagan lover took ship and arrived at a place in Cornwall called Trevelgue where the tyrant having intelligence of it pursued her and at a place called Ruthwas overtook her and refusing to renounce the Christian religion chopt off her head. At which place there is yet (about 1560) a well at this daie which beareth her name.'

14

THE WELLS
OF THE WEST

*Keeping the dreaded noose at bay—The work of the
Devil—The old priestess—The Magical Mount—A
primeval place—marvellous miracles and powers of
prophecy—to the end of the Earth*

ASSING by the rocky citadel of *Carn Brea* at Redruth, you
cannot fail to find the mind being teased back into childhood
awe of such an imposing spectacle. The great pinnacle scrapes
the sky in a way that nothing from our modern experience
could hope to compete with, the prehistoric air of the place
conjuring up images from a time when our imaginations would
run riot at the slightest stimulus. Castles in the air, secret rooms and
underground passages, caves and dragons crowd the brain threatening to
overload the conscious mind with a universe of fantastic creation. Thousands
of years ago this gargantuan rock-pile was the hub of a pagan empire that
influenced the life of an area that is still the most heavily populated in
Cornwall, and which, in its industrialization, demonstrates the sordid side of
the all-encompassing Machine Age. But Carn Brea stands aloof from such
matters, its head in the clouds, waiting for the aeons to pass with all the time in
the world.

The old hamlet of Carn Brea and its churchtown are situated at the foot of the
ancient fortress, significantly near the site of an old well that must have been
venerated by the inhabitants of this rock-strewn hill from time immemorial.
Hidden among the rugged moor-stones are the remains of *St. Euny's Well*, once
said to have had a stone cross close by, and much used by the locals in the last
century in preference to the water from the village pump. It may have been the
taste that they held in such esteem, or even some benefic attributes that have
now been forgotten, but the reputation of the waters would seem to have little
appeal in these days of less stringent methods of criminal punishment, for the
fame of this well is that whoever was baptized in it would never be
ignominiously hanged! It is perhaps a little fanciful to imagine large numbers
of Victorian convicts making pilgrimages to the old well in the hope that a late
baptism might thwart the tightening of the hangman's noose. And interesting
to note that near the slopes of that other Carn Brea, near Land's End, is yet
another well that bears the same name, a curious coincidence.

LEGEND TELLS US that during the night, crows removed every stone from a church being built near Helston, leaving only the porch which became Trelill Holy Well. The story is probably a folk-memory recalling the transfer of worship from an ancient sacred site to a new one as the old and new religions battled for supremacy.

Heading down towards Helston, that bastion of prim Victorian paganism with its annual 'Furry Dance' on May 8th, we come across an interesting old well whose legend is a folk memory of the removal of previously pagan worship to another site. Such stories are common in other parts of the country and especially in Brittany, when the incoming Christian faith for a variety of reasons, found it impractical or impossible to change the basic nature of an ancient sacred site and foist upon it the new religion. The Misses M. & L. Quiller Couch, seeking out the old holy wells after the death of Thomas, encountered an old woman of the parish who remembered visiting the spot in her childhood and dropping a pin, accompanied by a wish, into the magic waters. She told them that the tradition concerning the well was that 'many years ago, Wendron Church was being built upon the spot, but for some reason there were strong objections to the locality, and crows came by night and removed every stone, with the exception of the porch, which remaining portion now forms the covering of the well'.

Trelill Holy Well, as it is called, is a fifteenth century building at the edge of a field near the hamlet of Trewennack, and may well be the only holy well in Cornwall to feature on the motif of the local Women's Institute banner! Inside the arched doorway are seats on either side, and at the back a niche for the figure of the saint. Canon Doble, who was vicar of this parish, suggests that St. Wendron must have lived in a hermitage near the well, which 'may have been an object of worship in heathen times before it was sanctified by its association with the Saint'. At the beginning of the fifteenth century a chapel stood near, but all remains have now disappeared. What does remain, however, is the local feast day on October 27th, a date which may well go back beyond the times when the crows carried their nocturnal burden over the hill to Wendron. Whether or not the waters had any curative properties is now forgotten, but the day I visited the well I refrained from sampling the copious fluid, thinking that I would be more likely to catch something undesirable from the cattle that drink there than be protected from the ravages of scrofula or rickets.

Lizard point being the most southerly tip of England, it would seem to follow that *St. Ruan's Well* is the most southerly holy well, although there is a small spring at the bottom of a hill between Grade and Cadgwith that seems, as far as I could gather, to have been used solely for domestic purposes, and mention of another well in the last century, with rough steps leading down to it close to Grade Church, of which I could find no trace. A simple building made from local serpentine with a granite archway, there was once a cross on the roof which now resides in the local church. St. Ruan, or St. Rumon, as he was called in the old days, was reputedly an Irish saint who came to Cornwall and 'made an oratory for himself in the Nemaean wood', a place that was 'formerly very full of wild beasts'. The original chapel that was said to have stood on the spot is recorded as having sunk under the weight of its own antiquity, and

St. Ruan's Well,
near Grade Church

crumbled to ruins. The saint died at his cell, and was buried in the oratory, which became a centre of veneration so famous, that Ordulph, Duke of Cornwall, had the relics transported to his monastery at Tavistock in the tenth century. Originally very much like Trelill Holy Well, the present building is a plain and simple structure standing near to the side of the road, but brimming full with the most delicious, cool water throughout the summer.

St. Ludgvan's Well is said to have been founded by yet another missionary from Ireland, that great centre of Druidism and early Christianity. The legend of the well cannot be better told than by quoting Hunt's 'Romances of the West of England';

> *'St. Ludgvan, an Irish missionary, had finished his work. On the hill-top, looking over the most beautiful of bays, the church stood with all its blessings. Yet the saint, knowing human nature, determined on associating with it some object of a miraculous character, which should draw people from all parts of the world to Ludgvan. The saint prayed over the dry earth, which was beneath him, as he knelt on the church stile.*
>
> *His prayer was for water, and presently a most beautiful crystal stream welled up from below. The holy man prayed on, and then, to try the virtues of the water, he washed his eyes. They were rendered at once more powerful, so penetrating, indeed, as to enable him to see microscopic objects. The saint prayed again, and then he drank of the water. He discovered that his powers of utterance were greatly improved, his tongue formed words with scarcely any effort of his will. The saint now prayed that all children baptised in the waters of this well might be protected against the hangman and his hempen cord; and an angel from heaven came down into the water, and promised the saint that his prayers should be granted. Not long after this, a good farmer and his wife brought their babe to the saint, that it might derive all the blessings belonging to the holy well. The priest stood at the baptismal font, the parents with their friends around. The saint proceeded with the baptismal ceremonial, and at length the time arrived when he took the tender babe into his holy arms. He signed the sign of the cross over the child, and when he sprinkled water on the face of the infant its face glowed with a divine intelligence. The priest then proceeded with the prayer; but, to the astonishment of all, whenever he used*

the name of Jesus, the child, who had received the miraculous power of speech from the water, pronounced distinctly the name of the Devil, much to the consternation of all present. The saint knew that an evil spirit had taken possession of the child, and he endeavoured to cast him out; but the devil proved stronger than the saint for some time.

St. Ludgvan was not to be beaten; he knew that the spirit was a restless soul, which had been exorcised from Treassow, and he exerted all his energies in prayer. At length the spirit became obedient, and left the child. He was now commanded by the saint to take his flight to the Red Sea. He rose, before the terrified spectators, into a gigantic size; he then spat into the well; he laid hold of the pinnacles of the tower, and shook the church until they thought it would fall. The saint was alone unmoved. He prayed on, until, like a flash of lightning, the demon vanished, shaking down the pinnacle in his flight. The demon, by spitting in the water, destroyed the spells of the water upon the eyes and the tongue too; but it fortunately retains its virtue of preventing any child baptised in it from being hanged by a cord of hemp. Upon a cord of silk it is stated to have no power.'

Evidently, many years after these strange happenings, the reputation of the old well was in great jeopardy, for a Ludgvan woman was convicted of murder, and very successfully hanged with a hempen cord. This was a terrible shock to the people of Ludgvan, who began to have horrible misgivings for their safety, not to mention the safety of their children also, from the hangman's hempen rope. But after much anxious and diligent searching in the parish records, it was found that the woman had actually been baptised in a neighbouring parish, and the villagers, greatly relieved, were filled with joy at the discovery, their belief in the powers of the well firmer than ever.

But in wandering past the spring that rises a little to the north of Ludgvan Church, perhaps it would be wiser to avoid supping of the miraculous waters, for it may be more likely that a mild case of demonic possession might result than the laws of the land be changed to bring back the hangman, and put the old fable to the test once again.

In *Phillack* churchtown, a flight of old steps lead down to the holy well, but if you happen to have your dog with you, it may be wise to leave him tied up some way off. For the Rev. Lane-Davies, in his guide to the wells, tells a story taken from an 'Old Cornwall' magazine which may stand as a warning to those uncouth Philistines who do not approach the old shrine with the proper respect. Evidently, a certain Erasmus Pascoe, who was the sheriff of Cornwall in 1720, washed his mangy dog in the old well, and as a direct result of this sacrilegious act his wealthy family was reduced to poverty and became extinct in little more than twenty years. Erasmus himself, so we are told, died soon after his profane deed in the most dreadful manner, his son Thomas dying two months later, and his other children passed on soon after, his property and estate wasting away. Unfortunately, we have no way of knowing what became of the dog.

Gulval Well was once a famous well, attracting great numbers of people to drink the health-giving waters and to pry into the unknown future. It also had a tradition of curiously combining clairvoyant insight with the health of those not present, for the chronicler Hals writes in the seventeenth century ' . . . *to which great numbers of people, time out of mind, have resorted for pleasure and profit of their health, as the credulous country people do in these days, not only to drink the waters thereof, but to enquire after the life or death of their absent friends; where, being arrived, they demanded the question at the well, whether such a person, by name, be living, in health, sick or dead? If the party be living and in health, the still quiet water of the well-pit, as soon as the question is demanded, will instantly bubble or boil up as a pot, clear crystalline water; if sick, foul and puddled waters. If the party be dead, it will neither bubble, boil up, nor alter its colour or still motion.'*

He goes on to tell us of an old woman who was looked upon as the high priestess of the well, who understood both the mystic endowments of the fountain as well as the needs of those who wished to invoke them. She kept the well neat and clean, told everyone who passed of the miraculous powers of the waters, and dispensed them in return for a monetary offering. She is remembered as giving oracles to strangers, and whilst under the influence of the waters the old lady could also reveal the whereabouts of lost or stolen objects, including the local cattle. She was probably the last of her kind to be recorded in the county.

The village of Gulval is named after St. Gudwal, a saint with most impressive powers, almost Christ-like. Born in Wales, he became a bishop but gave up the good life to retire to a cave by the sea, with just one disciple.

His rock was an island, and as the winter storms beat the Atlantic into a great fury, the foam rushed into his retreat, threatening to overwhelm the sanctuary. Prayers were necessary at this stage, and the saint prayed to God for a barrier to be thrown up, which had a remarkable effect. For thousands of fish appeared with grains of sand in their mouths and deposited them all in one place, forming a miraculous breakwater. Later on, he was noted for leading his collection of monks (who must have joined him after the fishy miracle) over the Bristol Channel in seven boats, while he himself guided them by walking on the water! On his arrival at what was to become Gulval, near Penzance, stories abounded with the fabulous workings of the saint, who had a way with other animals as well as fishes, for he was famous for pulling a thorn from the foot of a wolf that came to him for healing.

Of the saint, of the old 'priestess' of the well, of the well itself, all we have now are the stories, for not even the ancient spring rises to the surface in the field just south of the church.

Having travelled into the most remote parts of the Cornish landscape, isolated places which would never be idly visited by anyone other than an itinerant well-hunter, the weary pilgrim now enters an area that is famous for its solitude. Even in the depths of summer, when the narrow snaking lanes become clogged with those in search of peace, the massive promontary of West Penwith arches round Mount's Bay in a timeless sweep of prehistoric permanence. Great granite hills climb steeply from pastureland criss-crossed with ancient stone hedges, their summits crowned with the tumbled remains of huge cairns. Storm-blasted cliffscapes hide deep wooded valleys, thick with impenetrable undergrowth. Standing stones and relics of lost aeons loom out of the early morning mist at the turn of every corner, sharpening the senses to a fine realization of the transience of our modern world. Raw nature has, in this place, no sugar coating to cater for the taste of our civilized sensibilities, and the old wells that still exist in this haunted area possess the same elemental character. Each one is soaked in prehistory, no attempt having been made to hide the stark severity of such ageless shrines that must have been held sacred since the beginning of human habitation. Somehow, it reminds me of that old children's riddle;

> *The beginning of Eternity,*
> *The end of Time and Spuce,*
> *The beginning of the End,*
> *The end of every place.*

Wherever you travel in this tight, taut landscape, moving through a land where the houses and hedges are made from the biggest boulders that men could move, you seem to suddenly emerge at the top of some cairn or castle, surveying the scene from coast to coast. And wherever you stand, the gaze is magnetically drawn to that distant shrine of shrines, the turreted outline of St. Michael's Mount, basking in the sweeping curve of the bay that shelters it from much of the Atlantic blast. The sharpness of the light deludes you into thinking that you could almost reach out and touch these tiny foibles of mankind, you begin to feel like some vast giant possessed of limitless power, the sort of giants that still abound in the legendary landscapes that fall away on either side. Like the giant Cormoran, who not only used to live on the famous Mount, but built it himself from the granite masses of these very hills. Legend tells that his wife, Cormelian, disobeying his instructions, attempted to carry a huge greenstone rock across to the Mount, but dropped it from her apron when kicked by the irate colossus in a fit of fury. When the giantess died, the mass of greenstone became her monument, and later, 'a lytle chapel' was built upon the revered rock giving it the name of 'chapel rock'. Cut in the living rock of the Mount is a well that was once known as *'Giant's Well'*, but is sometimes referred to today as 'Jack the Giant Killer's Well', as a tribute to the clever youth who succeeded in ridding the mount of its monstrous inhabitant.

A well of great fame throughout the area that was also once referred to as 'Giant's Well', but is more commonly known now as *Chapel Euny Well*, is to be found about a mile and a half from Sancreed. Once covered by a building, with a chapel nearby, it is now a rough structure built over with weathered moorstones, evoking a crude primitive feeling that would seem to be in total sympathy with the nearby prehistoric village of Carn Euny, with its mysterious underground passage, or fogou, sixty-six feet long, and leading to an unusual circular side chamber that once had a corbelled roof. Dr. Borlase gives a good account of this well in his 'Natural History of Cornwall', in the latter half of the eighteenth century;

> 'As a witness of its having done remarkable cures, it has a chapel adjoining it, dedicated to St. Eunius, the ruins of which, consisting of much carved stone, bespeak it to have been formerly of no little note. The water has the reputation of drying humours as well as healing wounds. The common people will not be content to attribute the benefit they receive to ordinary means; there must be something marvellous in all their cures. I happened, luckily, to be at this well upon the last day of the year, on which, according to vulgar opinion, it exerts its principle and most salutary powers. Two women were here who came from a neighbouring parish, and were busily employed in bathing a child. They both assured me that people who had a mind to receive any benefit from St. Euny's Well must come and wash upon the first three Wednesdays in May. But to leave folly to its own delusion, it is certainly very gracious in Providence to distribute a remedy for so many disorders in a quality so universally found as cold is in every unmixed well water.'

A later chronicler notes that to take full advantage of the many miraculous virtues, especially in the cure of infantile mesenteric disease, children should be drawn through the pool three times against the sun and three times on the surrounding grass in the same direction.

Thomas Quiller Couch wrote that to form a bath for the dipping of the diseased, turves were cut from the surrounding moor, and he commented that the waters do not contain any mineral impregnation, but probably rely on the tonic effects of the cold, and the firm faith of the devotees. On my last visit to this place, which is best seen after soaking up the atmosphere of the nearby prehistoric village, just a short walk away, there was evidence that well-worship is still very much alive in the far west. Curious tokens, offerings to the well-spirit, I supposed, were implanted in the ground at the side of the well. They somehow had a Nordic quality about them, or perhaps an American Indian influence. Bright feathers were tied together with coloured cords that appeared to have some special significance, the shape of the fetish being obviously carefully contrived and skilfully executed. It was fascinating proof that well-magic still goes on at these ancient shrines, melting the millennia away, pushing us back to lost times.

While still in the mood of such prehistoric reverie, we should leave this ancient site and visit another not far away, where *Sancreed Holy Well* is to be found along a narrow footpath opposite the old church, by walking through a farmyard and up to a grassy mound, sheltered by a distinctive fir tree that is visible for miles around. This well, out of all the sites I have visited during this strange odyssey, possesses the most potent atmosphere of extreme antiquity, something that is beyond the range of words and the conscious levels of the mind. Even the Rev. Lane-Davies says 'The spot always seems to me to possess a greater air of mystery and sanctity than any other in Cornwall', and for once, despite our differing viewpoints, I agree with him most wholeheartedly! It seems that it was rediscovered by the Vicar of Sancreed in 1879, lost in a tangle of brambles.

The path leads down into a deep well, and as you stand below the level of the surrounding land, the long flight of granite steps lead to a cascading pool of water. The large mossy boulders that form the round curve of the wall exude a penetrating air of distant, primeval times and earthy, womb-like peace. In between the cold boulders, small holes appear, forming miniature caves where water drips onto a luminous lichen that glistens green like polished malachite. This truly ancient shrine is beyond all others in its peculiarly elemental essence, evoking strange thoughts that lie beneath the surface, like the well itself. It is like returning to some rare haven of tranquillity, at home in the womb of the Earth after many long and tiresome adventures enacted in a state of partial amnesia. Something inside screams 'Yes! I remember!'

Mossy turf creeps over the stones of the ruined chapel that lie above and behind the well, and swathes of Montbretia sway in orange glory in this harmonious place, a delicious and delicate balance between the works of Man and the works of Nature.

The careful and sympathetic tending of this sacred spot is due to a certain Juliot Shanks, who obviously felt the mysterious magic of the place and left provision in her will that it should be kept in a manner 'as befits a holy place'. One cannot imagine a more perfect memorial to the miracle of Life.

Madron Well is in what can only be described as an enchanted wood. A meandering path leads past green pools and tortuous trees to a boggy pond that is the well, where rough chunks of granite lie about covered in a thick carpet of moss. Despite its outward appearance, for no remains of a building now exist, the place is much visited by sightseers and those who come for more positive purposes. A newly-planted Rowan tree stands beside the pool, and all around the trees are festooned with small pieces of rag tied among the branches, fluttering strands of wool and tatters of coloured cloth that give life to the autumn breeze. Pieces of tartan, shiny faded ribbon and even scraps of tissue paper from those who could find no small offering of cloth, wave limply in the wind. Almost at the top of the tree, ancient faded scraps tied well out of the way of other humans assume the colours of the gnarled wood, lichen green and dripping with old man's beard. A shoe hangs from a lower branch, and two feathers flutter in the wind, tied together with a piece of knotted thong. The trees in the wood creak and groan as they bend to the will of the wind.

This old practice of leaving some article behind that has had intimate association with the diseased part, is a ritual that is as old as man himself, and is to be found in every corner of the globe. The rationale for the practice is contained in elementary sympathetic magic, working on the principle that as

TIED TO A TREE are white feathers, left as a fetish at Madron Well. The trees around are festooned with pieces of rag and clothing, left by those who wish to be healed by the power of the well. This old superstition, in the best tradition of sympathetic magic down the ages, is to be found in all parts of the globe.

the rag or article decays, so the diseased part heals naturally, in much the same way that wart-charmers sometimes rub a piece of meat against the wart and then bury it to decompose. The practice is still widespread in Ireland and is common amongst the Shintoist devotees in Japan. Even in the interior of Africa, travellers have been amazed to find trees covered with innumerable shreds of cloth fastened there by afflicted wayfarers. Throughout Asia, the ancient ritual is still followed by the countless followers of various religions, all utilizing a belief that predates them by thousands of years. An old man who lived near Castlereagh, Ireland, at the beginning of the nineteenth century, threw light on the beliefs of his time when asked what possible advantage he expected to gain from the singular custom of sticking rags to the branches of trees near such a well, and sometimes spitting on them. His answer was that his ancestors always did it, that it was preservation against 'Geasa Draoidecht', the sorceries of the Druids; that their cattle were preserved by it from infectious disorders; that the 'Daoini Maithe', that is, the fairies, were kept in good humour by it; and so thoroughly persuaded were they of the sanctity of these pagan practices that they would travel bareheaded and barefooted from ten to twenty miles for the purpose of crawling on their knees round these wells, upright stones and oak trees.

In Cornwall, the old rituals often degenerated in the latter stages of well-worship into scenes that were so disorderly and unseemly that the magistrates were required to interfere, suppressing the miraculous cures and shutting up the well.

In Ireland, the collective pilgrimages to such wells were often the occasion of 'such heathenish orgies that pipers, fiddlers, free libations of whisky, wild dances, fighting, quarrelling, and all manner of debaucheries, wound up a ceremony begun with penance, and ending like the festivals once held in honour of Aphrodite'.

It is quite possible that such scenes were once enacted at various Cornish Holy Wells, especially one as famous as Madron, where much has been written about the miraculous cures that have taken place. One of the more circumstantial accounts of such a cure is recorded by an unknown author towards the end of the seventeenth century, and testified to by the then Bishop of Exeter;

> '*I will relate one miracle more, done in our own country, to the great wonder of the inhabitants, but a few years ago, about the year 1640. It was this; a certain boy of twelve years of age, called John Trelille, in the coast of Cornwall, not far from Land's End, as they were playing at football, snatching up the ball, ran away with it; whereupon a girl, in anger, struck him with a thick stick on the backbone, and so bruised or broke it that for sixteen years after he was forced to go creeping on the ground. In this condition he arrived at the twenty-eighth year of his age, when he dreamed that if he did but bathe in St. Maderne's Well, or in the stream running from it, he should recover his former health and strength. This is a place in Cornwall frequented at this time of year by many on the first Thursday in May, near to which well is a chapel dedicated to St. Maderne, where is yet an altar, and right against it a grassy hillock (made every year anew by the country people) which they call St. Maderne's Bed.*
>
> '*The chapel roof is quite decayed; but a kind of thorn, of itself shooting forth out of the old walls, so extends its boughs that it covers the whole chapel, and supplies as it were a roof. On the first Thursday in May, assisted by one Perriman, his neighbour, entertaining great hopes from his dream, thither he crept, and lying before the altar, and praying very fervently that he might*

regain his health and strength of his limbs, he washed his whole body in the stream that flowed from the well and ran through the chapel. After which, having slept for one hour and a half in St. Maderne's bed, through the extremity of pain he felt in his nerves and arteries, he began to cry out, and his companions helping him and lifting him up, he perceived his limbs and joints become stronger, insomuch that partly with his hands he went more erect than before. Before the following Thursday he got two crutches, resting on which he would make a shift to walk, which before he could not do; and coming to the chapel as before, after having bathed himself, he slept on the same bed, and awakening, found himself much stronger and more upright; and so, leaving one crutch in the chapel he went home with the other. The third Thursday he returned to the chapel; yea, grew so strong that he wrought day-labour among other hired servants; and four years after enlisted himself as a soldier in the King's army, where he behaved himself with great stoutness both of mind and body; at length in 1644 he was slain at Lyme in Dorsetshire.'

Madron Well was also much visited by young girls wishing to know the secrets of the future, and another writer of later date recalls 'here divination is performed on May morning by rustic maidens anxious to know when they are to be married. Two pieces of straw about an inch long are crossed and transfixed with a pin. This, floated on the waters, elicits bubbles, the number of which, carefully counted, denoted the years before the happy day'. It would seem that some similar form of superstition still lingers, for reed crosses are still to be seen in the well occasionally even today.

Children used to be taken to this well on the first three Sunday mornings in May to be dipped in the water, that they might be cured of rickets, or other disorders. Three times they were plunged into the water, after being stripped naked, the parent or person dipping them standing facing the sun. After the

The Doom-Well of St. Madron

dipping they were passed nine times round the well from east to west, then they were dressed and laid on St. Maderne's bed. If they should fall asleep, and the water in the well bubbled this was considered a good omen. Strict silence had to be observed during the entire performance, or the spell was broken!

The remains of the baptistry are now well-tended after two hundred years of utter ruin, the rounded walls enclosing a granite altar, seats, and a crude font that can be filled from the stream behind by the removal of a stone. All around water rises, forming limpid pools and sparkling streams, and the whole area is suspended in a thick cloud of supernatural expectancy that would seem to add weight to the innumerable stories of the miracles that have taken place at this magical site.

St. Levan's Well is romantically situated on the side of a cliff just over the headland from Porthcurno, its weather-worn stones that make up the remains of the building looming up from the cliff-top that looks out across the channel. Above it, along the valley, is St. Levan's Church with its remnant of a culture that was rooted in another age, a vast pagan boulder split asunder as if by some cataclysmic bolt of lightning, and below it in the rocky glen are the remains of the saint's cell. J.T. Blight in his book 'A Week at Land's End' gives an account of this well in the last century which is not far removed from what is to be found today;

> 'Standing on some elevated rocks on Porthchapel Point, the remains of St. Levan's Well are seen in a little glen beneath. Still, no sign of life, a deep solitude hangs around the great cliffs; the babbling of a little stream over its rough bed, blended with the murmurs of the waves below, is the only sound that breaks on the ear. This was the spot chosen by St. Levan for his chapel or hermitage, which stood on the verge of the cliffs; the well was farther back, but steps communicated from one to the other; these, however, have disappeared. The site of the chapel can only be guessed at, whilst the walls of the little baptistry are wildly overgrown by rushes and tall water-plants. Thus is the altar overthrown, the shrine deserted, and the place become a wilderness'.

On the road between St. Buryan and Land's End lies the tiny hamlet of Alsia, no more than a farm with a few nearby cottages. In a hollow down in the corner of one of the fields flows *Alsia Well*, a wishing well once of great repute, and one of the most beautiful of the old natural springs to be found, with no trace of any building to detract from its delicate charm. It is fenced around to protect it from animals, and is obviously tended to by other hands than that of its Naiad, for it is kept lovingly by some sympathetic human hand. The water wells forth from a small, dark, cavern, framed by water weeds, deep green

THE WEATHER-WORN ROCKS OF ST. LEVAN'S WELL look out across the channel from their isolated clifftop site. An ideal spot for an early hermit to seek enlightenment, it was chosen by St. Levan who built his small oratory down in the glen below, although the place may be far older than the early Celtic saints.

mosses and sprouting pennywort, to trickle down into a narrow gravelly bed that is kept free of obstruction. One is almost left with the impression that the guardian of the well is standing somewhere nearby, looking kindly on as the pilgrimage draws to a close.

One 'old Celt', William Bottrell, who diligently recorded the folk-lore of West Cornwall in his 'Traditions and Hearthside stories of West Cornwall' (Printed by W. Cornish, Penzance 1870), recorded his impressions of the well as follows;

> *'We know not if 'this fount' is still regarded as a holy well; but many years ago we have often heard an aged lady, who was born and bred near Alsia, and was well acquainted with legendary lore and old customs of the district, say that in her younger days the Saint's Well of Alsia was almost as much frequented on the first three Wednesdays in May as the noted well of Chapel Uny. Mothers came from far and near with their weak and rickety children that they might be strengthened by being bathed in its waters. Moreover, the same old lady to whom we are beholdened for many of the incidents of the legend, Nancy Trenoweth (the fair daughter of the miller of Alsia), informed us that it was not unusual for these pilgrimages to be the occasion of a fight between the women of Alsia and the pilgrim mothers, when the good housewives caught the strangers dipping their precious babes into the enclosed part of the well, or the place from which the neighbours drew their drinking water'.*

Thomas Quiller Couch also tells us that 'Of a summer's evening scores of maidens might be seen around it, eager for their turn to see what sweethearts would be united or parted, which they discovered by the fall of pebbles or pins. As the articles sank near or apart so their future was foretold; and the number of the bubbles raised bespoke the number of years before the happy or unhappy issue could befall. Another method of consulting the spirit of the well was by floating bramble leaves upon it'.

Beyond Land's End, two and a half hours out from Penzance into the surging Atlantic swell, the fabled Isles of Scilly rise up from the Ocean floor. These remote islands are crowded around by treacherous dark rocks which foam and boil even on a serene day, and which have proved fatal to countless mariners in search of a safe haven. But the persistant winds that tear at the islands have not deterred human habitation over the millennia, and the history of these 'very peculiar scraps of England' has been long and eventful since, so the old legends tells us, it was connected to the mainland as part of the now lost land of Lyonesse.

Some of the islands are the wind-worn remnants of huge prehistoric cemeteries, large numbers of barrows and chamber-tombs dotted about the craggy hills, the Scillies earth and stone covering the bones and ashes of some

IN A HOLLOW AT THE BOTTOM OF A FIELD near St. Buryan rises Alsia Well, a wishing well once of great repute. 'Of a summer's evening scores of maidens might be seen around it, eager for their turn to see what sweethearts would be united or parted'.

of the earliest inhabitants. There are more of these great burial chambers in Scilly than in the rest of Cornwall, and some historians hazard that chieftains were brought from the mainland to rest for ever in the savage setting of the Isles. Visited by the Phoenicians and other early traders, the seabed must harbour all manner of rich treasures, and remnants of the old merchantmen of antiquity are still occasionally washed up on the beaches. Glass beads from a Venetian wreck are often ploughed up in the fields of St. Agnes, carried there in the seaweed used as fertilizer. Pieces of Roman statuary tell of a time when a temple of Diana stood on one of the smaller eastern islands, at a time when the sea level was far lower and you could walk from one island to the next.

Long after this romantic period of the Scillies' history, the legends tell of St. Warna, who crossed over from Ireland in a wicker boat covered with hides, and, fortunate enough to escape the fate of many others, landed in the bay that was afterwards to bear her name. Not surprisingly, this particular saint came to be revered by the islanders as having a supernatural association with shipwrecks, the lifeblood of the western isles. The five families of St. Agnes who, in later days achieved notoriety as the most unscrupulous and daring of the Scilly wreckers, would take themselves to *St. Warna's Well*, and dropping a crooked pin into the slightly salty waters, pray for the beneficent saint to send them 'a rich wreck'. The wreckers' days were numbered, though, and with improved navigation and the building of a lighthouse on the island (an extremely unpopular move with the locals), the well fell into disuse and a century ago was little more than a damp hole in the ground. Today it is a rugged little well, three steps lead down to the murky pool, surrounded and roofed over by slabs of worn, grey granite. In style it resembles one of its nearest neighbours, that of Chapel Euny at Sancreed on the mainland, a rough, raw place looking out across the boulder-strewn beach to the broken teeth of jagged rocks that jut out into the sea. And trapped between the boulders, jammed into the crevices of the sea-caves, is the wreckage of foundered ships, still resisting the pounding of the Atlantic, with its vast expanse of landless ocean stretching away beyond the horizon.

It is, perhaps, a fitting place to end our adventure, as it echoes the spirit of solitude of St. Morwenna's well with which we embarked upon this strange quest, far away on the north coast of Cornwall. Looking back, the search for the wells has in many ways become a personal quest for the Holy Grail, that brimming chalice of the life force which is the source of all inspiration and the vessel through which flow the subtle energies that give shape to our world. And, like that timeless quest that is symbolized in the mythologies of all races, we have followed the footsteps of those who have gone before, shaman, druid, hermit and priest, into little known regions of an unfamiliar landscape, peering back through the hazy veils of time to penetrate the mysteries of the past. And in contemplating the attitudes of our ancestors to the Natural world around them, we cannot fail to acknowledge that the essence of their beliefs goes much deeper than the modern world can currently grasp, although at the present time we are just beginning to realize that there is something far more significant to their beliefs than has previously been admitted.

In treading the mystic path of the ancients, our adventure has been taking place on different levels, for as our feet followed the trackways of antiquity to the old hallowed places, so our minds have explored and remembered old ways of thinking that may yet have some real purpose in the future. In travelling the old ways, we have been projected into something of a different dimension, where we have experienced exquisitely beautiful, often strange and even occasionally sinister fingers beckoning us to recall those lost times that still hang in the air at the old shrines. Like the venerable mystics of ages past, we have become different people, our awareness is more finely attuned to the subtle realms that give life to everything, and we know that we are one with the Earth.

THE END

OTHER WELLS
OF INTEREST

THE NORTH

NORTH TAMERTON

A picture of neglect. In the middle of a field opposite a row of modern houses, the well is sunk down below the lie of the land, just a hole in a field. It looks as if no-one has tasted the waters for years. The few steps that lead down are broken and brambles, nettles and weeds bar the way. A large slate blocks the opening to the brick-built chamber. The cows that trudge round the old well are destroying it, leaving a sad and sorry impression on the mind.

JACOBSTOW

An old, rough lane leads from the top of a hill on the main coast road, after the turning to the village. Over the first gate on the right is a marshy clump of trees and the derelict holy well dedicated to St. James, evidently a shrine on the ancient pilgrim route from Wales, across Cornwall to Compostela in Spain.

MINSTER, BOSCASTLE

A strikingly beautiful place that brings peace to the inner being. Once, the terraces that are now overgrown were alive with contemplating monks from the priory that was built on this spot and had an intimate connection with the monastery at Tintagel. It is indeed a place of haunting atmosphere. Flowing right under the church to emerge, trickling past the swathes of wild garlic, into a scooped-out hallow at the bottom of the churchyard, one cannot fail to be impressed with the piercing serenity of the place. Someone once told me that at certain times, from inside the church, the mellifluous cascade of the water sounds like some distant, other-worldly choir, celestial voices just barely raised above the heavy sound of silence.

EGLOSKERRY

A fairly miserable brick-built affair with a large slate over the top, with little to interest the well-seeker. It is in a field over the road from the church, over a wooden stile. My reaction to it was no doubt influenced by the fact that on the day I visited it, a chain-saw gang were busy destroying a hedge of trees behind the well, while the incessant churn of a cement mixer filled the air as builders threw up a quick bungalow not far away.

LEZANT

Three wells can be found at Lezant, one interesting building on Rezare village green, another just north of the church and another at a small farmhouse that has been built on the site of a Chapel of St. Lawrence, half-a-mile to the north of the village. The well here is in the orchard just a few yards from the building, a mixture of masonry ancient and modern. In the farmhouse is a carved niche which must at one time have been a piscina.

FENTONADLE

All that remains of this old well, mentioned as a boundary marker in 1613, is a pipe protruding from the stone hedge on the road to St. Breward, through which flows a veritable river of water.

PADSTOW

Various wells remain, remnants from the days before the Reformation when Padstow abounded in chapels and holy wells. Lady Well, in Lanadwell Street may be one that survived the ravages of time. Below Prideaux Place is Fenton Luna, thought by some to be the true holy well of Padstow, with a 16th century stone archway next to the old pump, and mentioned in 1552. One of the legends that are common to many wells, that of the saint striking the ground with his staff, giving miraculous rise to a spring, is connected with this well. A simple spring under a rock half-way down the cliff at Stepper Point is all that is left of St. John's Well, below a site that once boasted a chapel and a beacon. Among the rocks near St. George's Cove is yet another well, with the scant remains of old stonework providing the only clue to the old site.

HARLYN

Near Harlyn Bay, the farm of St. Cadoc's takes its name from the famous chapel and holy well that once stood on the spot. One of the most famous in Cornwall, this well was mentioned twice in the life of St. Cadoc and also again three centuries later by William of Worcester. Now, nothing remains except an overgrown marsh and a collection of ancient stones to remind us of the sanctity of the place.

PORT ISAAC

On a site where a chapel of St. Electa stood in medieval times was a well that was protected by a warning to those who would harm it, a dim memory of the powers of the spirit of the well, which could withold its beneficence and turn the elemental force against those who might desecrate the shrine. Roscarrock writes 'There was a tree over her well wch those that attempted to cutt downe had ever harme so as they gave over to cut it. Till one more bold than the rest did cutt it downe whoe hurting himself was noted to dye shortly after'.

ST. ENDELLION

Perched on a hill, its church tower visible for miles around, the tiny hamlet of St. Endellion possesses one of those ancient wells that has no structure to show if it was once a place held sacred. Even a century ago, it was unfrequented except for the villagers who came to draw water for domestic purposes. But legend has it that it was used by the saint herself, one of the many offspring of King Brychan. What remains there are can be found beyond a cottage at the end of a lane near the church, a muddy and overgrown patch of wasteland.

THE EAST

MENHENIOT

A restored stone-built well to be found against the south wall of the Vicarage garden, with no legend or myth to stimulate the imagination.

NORTH HILL

A difficult well to find, but explicit directions are given in J. Meyrick's guide to the old wells. It is near Berriow Bridge, past an old mill next to the banks of the River Lynher. An ancient building covers the spring, where the water was collected for baptisms within living memory.

CHAPEL HALTON

Neglected for years, this little holy well was once connected with one of the ancient chapels that stood nearby, which gave its name to Chapel Farm. It has been restored with a statue of the Virgin Mary and a wrought iron gate, and is situated by the side of the road leading from the farm to the River Tamar, a few hundred yards below. Old stones from the chapel are built into the walls of the farmhouse, but this pleasant well is all that remains of the old days.

BOTUS FLEMING

An old stone building with no water. It dried up many years ago, and even the iron door that now protects the entrance could not keep the Naiad from seeking a new spring. To be found near the school.

ST. ERNEY

Some confusion reigns as to which is the original well that is remembered in the name of the hamlet of Markwell. I was pointed to a rough building in between the two farms, and which supplies them with water, but others have thought that the true site is in a clump of trees in the middle of a nearby field. In the old days it was variously known as St. Mark's Well, Earls Well and Earl of Cornwall's Well.

POLPERRO

Once a well-known wishing well, all that is left of it today is a trickle of water at the side of a steep hill leading to Lansallos, where there was once a chapel to St. Peter. The building itself seems to have disappeared during road improvements. In its heyday it was one of those wells that was considered a 'site for sore eyes'.

BODMIN AND THE MOOR

LANLIVERY

A practically invisible and overgrown well with a well-preserved stone building and a clear, cold stream issuing from it. Down a path from the 'Crown' inn, a good pair of wellingtons are necessary for this expedition.

CARADON

Down below the eastern slopes of Caradon Hill, with its towering television mast and collection of prehistoric cairns and tumuli, a reconstructed well can be found near the ruins of an old chapel in the hamlet of Caradon Town.

LANHYDROCK

To be found nestling between the sumptuous shrubs and trees of the magnificent Lanhydrock gardens, a few hundred yards west of the church tower. The medieval building, sunk below ground level, was discovered some years ago, and although nothing appears to be known about it, it may well have been important when the monks from St. Petroc's Priory at Bodmin owned the estate.

Altogether an exquisite well, with spirals carved on corbel-like projections that echo the energy spirals found by dowsers at such springs.

MID-CORNWALL

ST. JUST-IN-ROSELAND
As well as the 'true' holy well down below the church, there is yet another beautiful stone well in the famous churchyard, swathed in water weeds and with fuschias and ferns growing from the masonry. Much has been written about the atmosphere of mystical tranquillity in this peaceful place.

RUAN LANIHORNE
The remains of an old well are in a wood down behind the church, the water flows in a stream to the road below where there was until recently a large granite trough.

PROBUS
The remains of various wells exist at Probus, one being at the side of a lane that leads away from the church and the main road, and is now the rusting remnant of the Victorian village pump. Another well exists on a farm about a mile away, called Fenton Glidder, and yet another near the remains of the 15th and 16th century ruins of dwellings where the Jesuit priest Cuthbert Mayne was captured in 1576.

CARNANTON
A small arched well stands on the left of the road that leads to St. Mawgan airfield, solitary but with a copious supply of water. It is known locally as 'Nun's Well'.

FOWEY
A hitherto unrecorded well, as far as can be found. Behind a quaint gift shop called 'the old house of Foye', an atmospheric place and genuinely ancient, is a

beautiful well. Built into the side of the cliff is a granite entrance with a niche, and a reservoir brimming with cool, clear water from the rock-fed spring. Old carved stones lie around in a mood of timeless tranquillity, secret from the busy summertime streets of this delightful old Cornish port.

THE WEST

LELANT

The village of Lelant takes its name from an ancient chapel which perched on a rock at the mouth of the haven, and St. Euny has been the saint of the parish from a very remote period. The saint's well is a rock cut basin into which the spring flows before continuing in its seaward journey down the cliffs. Its old name was the 'Fairy Well', but it is now known as a wishing well. Another well, known as Abbey Well is in the grounds of an old house called The Abbey, and may well have been a site of some sanctity considering the ancient connection of the place with Syon Abbey.

ST. IVES

St. Ia gave her name to the town of St. Ives, and her well stands somewhat incongruously below the graveyard overlooking Porthmeor Beach, where its far from crystal waters fulfil the role of litter-bin in the holiday season.

BOSCASWELL

In between Pendeen and the sea are the remains of an old well that also once had a chapel. Stones have been piled up around the now dry spring like some prehistoric cairn, giving it a false air of antiquity. The Rev. Lane-Davies tells how the well was noted for horse leeches, which were often found attached to the lips of horses who drank there, and which were caught for medicinal use on cattle and human beings. They seem to have been particularly well-behaved leeches, for although they were always caught by hand, they would never bite any but the diseased part!

ZENNOR

A ruined chapel stands overlooking the sea at Gurnard's Head, and nearby is Chapel Jane well, situated, like St. Levan's, in a dramatic and desolate position. Time has taken its toll, for all that remains are a few rough stones around the spring, which is about a quarter of a mile from Zennor cairn.

TRESCO ABBEY

A beautiful, traditional round well sunk into the rock and built in Scilly granite with walls almost two feet thick. This must have been a spring of considerable importance, for fresh water was practically non-existent on the island in the old days. The ruins of the original abbey are all that is left of the ancient refuge and retreat for the only such gathering of monks on Scilly, although each island had its solitary hermit. Now it is set in the dreamlike atmosphere of the sub-tropical gardens, with a cool, walled garden all to itself. Across the top lies an old iron cartwheel, an ancient symbol of the wheel of fortune. It is a place of delicious tranquillity, even amongst the swarms of summer visitors, for it is away from the more spectacular gardens and missed by most people.

TRESCO ABBEY WELL

Books referred to

Ancient and Holy Wells of Cornwall, M. & L. Quiller Couch. (London 1894)

Ancient Crosses and other Antiquities in the East of Cornwall, J. T. Blight. (Simpkin, Marshall, London 1858)

A Pilgrim's Guide to the Holy Wells of Cornwall, J. Meyrick. (Falmouth 1982)

Holy Wells of Cornwall, the Rev. A. Lane-Davies. (Federation of Old Cornwall Societies 1970)

Traditions and Hearthside Stories of the West of Cornwall, William Bottrell. (1870, Frank Graham 1970)

Popular Romances of the West of England, R. Hunt. (Chatto & Windus 1923, Benjamin Blom 1968)

Cornish Feasts and Folklore, M. A. Courtney. (Penzance 1890, E. D. Publishing 1973)

A Week at Land's End, J. T. Blight. (London 1861)

Cornish Saints Series, the Rev. G. H. Doble. (King's Stone Press 1936, Parret and Neves Ltd 1960)

The Earth Spirit, John Michell. (Thames & Hudson 1975)

The View over Atlantis, John Michell. (Sago 1969)

Feng Shui; The rudiments of Natural Science in China, E.J. Eitel. (Trubner & Co. 1873, Pentacle Books 1979)

Celtic Mysteries, J. Sharkey. (Thames & Hudson 1975)

Geomancy; a Synthonal Re-appraisal, Anthony Roberts. (Zodiac House 1981)

The Pattern of the Past, Guy Underwood. (Pitman 1970)

Rambles beyond Railways, Wilkie Collins. (Richard Bentley 1851, A. Mott 1982)

A Short Life at the Land's End, John Michell. (Compton Press 1977)

The Druids, Ward Rutherford. (Aquarian Press 1978)

Meyn Mamvro Magazine

Cornish Life Magazine.

Index

List of Subscribers

Charles Connon, *Egloskerry, Cornwall*
Hamish Miller, *Trencrom, Cornwall*
Nanette & Roger Irving Little, *Boscastle, Cornwall*
Professor Charles Thomas, *St. Clement, Cornwall*
Godfrey Rehaag, *North Hill, Cornwall*
Graeme Broadhurst, *Launceston, Cornwall*
Marjorie Bunt, *Seaford, Essex*
Janet & Colin Bord, *Corwen, Clwyd*
Robin Hanbury-Tenison, *Cardinham, Cornwall*
Thelma & Barry Webb, *Llanhilleth, Gwent*
Gordon & Jacinth Jones, *Nelson, Wales*
Mrs P.M. Robbins, *Trebullett, Cornwall*
Chris Street, *Southgate, London*
Paul Riley, *Brentford, Middlesex*
Donald Vage, *Truro, Cornwall*
Brian Tuck, *Redruth, Cornwall*
Daniela Gerling, *Köln, West Germany*
Cecil Williamson, *Witheridge, Devon*
Brian Fleming, *Edinburgh, Scotland*
Mr & Mrs A.C. Berry, *Widemouth Bay, Cornwall*
Jamie George, *Glastonbury, Somerset*
Cecilia Boggis, *London*
Geoffrey Jelbert, *Lelant Downs, Cornwall*
Thomas Neurath, *Bloomsbury, London*

James Colville, *Penheale Manor, Cornwall*
Sheila & Trevor Nevins, *Perranuthnoe, Cornwall*
Pamela & Kent Stanton, *Launceston, Cornwall*
Nancy Bailey, *Penhallow, Cornwall*
James Aldrich, *Massachusetts, U.S.A.*
Anne Blackburn, *Massachusetts, U.S.A.*
Mark Valentine, *Southampton, Hampshire*
Michael Newman, *Plymouth, Devon*
R.F. Edward-Collins, *Little Petherick, Cornwall*
Revd. Barry Kinsmen, *St. Issey, Cornwall*
John Clarke, *Launceston, Cornwall*
Craig Sams, *Portobello, London*
Simon Swale, *Otterham, Cornwall*
David Lister, *Grimsby, Lincolnshire*
Bruce Burley, *Bude, Cornwall*
James-Carol Ivey, *Stithians, Cornwall*
Janet Ivey, *Stithians, Cornwall*
Donovan Wilkins, *Chacewater, Cornwall*
Mr & Mrs M.H. Daniel, *Tregadillett, Cornwall*
Mary Poulter, *Gunnersbury Park, London*
Graham Ovenden, *Mount, Cornwall*
Major S.E. Bolitho, *Trengwainton, Cornwall*
Ian Cooke, *Bosullow, Cornwall*
Breyan Gilyead, *Launceston, Cornwall*
Jill Wellby, *Morwenstow, Cornwall*
Stephen Havery, *Cheltenham, Gloucestershire*
Penzance Library, *Penzance, Cornwall*
Sarah Foot, *Saltash, Cornwall*
Austin Arnold, *Vaud, Switzerland*
Simon J. Wooders, *Wokingham, Berkshire*
Cornwall County Library, *Truro, Cornwall*
Lord Londonderry, *Shaftesbury, Dorset*
Hilary Evans, *Tranquil Lane, London*
Patricia Cox, *Halesowen, Worcestershire*
Alwyn Ladell, *Bournemouth, Dorset*
Donald & Lesley Holmes, *Bath, Somerset*

Agnes Hunt, *Paignton, Devon*

J. Malcolm Allan, *Bridge of Allan, Stirling*

Dr. R.W. Morrell, *Nottingham*

Barbara & David Russell, *Ashurst, Sussex*

Erica Evans, *Walsall, Staffordshire*

P.S. O'Flynn, *Truro, Cornwall*

Sylvia Clarke, *Illogan, Cornwall*

Sally Anne Roberts, *Egloskerry, Cornwall*

James P. Whittall, *Massachusetts, U.S.A.*

Jean & Reg Stanton, *Padstow, Cornwall*

Aline Salisbury, *St. Breock, Cornwall*

Philip Taylor, *St. Ives, Cornwall*

Timothy Wyllie, *London*

A.J. Lyne, *Truro, Cornwall*

Anne & Seaver Leslie, *Maine, U.S.A.*

University of California, *San Diego, U.S.A.*

Bart C. Alkemade, *Haarlem, Holland*

S.W. Henley, *Carlton, Nottingham*

L.H. Sanders, *Wadebridge, Cornwall*

Cheryl Straffon, *St. Just-in-Penwith, Cornwall*

Dale Chihuly, *Washington, U.S.A.*

A.J. Dixon, *Sittingbourne, Kent*

G.B. Goodman, *Tywardreath, Cornwall*

Kenneth R. Emmett, *Anglesey, Gwynedd*

Dr. P.O. Leggat, *West Looe, Cornwall*

Venetia Howard, *Blisland, Cornwall*

Nick Lilley, *Blisland, Cornwall*

David Mlinaric, *London*

A.R. West, *Kelvedon, Essex*

Josephine Rundell, *Eldon Grove, London*

Dominic Sasse, *London*

Revd. Brendan O'Malley, *Haverfordwest, Dyfed*

Glynne Welby-Everard, *London*

Dr. & Mrs R.W. Shillitoe, *Ilkley, Yorkshire*

Devon County Library, *Exeter, Devon*

Jonathan Foster, *Haslemere, Surrey*

Frank Hoppé, *Week St. Mary, Cornwall*
Jim & Beryl Pym, *Carshalton, Surrey*
Lord Eliot, *St. Germans, Cornwall*
John Lane, *Beaford, Devon*
James V. Cornish, *Pennsylvania, U.S.A.*
George Alexander, *Ewell, Surrey*
Michael Colmer, *London*
G. Bayfield, *Trethevy, Cornwall*
Richard T. Crowe, *Chicago, U.S.A.*
Moira Wilson, *St. Just-in-Penwith, Cornwall*
Sig Lonegren, *Vermont, U.S.A.*
Tony Foxworthy, *Shooters Hill, London*
John King, *Camborne, Cornwall*
David R. Fideler, *Grand Rapids, U.S.A.*
Margaret Venator, *Boston, U.S.A.*
Rose Heaword, *London*
Vita de Waal, *Forres, Scotland*
Mrs George Foley, *Massachusetts, U.S.A.*
Gordon McLellan, *Erskine, Renfrew*
Leonard H. Truran, *Trewirgie, Cornwall*
John Blowey, *Tuckingmill, Cornwall*
Fredric Lehrman, *Washington, U.S.A.*
Dr. A. John Rostron, *Edinburgh, Scotland*
S.M. Satchwell, *Feock, Cornwall*
Mrs L. Hawke, *Roche, Cornwall*
A.E. Brown, *Longstanton, Cambridge*
Mrs A.C.M. Long, *St. Just-in-Penwith, Cornwall*
Hugh Pincott, *Frome, Somerset*
Ivor S. Lander, *Liskeard, Cornwall*
Ed Prynne, *St. Merryn, Cornwall*
Mrs L. Juleff, *Whitemoor, Cornwall*
Joan Vincent, *Stenalees, Cornwall*
P. Tonks, *Lelant, Cornwall*
Paul Caponigro, *New Mexico, U.S.A.*
Alison Ross, *Menheniot, Cornwall*
Mrs J.A.F. Trier, *Solva, Dyfed*

J.M. Henwood, *Padstow, Cornwall*
Walter-Joerg Langbein, *Lugde, West Germany*
Eric J.S. Rapley, *Crowborough, Sussex*
Mrs I. John, *Whimple, Devon*
Paul S. Thompson, *Altarnun, Cornwall*
Richard Gerrard, *New Malden, Surrey*
Bill & Anne Mills-Roberts, *Bristol*
Betty Hill, *Heamoor, Cornwall*
Mrs Cherry Scott, *Isle of Mull, Argyll*
D.G. Amy, *Bodmin, Cornwall*
Robin Thomas, *Redland, Bristol*
Jane Osborne Fellows, *Shortlanesend, Cornwall*
Barbara Done, *Appledore, Devon*
Joyce M. Warner, *Layer Breton, Essex*
Lesley Whittaker, *Cheltenham, Gloucestershire*
E.T. James, *Calstock, Cornwall*
George & Dorothy Dann, *Torquay, Devon*
Ronald K. Trethewey, *Boston, U.S.A.*
Tim Whiting, *Marblehead, U.S.A.*
Kurt Jackson, *Boscastle, Cornwall*
Grant Rainford, *Worthing, Sussex*
P. Constable, *Ashford, Kent*
Anna Lardon, *California, U.S.A.*
Jeff Grace, *White City, London*
Ray Batchelor, *White City, London*
Dr. David Guy Healey, *Woodbridge, Suffolk*
Miss Joan Rendell, *Werrington, Cornwall*
Robert D.L. Lyle, *Bonython Manor, Cornwall*
Henry Goulden, *St. Cleer, Cornwall*
Pamela H. Goulden, *St. Cleer, Cornwall*
Rosemary Stratton, *Eastbourne, Sussex*
John Baxter, *Trebetherick, Cornwall*
Michael Whitmarsh, *Par, Cornwall*
Elaine Dunning, *Chalgrove, Oxford*
Ann Rodda, *Trevalga, Cornwall*
Richard Bowden-Dan, *Greenwich, London*

R.J. Commons, *Burslem, Stoke-on-Trent*
Mark & Marga Thomas, *Penzance, Cornwall*
Robert & Janet Farrah, *Appleby, Cumbria*
Rule Memorial Library, *Truro, Cornwall*
Wendy Winstanley, *Truro, Cornwall*
A.M. Robathan, *Goonhavern, Cornwall*
Lorna West, *Mawnan Smith, Cornwall*
R.G. Lindfield, *St. Leonards-on-Sea, Sussex*
L. Norwood, *St. Leonards-on-Sea, Sussex*
Alice & Julian Van der Schuit, *Gosport, Hampshire*
Colin Gregory, *Truro, Cornwall*
Bruno & Jane Clements, *Bishopston, Bristol*
Sally Cooper, *Newport, Isle of Wight*